THE *REAL* HOUSE OF GOD

THE *REAL* HOUSE OF GOD

Unleash the Full Power of God's Spirit Within You

H. DELE DAVIES, MD

WESTBOW
P R E S S
A DIVISION OF THOMAS NELSON

WestBow Press books may be ordered through booksellers or by contacting:

WestBow Press
A Division of Thomas Nelson
1663 Liberty Drive
Bloomington, IN 47403
www.westbowpress.com
1-(866) 928-1240

ISBN: 978-1-4497-7793-7 (e)
ISBN: 978-1-4497-7794-4 (sc)
ISBN: 978-1-4497-7795-1 (hc)

Library of Congress Control Number: 2012922675

Printed in the United States of America

WestBow Press rev. date: 2/13/2013

For my wife and best friend, Arike, and God's very special gift to us—our wonderful children, Toluwanimi (Toluwa), Temiloluwa (Temi), and Oluwalademi (Lademi).

FOREWORD

God is not far away. Since the time man became separated from God, He has tried to draw near to us. Although He is everywhere, He has chosen to manifest Himself in particular places. In the Old Testament, that was the tabernacle followed later by the temple. The presence of God in these structures had a powerful impact upon His people. Asaph said, "But as for me, the nearness of God is my good" (Psalm 73:28, New American Standard Bible). God was not far removed but chose to come close and dwell among His people.

In the New Testament, that place is the heart of His children. This is a real and personal manifestation, one that was promised by Jesus. "I will ask the Father, and He will give you another Helper, that He may be with you forever; that is the Spirit of truth, whom the world cannot receive because it does not see Him or know Him, but you know Him because He abides with you and will be in you" (John 14:16–17, NASB). Every born-again believer becomes a temple of the Holy Spirit.

Paul had to remind the early church of this fact. He wrote, "Or do you not know that your body is a temple of the Holy Spirit who is in you, whom you have from God, and that you are not your own?" In the New Testament, the desire of God to dwell among us is taken a step further, in that He not only walks among us as a people—the church—but also has chosen to live within us as individuals.

In this volume, Dele Davies has combined his skill as a researcher with his love for the Word of God to give us a detailed picture of the habitation of God. You will learn what kind of place the house of God was, how this knowledge has parallel effects and obligations on us today, and the implications of what it means to personally be a dwelling place for God. In the detailed study of the temple as the house of God, Dele has provided us with an understanding of the symbols of temple worship and how

God wants to operate within the believer as a temple of the Holy Spirit. Each part of this symbolism becomes a mnemonic device, helping us to remember all that God has done for us and wants to do through us.

In the years that I have known Dele Davies, I have found him to be a faithful friend and a trustworthy follower of the Lord Jesus Christ. May his work be as much a blessing to you as it has been to me.

Curt Dalaba
Pastor, First Assembly of God of Greater Lansing
East Lansing, Michigan

ACKNOWLEDGMENTS

A special thanks to the following people:

My Lord and Savior, Jesus Christ, who makes all things possible for me.

My wife and best friend, Arike, and our children, who exhibited extraordinary patience and voiced no complaints about the time I spent time on this book—thanks guys!

My mother, Yewande, whose gift to me is prayer, and to my father, Hezekiah Oladipo, who has long gone on to be with the Lord but managed to lay the foundation of love and generosity that made me who I am today.

My Canadian "parents" John and Marj Koop, who have constantly lifted me up in prayers and were extraordinary role models with almost sixty years of what God intended a marriage relationship to be like until John was called home to be with the Lord in March 2011.

My senior pastor in Michigan, Pastor Curt Dalaba, for always preaching God's word with clarity and truth straight from the Bible, and for taking the time to review and give constructive comments on the draft of *The Real House of God.*

Pastors Tim Covert, Buzz Barr and Jo Mason for conducting themselves always with a spirit of excellence and the Pastors' spouses, Anne Dalaba, Lynn Covert, Kelly Barr and Janice Mason for being such great partners.

My current pastors in Omaha, starting with Senior Pastor Walt DeVries, for his obvious love for God and his courage and determination to live a life pleasing to Jesus Christ.

Pastors Jason Carter, Rafael Aristy, Bobby Clarke, Chris Ford, Pam Franks and Mark Stevens for their daily living examples of dedication to Jesus.

Robert Nelson, who worked patiently and carefully with me in designing the front cover of the book, ensuring that the image projected the desired meaning.

Enonche Ameh who was diligent in researching and portraying elegantly simple but clear concepts in the illustrations of the Tabernacle used in the manuscript.

Stephen Chittenden, for careful review and editing of the manuscript.

My Sunday school teachers over the years, especially John Schafer, for his deep spiritual insight and modeling of humility.

Cecil Copeland, for encouraging me to write about this topic.

My prayer meeting teams and others who have diligently provided mutual prayer support and counsel over the years, including Nicholas and Ade Olomu, Francesca and Ben Dwamena, Sonia Diallo, Elna Saah, Doug and Donna Carr, Kobina and Gretchen Inkumsah, Jennifer Elizondo, Funmi Idowu, David Townsend, Bisola Santos, Stephen and Monique Chittenden, Tracy Bowden, Jumoke Lambo, Pastor Keith D'eall, Kristina Johnsen, Jeromey and Nicole Martini, Don and Amay Dufault, Modupe Awonuga, Zipporah, Agheneza, Tambu Hove, Kunle and Jade Adedeji, Bode and Ajike Oladoyin, Michael and Bola Oladosu, Tunde and Diekola Oshinubi, Ayopo and Kikelomo Odunuga, Peter and Bola Mebude, Don and Shirley Elliott, Femi and Ola Awodele, Eric and Sheree Gilmore, Jerome and Sonia Teveodjre, Bunmi and Solape Dada, and Mona Yath. I love you guys!

CONTENTS

INTRODUCTION

To discover where God lives and how easily accessible He is to you is to be transformed from a life of daunting challenges and hopelessness to a life of boundless possibilities.

Don't you know that you yourselves are God's temple and that God's Spirit lives in you?—1 Corinthians 3:16

Where Does God Live?

This is one of life's enduring mysteries. Even believers in a supreme Creator have debated for years the nature of God and where He resides. Perhaps *you* understand God to be living exclusively in heaven, isolated and far removed from your current reality in this life on earth. You may think of heaven as indescribably beautiful with pearly gates, seas like crystal, and streets paved with gold. You may even believe you'll one day be there with Him but can't see how that makes a difference here, right now, and *that* day seems so far away from the challenges facing you today! You may believe your only chance to be in the presence of God can only come within your reach after you die, when you will be rewarded or punished for the life you have lived while on earth. Perhaps you even feel insignificant with the realization that the fourscore or so years you will spend on earth barely register on the infinite timescale of eternity.

If this describes your situation, then you are probably wondering why anyone is asking you a silly question such as, "Where does God live?" The obvious answer is perhaps, "Who cares?" You might as well live your best or worst possible life now in total isolation from a God who lives in a remote and obscure place, who is far removed from the burdens you have to carry alone here on earth. After all, your only hope for escaping this broken world is contingent upon entering heaven after you are dead, when you will meet God and all your troubles will disappear. Even heaven may be a farfetched concept for you, or you may not be confident that you have done enough to make it there.

Well, I am here to tell you from personal experience that God does not only live far away in heaven, controlling events on earth by "remote control." God is actually very close to you, such that there is nowhere you can go on earth where He is not present. He is on the mountains, and He is in the plains. He is in the oceans and He is on the land. He is in the mega-cities as He is in the small towns, the countryside, and in the suburbs. He is in the air you breathe and in the physical structures around you. Indeed, He is so close to you that when you get to know Him, you can reach out and feel His presence any time you want and develop a very close and personal relationship with Him. You do not need to wait to die and get to heaven to have a close relationship with God your Father!

While heaven remains the ultimate eternal target and the final destination for all children of God, God has made it possible for you to interact closely with Him while you roam the precincts of this current world. In fact, He has given you a specific blueprint and instructions on how to relate to and interact with Him. Nonetheless, only a few people during their lives ever tap into this most incredible of opportunities offered by the Creator of the universe. You can be one of those few truly successful people by God's measure. Alternatively, you can be part of a majority that chooses to live life apart from a relationship with God, chasing after worthless goals that will never fully satisfy or endure, even if you are a successful person by all human measure.

A close relationship with God is possible!

A life apart from a close relationship with God is as empty as a poor man's pocket. By contrast, a close relationship with God will lead you to attain supernatural peace and joy no matter what your circumstances are in life. If you have ever desired this peace and joy, it is likely you have been inspired by the Holy Spirit to pick up this book, which will give you a glimpse into how God the Father operates and how He wants you to operate. It is the deepest desire of my heart that you would know that you can live the life He has planned for you and that you can have a closer relationship with Him.

As you read further, let me declare up front that God is in the center of all the arguments I will develop in this book in connection to growing a closer relationship with Him. It is my firm conviction that the only person who can change your life and make it meaningful is God, through belief in His son, Jesus Christ, and the transforming power of His Holy Spirit. This is based on my own personal experiences, where the transforming power of Jesus Christ has impacted my life.

When you are ill, you go to a doctor for healing. You would not wait until you feel better because you are embarrassed by what the doctor may think of you while you are ill. Similarly, if what you desire is spiritual change or fulfillment in your life, you have to go as you are to the master changer. The only sustainable changer of your spiritual condition is God, and He is waiting and ready and willing to accept you as you are and to change you for good today, not some time in the future when your life may or may not have improved.

There is no condition too difficult for God to change, nor is there any sin you have committed that is too grave or embarrassing for Him to forgive. You only have to draw close to Him with a repentant heart and He will touch you with a healing and loving and joyful touch that will calm all the storms raging in your life. He will transform your life from one of daunting challenges to one of boundless possibilities.

Before you can accomplish this transformation, though, you first have to find God. Throughout this book, I have written prayers I want to pray with you, and I strongly encourage you to join me and read each one out loud, because according to the Lord Jesus, the prayers where we stand together in agreement are especially blessed by God: "Again I say unto you, that if two of you shall agree on earth as touching anything that they shall ask, it shall be done for them of my Father which is in heaven"[1] (Matthew 18:19, KJV).

Each two chapters constitute a "session" relating to a specific theme in the book. Each session has been written to be interlinked and can be used either for contemplation alone or for you to get together with others in your church's Sunday schools, home fellowships, or other places of gathering for discussion. At the end of each session are "Questions to Ponder" that can be used as the basis of your discussion or private contemplation. There are also specific prayer points for you to pray, either individually or as a group, following each session.

You will notice that throughout the *Real House of God*, all references to God the Father, Jesus Christ, or the Holy Spirit are capitalized out of respect for and recognition of their roles in the Creation and Rulers of the universe and of humanity. In contrast, all references to satan are deliberately in small letters, except when it begins a sentence. This is not a typographical error but done as a reminder that satan is a creation of God and is not due the same elevation.

Pray this prayer with me:

Dear Lord Jesus, As I read this book, I confess that I have a need for You and ask that You prepare my heart and my mind to be open to the truths You are about to reveal to me. May the words be a blessing to me, for the changing of my life and for the bringing down of any strongholds that are holding me back from having the close relationship You desire to have with me today. Amen.

1. All verse references are from the New International Version (NIV) of the Bible unless otherwise specified. Where the author quoted from the 2011 edition of the NIV, and it differs from the 1984 edition, then NIV 2011 is displayed after the quote. If the quoted material is from the 1984 edition, or where there is no difference between the editions, no identification follows the book, chapter, and verse.

CHAPTER 1

God Desires a Close Relationship with You

(Session 1a)

What were we made for? To know God. What aim should we have in life? To know God. What is the eternal life that Jesus gives? To know God. What is the best thing in life? To know God. What in humans gives God most pleasure? Knowledge of Himself.—James I. Packer, British-born Canadian Anglican theologian.

"Return to me," declares the LORD Almighty, "and I will return to you." … Return to the LORD your God, for he is gracious and compassionate, slow to anger and abounding in love.—Zechariah 1:3; Joel 2:13

The Blessing That Is America

Americans are an ingenious people. They have made numerous and substantial contributions to improving the standard of living enjoyed by billions of people around the world that touch just about every aspect of daily life. Examples of these benefits include inventions as basic as the incandescent lightbulb; health benefits such as the eradication of polio and smallpox; the invention of more sophisticated items, such as the automobile, airplanes, personal computers, the Internet, and social media; and of course the worldwide spread of democracy. With all these accomplishments, personal wealth, human knowledge, and freedom have exploded to a historic level, even with the recent global economic downturn.

Unfortunately, as a result of this wealth and comfort, an increasing numbers of Americans now believe all the accomplishments of this great nation were based on the ingenuity of the people and have forgotten the fundamental role God played. God's role in making America great is being increasingly questioned and denied, and He is no longer viewed by many as relevant. This cycle is one that has been seen repeatedly in many of the great nations in history after the nations are blessed and become prosperous as a result of following God. After one or more generations, the people, in their blessed state, forget about God's role in their success and no longer feel the need for Him. They believe it was the result of their own doing, and they ultimately lose the benefits that come from being under God's cover.

God is smarter than you and I

All the nations that have followed this pattern have typically gone into decline—and their people along with them. The truth is this: a life lived without God on earth will ultimately lead to emptiness and futility and one destined for eternal darkness and eternal separation from Him in the world after.[1] No amount of human ingenuity can approach the level of knowledge of the one who created the universe.

Consequences of a Life apart from God

What have been the consequences of pushing God aside in America? Marriage failures are at such an all-time high that almost half the population does not even bother going through with it anymore. Suicide rates are high, especially among the elderly[2]. Teenagers face overwhelming pressure from peers and the media to engage in premarital sex and other behaviors that would not have been considered remotely acceptable in recent history. Addictions to alcohol, drugs, pornography, and gambling are commonplace and have deprived many of the productive lives God intended for them. Credit card debt and personal bankruptcies peaked at a historic high binding men and women in a new kind of "slavery" until new stricter preventive laws were introduced in 2005[3]. Selfishness and self-aggrandizement are now portrayed in all the mainstream and alternative media as if they were honorable standards and attitudes to be desired. At the same time, the number of Americans living in constant fear of attack appears to have surged with a record 300 million firearms estimated to be in circulation in 2012 compared to 200 million in 1995 - a 50% increase[4].

During the same period, the US population only grew by 20%. There are now almost as many firearms in circulation as there are people. It is almost as if a segment of Americans have replaced the slogan of "In God We Trust" with a new one of "In Guns We Trust." In 2012 especially, the nation was repeatedly horrified with the rash of mass shootings and massacres of innocent little children and of adults in Oakland, California; Minneapolis, Minnesota; Aurora, Colorado; Oak Creek, Wisconsin and Sandy Hook, Connecticut among others.

Why the grim statistics? They are a direct consequence of you and me trying to go through life without a close relationship with the one who designed us. But there is a better way. Bear with me while I reintroduce the well-known history concerning the beginning of God's relation to man.

The Cost of Your Sin Is Separation from God

In the beginning of the world, when God created Adam, the first human being, God gave him a beautiful home within the Garden of Eden and freely communicated with him on a daily basis. God spoke directly with Adam and Eve, the partner He later gave Adam (Genesis 2:4–25). There was no need for intermediaries, priests, or prophets to interpret or determine God's intention for either Adam or Eve's lives. God was right there, always available to them in a harmonious relationship. It was always God's intent to live with you and me in this way, directly communicating His love and presence with us daily. That is why He made us in His own image and gave us complete authority over every living creature and every plant and seed on earth (Genesis 1:26–30).

God created us out of love to serve Him and to reign as His ambassadors on earth. He desires to have a close relationship with us, just as every parent seeks a close relationship with his or her children. However, there was an early falling out between God and man as a result of Adam and Eve's disobedience—a separation that is responsible even today for the current state of our relationship with our Creator. It explains why many people cannot feel or find the true God or have the full relationship He desires for them. Many end up chasing after false gods and material security blankets that inevitably lead to emptiness.

God created you out of love

This falling out stemmed from Adam and Eve disregarding God's command by eating the fruit from the only tree in the Garden of Eden that God had specifically forbidden them from eating. There were several trees in the garden of Eden, and all were freely available—except for the fruits from one tree known as the Tree of the Knowledge of Good and Evil (Genesis 2:8–17). However, Adam and Eve, under subtle deception from satan—God's enemy, who was disguised as a serpent—could not resist the temptation to eat the fruit in direct disobedience to God.

> Now the serpent was more crafty than any of the wild animals the LORD God had made. He said to the woman, "Did God really say, 'You must not eat from any tree in the garden'?" The woman said to the serpent, "We may eat fruit from the trees in the garden, but God did say, 'You must not eat fruit from the tree that is in the middle of the garden, and you must not touch it, or you will die.'" "You will not certainly die," the serpent said to the woman. "For God knows that when you eat from it your eyes will be opened, and you will be like God, knowing good and evil." When the woman saw that the fruit of the tree was good for food and pleasing to the eye, and also desirable for gaining wisdom, she took some and ate it. She also gave some to her husband, who was with her, and he ate it. Then the eyes of both of them were opened, and they realized they were naked; so they sewed fig leaves together and made coverings for themselves. (Genesis 3:1–7, NIV 2011)

The Trickster and His Deception

This first rebellion on earth and all subsequent sin have been orchestrated by satan. Satan is a fallen angel who was kicked out of heaven for seeking to take over God's position.[5] Since then, he has been continuously opposing God on Earth, primarily by using counterfeit methods and arguments to entice men and women to disregard their unique and preeminent role as God's ambassadors and rulers of all of His creation. *Subtle and big deceptions are the hallmark of how satan works in trying to convince people they do not need to know or obey God.* Instead, satan convinces people they can be equal to God or that God does not even exist.

Satan masquerades as an angel of light

4

Satan, often masquerading as an angel of light, makes disobedience to God so attractive that it becomes a perilous snare to the unsuspecting.[6] As a result of this deception, generations of men and women have abandoned a relationship with their Creator, instead foolishly choosing to disobey or disavow God or to grasp at equality with Him—the person who owns everything and has always offered it all freely to them. Adam and Eve's act of disobedience to God should have resulted in eternal condemnation and death for all of humanity, were it not for God's grace (His unwarranted act of favor) toward humanity. Although God did not destroy man, the result of this original disobedience was separation; God and man could no longer freely coexist. This separation has led to mankind living without the blueprint from which the Creator made him, much like a human body functioning without its genetic code.

God will never give up on you

For this reason, millions of people struggle everyday with problems God never intended for them to be burdened with. Many live in complete denial of God; others acknowledge He exists but cannot trust Him to handle the very complicated problems they believe are unique to themselves. Some people believe in God but do not really take seriously what He says or think that any of His promises and miracles detailed in the Bible apply to them. Others want total control over their own lives and are convinced that giving themselves over to God would translate to a loss of freedom that would equate to death. Many others are just deep in sin and are either so hooked on the sin they cannot even imagine giving up its pleasures or feel God would only condemn them if they turned to Him, so they reckon, "Why bother?" As a result, millions cycle repeatedly on their life journeys, but their journeys never seem to get them where they want to go, and emptiness is often the only reward. Why? The simple answer is this: separation from God is equivalent to being a walking dead man or woman. The cost of your sin is continuous separation from Him, which leads to unnecessary pain and turmoil while you are alive and an eternity spent in darkness and torment after you die. Is this your situation?

A Close Relationship with God Is Possible

The irony is that God loves you so much, in spite of your sinful nature, that even when you do not acknowledge His existence, He is in no hurry to condemn you—or, for that matter, to condemn any nation, no matter how far it has drifted from Him.[7] In fact, He has never given up on having a close relationship with you, and as long as you are alive, He will never give up on you. God's love for you is so deep, wide, and unending that He has chosen to tolerate and overlook your sins as long as is necessary for you to come back to Him.

God has always had a plan to "buy back" all those who want to restore the fractured relationship with Him. His love is so strong for you and me that He freely gave up His only Son, Jesus Christ, to die for us so as to deliver us from the consequences of our rebellion, enabling us to reestablish the relationship that He always intended for us. This is the good news for everyone! Learning to develop and nurture a close relationship with God will transform your life and give you such peace and joy that no amount of personal trials or challenges can permanently overwhelm you. You cannot accomplish this fulfillment by doing things your own way—climbing corporate ladders, running after "obvious opportunities," seeking fame and fortune, or engaging in hedonistic or other behaviors that may initially seem to give freedom.

In order to understand how to develop this close relationship, we will explore in this book some specific clues God gave in His instructions for the construction of the Tabernacle and the temple during a time when He resided in a very close and direct relationship with the Jewish people who He originally chose to restore relations to humanity. These instructions were a mirror of how God wants you and me to relate to Him in our physical and spiritual beings and were preludes to how we can accomplish the close relationship He desires to have with us. Over the next few chapters, through the design of the structures and contents of the Tabernacle and temple, we will explore how to gain a close relationship with God.

Pray this prayer with me:

Dear Lord, I would like to have a positively transforming and close relationship with You. Help me to begin to understand the blueprints You have designated for my life and how I can be fully built based on these blueprints. I thank You for the privilege of a second chance. Amen.

1. Deuteronomy Chapter 28.
2. La Vecchia, C, Lucchini, F and Levi, F. Worldwide trends in suicide mortality, 1955-1989. Acta Psychiatrica Scandinavica 1994;90:53-64
3. Mishel, Lawrence, Jared Bell1stein, and Sylvia Allegretto, *The State of Working America* 2006/2007. An Economic Policy Institute Book. Ithaca, N.Y.: ILR Press, an imprint of Cornell University Press, 2007
4. http://www.motherjones.com/politics/2012/09/mass-shootings-investigation
5. Revelation 12:7–12; Isaiah 14:12–15.
6. 2 Corinthians 11:14.
7. 2 Chronicles 7:14.

CHAPTER 2

Where Does God Live?

(Session 1b)

The Christian is in a different position from other people who are trying to do good. The Christian thinks any good he does come from the Christ-life inside him. He does not think God will love us because we are good but that God will make us good because He loves us.—C. S. Lewis, British Christian theologian and author (1898-1963).

The God who made the world and everything in it is the Lord of heaven and earth and does not live in temples built by human hands.—Acts 17:24 (NIV 2011)

The verse above from the book of Acts in the New Testament of the Bible is a key to understanding where God does not "live." If you grasp this, it could be the first step toward enabling you to develop the life-transforming relationship He has planned for you from the time He made you. Perhaps you believe like many people do that the only place God lives is in churches on Sunday mornings. You may also be from a background that takes comfort in bowing down to idols carved by human hands and worshipping them as gods.

In the profoundly insightful verse above, the apostle Paul reminded us more than two thousand years ago that God does not live in houses built by human hands! Even as the world has recently witnessed the growth and explosion of different types of churches, including "mega-churches," home churches, Internet churches, and all kinds of other new ideas for churches, we are reminded that God does not actually *live* in any of them. Clearly, churches are an integral and important part of Christian worship and God's manifest presence can be found in many churches around the world today, whether they are simple buildings or magnificent cathedrals. Churches are an important and critical part of God's means of touching believers and building Christians as a body to unleash His power into the world.

However, God will only set up a temporary presence that is very contingent on the conditions and hearts of the people who form the body of the church. No amount of human effort or detail could entice Him to set up His *permanent* abode in any church or temple built by human hands. That was never His intent and never will be. *So then where does God live?*

The Jewish Tabernacle and Temple Were Models of God's Preferred Temple—You

You are God's temple, created and designed by Him to live and interact with you. However, you control God's ability to dwell and manifest in you conditional on how much you are willing to totally yield to Him in obedience.

There is a connection between the original Jewish Tabernacle (a large mobile tent of worship) and temple (a more permanent building on Mount Zion (also known as the Temple Mount or Mount Moriah in Jerusalem) and you. All were similarly designed to serve as dwelling places for God, the former two as temporary sites, while you were always the one He intended to be His permanent abode. Thousands of years ago, God adopted the Jewish people to draw the rest of humanity back to Himself and again live closely with man as was His original intent. Rather than remaining remote and aloof following the fall of Adam and Eve, God used the Jewish people to reintroduce Himself as the Creator to a world that had long forgotten Him and was blindly living apart from Him. He gave them instructions for building the two structures, initially the Tabernacle and later the temple, which were replicas of the place where He resides in heaven. Both the Tabernacle and the temple were places of worship and sacrifice dedicated to God. During these golden years for the Jews, "the Glory of the Lord" (God's Spirit) was physically present with them first in the Tabernacle as

You are God's preferred temple!

they moved from place to place and then in the temple once they became more settled in their permanent land (Exodus 35–40; 2 Chronicles 2–7).

God's presence with the Jewish people within the Tabernacle and temple meant substantial blessings to them in the form of provisions for all their needs, protection from their enemies, and the envy of their neighbors. However, "His Glory" was present and only accessible under very strict conditions, which He worked out with His people in an original covenant. The covenant simply said that if they followed His commandments and obeyed Him, God would make the Jews the light and salt of the earth, and they would possess the earth. "Now if you obey me fully and keep my covenant, then out of all nations you will be my treasured possession. Although the whole earth is mine, you will be for me a kingdom of priests and a holy nation."[1] Similarly, we will see that when God takes residence in you, the manifestations of His blessings will be numerous, but it is also conditional on your obedience and yielding yourself to Him.

"If you listen carefully to what (my angel) says and do all that I say, I will be an enemy to your enemies and will oppose those who oppose you … worship the Lord your God and His blessing will be on your food and water. I will take away sickness from among you, and none will miscarry or be barren in your land. I will give you a full life span" (Exodus 23:22, 25–26). God, in choosing the Jews to draw the whole of humanity back to Himself, raised many great Jewish leaders during history specifically for this purpose. To one such great Jewish leader, Moses, God gave precise instructions how the Tabernacle should be built.

Just more than four hundred years later,[2] He gave instructions to another great leader, King David, about how to build His residence in the more permanent temple format, which replaced the Tabernacle in Jerusalem once the Jews were settled into the land God had promised them. God was so concerned about ensuring His desired outcome of enriching His relationship with the Jews that He gave detailed and specific instructions regarding both the contents and activities of both places of worship, including which materials to use, the exact dimensions and architecture, who could enter into His presence, and under what conditions they could do so.

While King David worshipped God in the Tabernacle, he was not permitted by God to build the temple, so he passed on the specific instructions given from God to his son, King Solomon, who completed the task. King Solomon, even as He was building it, recognized that God was bigger and greater than the temple being built by his human hands and could not be contained in it. This is what the king had to say: "But will God really dwell on earth with men? The heavens, even the highest heavens, cannot contain you. How much less this temple I have built" (2 Chronicles 6:18).

God used these structures as a glimpse for all humanity into how He chose to have us develop a relationship with Him.[3] His instructions were somewhat of a blueprint for future generations of believers seeking to draw close to Him. We will discuss in more detail the overall design of the Tabernacle and the temple in the next chapter.

God's Been Thinking about You for a Long Time!

Let us explore for a moment the statement by one of God's most ardent followers in the Bible, the apostle Paul, about the relationship between you and God's Spirit: "Don't you know that you yourselves are God's temple and that God's Spirit lives in you?" (1 Corinthians 3:16)

Think about this. You are being told by Paul that when you become a follower of Christ, you become God's temple and that His Spirit (who is in fact, God Himself) lives in you! (If you are not a follower of Jesus, you will be shown how and receive the opportunity to become one in the next chapter.)

God's always thinking of you

Amazingly, God was thinking of you when He designed the original manmade structures because the sole purpose for His creating you was so that He could live within you and have a close relationship with you, as much as you would allow Him to through His Holy Spirit. Your body as the desired temple of God is designed along the same model as He designed the Tabernacle and the temple. The conditions God demanded of the Jews in the Tabernacle and temple in order for Him to have a close and fruitful dwelling with them are the same conditions that He demands today in order to have a close and fruitful dwelling within you, except that He has made it much easier for you to fulfill these conditions. These are the same conditions that exist in heaven, where the omnipresent God also lives. God's conditions for living among His people in the Tabernacle and the temple were freedom giving and revolved around three principles: *love for Him, faith in Him, and obedience to His commandments.*

In contrast to what your human instincts may tell you, God's primary purpose for every rule and command He gives are borne out of a great love for you. His desire is to stop you from experiencing all the negative consequences of disobedience that He as your Creator knows will come.[4] Contrary to human thinking, the results of obeying God are freedom from the bondage of sin and the devastation it brings, along with a resultant inner joy and peace as you gain the unparalleled pleasure of a close relationship with Him. As long as the Jews were faithful and obedient to God's covenant with them, according to God's plan they flourished, subdued their enemies, and lived in peace and prosperity. Unfortunately, as is the case with all humanity, disobedience and sin ultimately showed up among them, with leader after leader of Israel ignoring God's plans and commands.

Ultimately, there was even deliberate desecration of God's temple, similar to how many people desecrate their own bodily temples today through all kinds of hedonistic behaviors. After many generations of continuous disobedience, even with His patience and love, the defilement of the Jewish temple and ultimately of God became so great that God, in spite of His great desire, could no longer reside in the temple.[5] "Then the glory of the Lord departed from over the threshold of the temple and stopped above the cherubim" (Ezekiel 10:18). With God no longer present, the history of the Jews became one of frequent calamity, bondage, and despair.

Jesus died for you

Without God in your life, you too are destined to the same result of continued bondage to the enemy, and you may already be feeling the consequences or the precursors to the consequences of such a life. When you open the door to desecration of your temple, God's temple, you are setting the stage for devastation. Understand that there is no shred of condescension or haughtiness in this statement. Every one of us human beings has sinned in some fashion in this way and has fallen short of the glory of God, and by God's law we all deserve eternal separation from Him as a result. However, because of His great love, God sent His only son, Jesus Christ, who was without sin, to earth to die in exchange for you and me so that whoever believes in Jesus Christ would not die but have everlasting life. This is the most wonderful news for you today. Adam's sin led to your separation from God. Jesus Christ bridged the gap of separation between you and God, allowing God to come and reside in you!

> Consequently, you are no longer foreigners and strangers but fellow citizens with God's people and also members of His household, built on the foundation of the apostles and prophets, with Christ Jesus himself as the chief cornerstone. In Him the whole building is joined together and rises to become a holy temple in the Lord. And in Him you too are being built together to become a dwelling in which God lives by His Spirit. (Ephesians 2:19–22, NIV 2011)

This means that you can take God's Spirit with you everywhere you go! While churches are important and are key parts of Christian fellowship, growth, and are places of worshipping God, you do not need to wait before you can meet God in church—you carry Him everywhere you go in your body.

Once you accept Jesus Christ as your Savior (the mediator between you and God), God's Spirit dwells in you. If you cooperate with Him, He will overhaul your life in a beautiful way. His Spirit can calm the raging storms of your life so you will have peace even in the midst of any chaos. He will provide an oasis of peace and security for you in the midst of black thunderstorms that threaten to engulf everything you have put your hope on. He will guide you in the path of righteousness, for His name's sake. You will be under His protection, such that no enemy can get at you. As long as you cooperate with God, you will flourish even when the odds are extraordinarily stacked against you.

On the other hand, if you repeatedly continue to ignore God or deliberately and knowingly oppose Him with your body and mind, even if as a Christian you have His Spirit dwelling in you, God will eventually turn away His Spirit and ultimately lift Himself away from you. When this happens, you will appreciate and experience—in a bad way—the difference between peace and chaos, between day and night, between light and darkness, between order and disorder, and between being a child of God or living like you are a slave of satan.

You will discover that when you prepare and care for yourself as a temple the way Moses, Joshua, and David cared for and respected the Jewish Tabernacle and the temple as God's dwelling places, your life will be transformed and you will experience joy, love, and peace that no relationship other than God in your life could give you. This is God's plan for you, and He is ready to help you get there. In the next chapter, we will learn how to accomplish the first prerequisite for accomplishing this goal—receiving the free and unconditional gift of Jesus Christ as your savior.

Pray this Prayer with Me:

Dear God, I strongly desire and hunger for the type of relationship with You that will enable You to come and reside comfortably within me. Please open all the doors of my heart and mind so that I can be ready to fully welcome You, and remove any obstacles or barriers that will stop me from fully becoming Your preferred temple. Amen.

Questions to Ponder

- What are some of the blessings and consequences you can think of for a nation to follow God?
- What are some blessings you can think of for having God in your life?
- What are the consequences of turning away from God?
- Can you think of areas in which you have turned away from God?
- What have been the consequences of your turning back from God in this area?
- Is it too late for anybody to turn back to God?
  - See Joel 2:13

Pray for America and for everyone there who has turned away from God. Pray for a revival in this great nation so that people will turn back to Him and that America will always be great.

Pray for the president and his cabinet, the Senate and the House, the two major parties, and those in authority over us that they will turn to God and use Him as the guide for making decisions that will bless America, and that ultimately will bless you and me.

Pray for yourself that God will show you how to remain steadfast in Him and help you to learn to never turn your back on your Creator.

1. Exodus 19:5.
2. 1 Kings 6.
3. Hebrews 8:2, 5; 9:24.
4. Deuteronomy 28; Galatians 6:7–8.
5. Ezekiel 8–9.

CHAPTER 3

Your Current Life Is an Audition for Where You Will Spend Eternity

(Session 2a)

The blood of Jesus washes away our past and the name of Jesus opens up our future.—Jesse Duplantis, American evangelical Christian minister.

You also, like living stones, are being built into a spiritual house to be a holy priesthood, offering spiritual sacrifices acceptable to God through Jesus Christ.—1 Peter 2:5

God's Perfect House

God, in designing the Jewish temple, was looking forward to the time after Christ when He would no longer need to live separately from His creation but would have an intimate relationship with you and me. The best way to have a close and wonderful relationship with God is to prepare yourself to becoming the perfect temple (home) for Him to reside in. Back to our key verse: "Do you not know that your body is a temple of the Holy Spirit, who is in you, whom you have received from God?" (1 Corinthians 6:19)

Jesus himself noted that the kingdom of God is within you[1] and described His own body as a temple: "Jesus answered them, 'Destroy this temple, and I will raise it again in three days.' The Jews replied, 'It has taken forty-six years to build this temple,[2] and You are going to raise it in three days?' *But the temple He had spoken of was His body. After He was raised* from the dead, His disciples recalled what He had said. Then they believed the scripture and the words that Jesus had spoken" (John 2:19–22; emphasis added).Jesus understood with great clarity that everywhere He went, He took the temple of God with Him. As a result, He was in constant communication with God and able to be totally obedient to Him and fulfill His destiny for eternity.

The perfect home for God is one that is built and kept in total obedience to God's explicit instructions. God had a reason for designing the Jewish Tabernacle the way He did; it was a replica and a "shadow" of what He has created in heaven and a precursor to your becoming His temple. Jesus is now our high priest in the real tabernacle in heaven: "Now the main point of what we are saying is this: We do have such a high priest, who sat down at the right hand of the throne of the majesty in heaven, and who serves in the sanctuary, the true tabernacle set up by the Lord, not by a mere human being. Every high priest is appointed to offer both gifts and sacrifices, and so it was necessary for this one also to have something to offer. If He were on earth, He would not be a priest, for there are already priests who offer the gifts prescribed by the law. *They serve at a sanctuary that is a copy and shadow of what is in heaven.* This is why Moses was warned when he was about to build the tabernacle: 'See to it that you make everything according to the pattern shown you on the mountain'" (Hebrews 8:1–5, NIV, 2011, emphasis added).

God has a blueprint for your life

The Blueprint for the House of God

God gave Moses and then King David the blueprints for how to build His Tabernacle and His temple, and He came and lived in each structure due to their obedience to His instructions. Similarly, building yourself and your life following God's blueprint for preparing yourself as the temple for the Holy Spirit is what this book is all about. Then God can come and live in you. This blueprint can be found in the written Word of God, the Bible. "And in Him you too are being built together to become a dwelling in which God lives by His Spirit" (Ephesians 2:22).

The following chapters of this book are devoted to examining and learning from this blueprint. However, there is some business to take care of before then.

God Is Searching for You!

God is searching for you! He is knocking on your door and wants to have a close relationship with you. "Here I am! I stand at the door and knock. If anyone hears my voice and opens the door, I will come in and eat with that person, and they with me" (Revelation 3:20, NIV 2011).

God wants nothing more than to have a close relationship with you through His Holy Spirit. This is the explicit purpose for which you were created. You were made in God's image to be His hands and feet and close friend on earth, and God desires to have a continuous kinship with you, not one in which He is separated from you by physical barriers. The sole precondition for this close relationship with God is recognition of your sinful nature and acceptance that God gave up His one and only son, Jesus Christ, to die so that you could become His adopted son.

In Christ, no sin is unpardonable

Unfortunately, as noted in the first chapter, as a result of the fall of man during the time of Adam and Eve, sin entered the world. Your sins as a human being now separate you from God. "For all have sinned and fall short of the glory of God" (Romans 3:23). As a result of your sin, what you deserve is death, but God has always had another plan, a better plan for you—a plan of redemption through Jesus Christ.

"For the wages of sin is death, but the gift of God is eternal life in Christ Jesus our Lord" (Romans 6:23).

Before Jesus came to the world, animals such as rams, goats, and lambs had to be sacrificed in place of sinful men and women so God could spare their lives.[3] These animals always had to be physically pure, without any defects, symbolizing God's purity and the understanding that symbolically, only the blood of physically pure animals could be shed to atone for human sin. However, God instituted this form of atonement only temporarily until He could send Jesus to replace the need for animal sacrifices once and for all. Jesus Christ was sent and lived as a man on earth more than two thousand years ago and is the only man who has ever been credited with having been pure (without sin). He totally removed the need for sacrifices of lambs by Himself becoming the "Lamb of God" and shedding His blood for you and me. He was perfect (without any moral or spiritual defects) in His nature and yet chose to die as a sacrificial lamb on a cross for crimes

He did not commit.[4] He also chose to forgive those (including you and me) whose sins condemned Him to death.

After He was killed, God raised Jesus from the dead, and as a reward for His sacrifice and obedience on earth, all authority in heaven and on earth has been given to Him. "Therefore God exalted him to the highest place and gave Him the name that is above every name, that at the name of Jesus every knee should bow, in heaven and on earth and under the earth, and every tongue acknowledge that Jesus Christ is Lord, to the glory of God the Father" (Philippians 2:9–11, NIV 2011).

He is called the Savior of the world because those who believe in Him no longer have to worry about eternal condemnation to hell and separation from God. God effectively replaced the law that says if you sin, you must die (*the law of sin and death*), with a superior law (*the law of life in Christ Jesus*), in which your sins are forgiven if you believe in Jesus. "Therefore, there is now no condemnation for those who are in Christ Jesus, because through Christ Jesus the law of the Spirit who gives life has set you free from the law of sin and death" (Romans 8:1–2, NIV 2011).

The average human life expectancy is about eighty years. If you live more than one hundred years, you will be considered to have lived an extraordinarily long life by earthly standards. Consider this then: after life on earth ends, life in eternity begins. Eternity goes on year after year after year—there is no end to it. One hundred years spent on earth does not even register as a second spent in eternity.

The implications of this reality should be obvious to anyone. Your current life is only an audition that determines where and how you will spend eternity. God is clear that there are only two places where you will spend eternity: either a beautiful place built with precious stones where you will forever be in the presence of a beautiful and kind God, or a place of constant torment of blazing fire and torture where you will be forever separated from God.[5] The choice is yours to make. A life lived in sin can only lead to death and eternal separation from God.

However, the greatest news is that Jesus has earned the authority to determine who enters into God's presence in heaven, and He is the lens through which God examines you and me. If you accept Jesus Christ as your Savior and choose to obey His commandments (with help from His Holy Spirit), God no longer sees your sins because He only sees you through Jesus, who is perfect and pure, and thus God receives you as perfect and pure. This offer is open to anyone regardless of your religious background, race, gender, ethnicity, or how "bad" the life you have already lived may have been. The gift of Jesus Christ is not exclusive to anyone. If you do not accept Christ, then God continues to see you exactly as you are, as we all are as human beings since the fall of Adam—a hopelessly doomed sinner. When you accept Christ, you become born again and a member of God's immediate family. Since God is the king, you become royalty, God's royal priest!

"But you are a chosen people, a royal priesthood, a holy nation, a people belonging to God, that you may declare the praises of Him *who called you out of darkness into His wonderful light*" (1 Peter 2:9–10, emphasis added).

"This is the message which we have heard from Him and declare to you, that God is light and in Him is no darkness at all. If we say that we have fellowship with Him, and walk in darkness, we lie and do not practice the truth. But if we walk in the light as He is in the light, we have fellowship with one another, and *the blood of Jesus Christ cleanses us from all sin.* If we say we have no sin, we deceive ourselves, and the truth is not in us. If we confess our sins, He is faithful and just to forgive us our sins and to cleanse us from all unrighteousness. If we say we have not sinned, we make Him a liar, and His word is not in us." 1 John 1:5-10, emphasis added)

When you receive Christ, you will no longer be in darkness because the light of Jesus Christ and the Holy Spirit comes and lives within you. There is no sin you have committed, no matter how heinous or grave, that is too difficult for God to forgive. He loves you exactly as you are, but you must receive the gift that He is offering to you in order to become a temple suitable for His Spirit to live in. If you have never had the opportunity to receive this gift, I offer you this opportunity now. Take it so you can become a temple of the living God.

Pray This Prayer with Me:

Dear God, I confess I am a sinner and that the punishment I deserve is eternal separation from You. I thank You for the free gift of Your son, Jesus Christ, whom You sacrificed to bear the punishment for my sins so I will not personally need to suffer eternal death if I receive this precious gift of salvation. I thank You that You have chosen to adopt me into Your family with all the full rights associated with Your kingdom when what I deserved was condemnation. I am eternally grateful to You for this and want to act in accordance with Your rules for being a member of Your royal family. I now receive this gift freely and ask Jesus to become my Lord and Savior. I seek to better understand what it means to be Your temple and how I can establish myself as a desirable place of abode for Your Holy Spirit. Help me to set up the conditions of transformation of my life into one where I have an inseparable relationship with You. Help me to learn how to use the light of Your Holy Spirit resident within me to live an extraordinary life. Amen.

If you have prayed this type of prayer for the very first time, congratulations! There is rejoicing in heaven as a result of your confession of faith. Listen to the words of Jesus Himself: "I tell you that in the same way there will be more rejoicing in heaven over one sinner who repents than over ninety-nine righteous persons who do not need to repent" (Luke 15:7).

All your sins are now forgiven, and you are a new creature in Christ and a member of His family. Now I strongly encourage you to join a local Bible-believing church where you can learn more about God and meet other members of God's family who can encourage you in your new walk of faith and where you can learn more about God's plans for your life and receive water baptism as a public confession of your faith in Jesus Christ.[6]

In the following chapters we will explore how you can walk in the light of Christ and use it to live an extraordinary life.

1. Luke 17:21.
2. The first temple (King Solomon's Temple) was destroyed in 586 BCE by the Babylonians, who captured Jerusalem and exiled the Jews to Babylon. The temple referred to here is the second temple, which existed between 516 BCE and 70 CE. The original temple took seven years to complete.
3. Leviticus 1–8; Hebrews 9:19–22.
4. Hebrews 9:11–15.
5. Revelation 21:10–21; 20:10, 14–15.
6. Acts 2:38.

CHAPTER 4

Design of the Jewish Tabernacle and Temple in Relation to You

(Session 2b)

Don't you know that you yourselves are God's temple and that God's Spirit lives in you? —1 Corinthians 3:16

The Overall Design of the Jewish Tabernacle and Temple

In this chapter, we will begin to examine in greater detail the structures of the Tabernacle and temple and how they relate to you as a temple of God.

Both the Tabernacle and temple were divided into three main areas: an *outer courtyard*, a middle room (or *Holy Place*), and an inner room—known as the *Most Holy Place* or the *Holy of Holies*.[1] (See Figure A, Tabernacle as example) Each inner room was progressively limited in terms of access by the public. The outer court was where all the Jews gathered regularly to worship God and where the sacrifice of animals to God occurred. The Holy Place was a place of continual worship and sacrifice to God with entrance limited only to the priests (the Levites). The Most Holy Place was where the "Glory of God" or God's Spirit resided and was restricted to entry only once every year by a single "high priest." Due to its sacredness, the Most Holy Place was also separated from the other two chambers by a large curtain, or "veil," in the Tabernacle, and by a large door in King Solomon's Temple.[2]

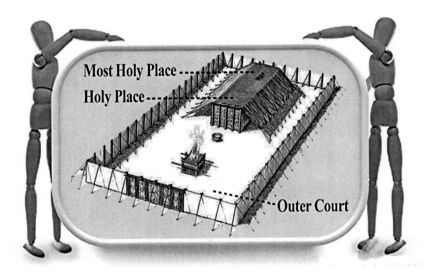

Figure A: Design of the Jewish Tabernacle

You Also Are Designed with Three Parts as God's Temple

Similar to the Tabernacle and temple, you as a person are analogous in that you consist also of three compartments: your body (flesh), soul (mind), and spirit, each with its own purpose. The outer court of the Tabernacle and temple is analogous to your flesh. The Holy Place is equivalent is your mind (or soul) and your Most Holy Place is a hidden place within you (sometimes referred to as your "heart") where your spirit resides and where the Holy Spirit comes and dwells when you give your life to Christ. (Figure B)

You're made of flesh, soul and spirit

There are several references to each of these compartments of your temple in the Bible: "For the word of God is alive and active. Sharper than any double-edged sword, it penetrates even to dividing soul and spirit, joints and marrow [body]; it judges the thoughts and attitudes of the heart" (Hebrews 4:12; NIV 2011); "May your whole spirit, soul, and body be kept blameless at the coming of our Lord Jesus Christ" (1 Thessalonians 5:23); and "My body is clothed with worms and scabs, my skin [flesh] is broken and festering ... therefore I will not keep silent; I will speak out in the anguish of my spirit, I will complain in the bitterness of my soul" (Job 7:5, 11).

As we will learn later, while the soul and mind are closely interrelated, your soul incorporates more than your mind. However, for the purposes of simplicity, the mind and soul will be mostly used interchangeably in this book unless the point being made demands a separation of the two. Your body (outer court) and spirit (Most Holy Place) are separated from each other by your soul (Holy Place) and are constantly in conflict with each other over control of your soul. This conflict will be explored in detail in the following chapters, but we will first examine some aspects of the overall design of the Tabernacle and temple and how they relate to your body, spirit, and soul.

There's a battle for your soul

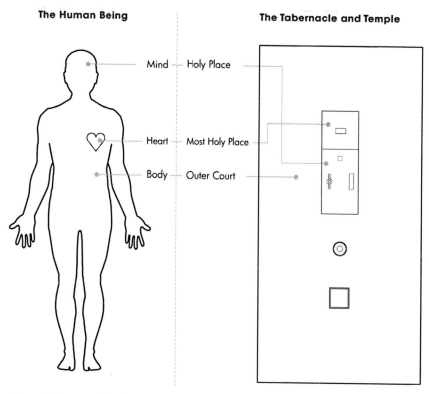

The Human Being

The Tabernacle and Temple

Mind — Holy Place

Heart — Most Holy Place

Body — Outer Court

Figure B: Corresponding Compartments of Human Beings and the Jewish Tabernacle and temple

The Jewish Tabernacle

The main part of the Tabernacle (the part housing the Holy Place and the Most Holy Place) was a tent-like structure covered with a combination of finely twisted linen and blue, scarlet, and purple yarn with angels (cherubim) woven into it[3] (see Figure A). It was a simple yet elegant structure that inspired reverence in all those who came near it. The carefully chosen colors of the tent symbolized *the deity, atoning power, and royalty of God*, concepts we will explore in greater detail in chapter 13.

The walls of the Tabernacle measured 45 feet long by 15 feet wide and were made of acacia wood boards and crossbars fitted together and overlaid with gold. The coverings over the roof and sides consisted of four layers of very durable materials. The first three outer layers consisted of a plain but very durable leather curtain on top followed by an inner layer of red dyed rams skins, and a third layer of tough goat's hair underneath. The innermost fourth layer (directly covering the walls) was made of finely twisted linen that was embroidered with figures of cherubim. The four layers of curtains were pinned to the ground with hooks and clasps. The tent was separated from a surrounding 7 foot high fence by a courtyard (outer courtyard) that measured 150 feet by 75 feet (Figure A).

Symbolism of the Tabernacle Roof Layers

Each layer of the roof symbolized an aspect of the Jews' relationship with God. The plain outermost layer of durable leather symbolized God's *protection* over them. While not very attractive on the outside, the leather protected against rain, sunlight, storms, and the heat of the desert.

Similarly, with God in your temple, God promises to protect you from all the uncomfortable elements and storms of life that constantly threaten you. "The LORD watches over you—the LORD is your shade at your right hand; the sun will not harm you by day, nor the moon by night. The LORD will keep you from all harm—He will watch over your life; the LORD will watch over your coming and going both now and forevermore" (Psalm 121:5–8).

The second layer, ram's skin, was dyed red and was symbolic of the *substitution* of ram's blood for the blood needed to atone for the sins of the Jews. Later on, Jesus Christ, the only sinless man and Messiah, shed His own blood once and for all as atonement for all sinners, including you and me, such that there would be no need for further sacrifice of blood for those who believe in Him.

The next layer of goat's hair was symbolic of the goat being used as a *sin offering*[4] and a means of *provision*.[5] Goats were an important source of meat and nutrition for the Jews and their abundance was associated with wealth. Similar to rams, goats were also sacrificed to atone for the sins of the Jews. As God's temple, Jesus Christ has become a sin offering for you, and He is the greatest source of provision you can ever have in this life.

God promises to protect you

The final layer closest to the internal structures of the Tabernacle consisted of fine linen embroidered with images of cherubim and symbolized the *kingship* of God (fine linen) and His *protection* (cherubim). As the material closest to the dwelling place of God, the linen had to be of the finest material as fit for royalty and the cherubim represented a different type of God's protection over the Tabernacle—that of His angels. Similarly, as a temple for the Most High God and an adopted member of His kingdom, you are also part of His royal family and are a royal priest. Furthermore, you also have the benefit of His angels to serve you, as we will discuss in greater detail in chapter 11.

The Tabernacle Gate

The fence surrounding the outer court of the Tabernacle was made up of linen held up by several pillars made of acacia wood. There was only one entrance through the fence, a thirty-foot wide gate made up of a curtain of finely twisted linen of blue, scarlet, and purple yarn located in the center of the east end, so that worshippers always faced the west upon entering. This was in stark contrast to most other religions during the time of the Tabernacle where the worshippers typically faced the east to worship their pagan gods. This was particularly true for sun worshippers who faced the east where the sun rose each day. The location of the gate and the direction it faced in relation to the Tabernacle symbolized the desire of the Jewish people to turn their backs on other gods and face the only true God. Similarly, when you turn your temple over to the living God, you make a conscious decision to turn your back on other gods in your life. The Tabernacle's single gate also symbolized that there is only one way to God. Jesus Christ, the long-awaited Messiah, has become this gate for everyone seeking to find God.

"Jesus answered, 'I am the way and the truth and the life. No one comes to the Father except through me'" (John14:6). The location and single entry point into the Tabernacle gate was a declaration by God of His willingness to let everyone into His presence who so desires, but also that those choosing to come to Him need to do so by the gate He has provided. Today, that gate is Jesus Christ. If you put your trust in Him, He will willingly bring you into the presence of God. We will discuss the contents of the Tabernacle in the following chapters, but first let us turn to the structure that ultimately replaced the Tabernacle.

The Temple Built by King Solomon

The temple conceived and planned by King David, but built by his son, King Solomon, as a permanent replacement for the Tabernacle was a magnificent work of architecture, considered one of the marvels of its time. (Figure C) It took seven years and massive investment of human and natural resources to complete the building. Here are the instructions King David gave his son in relation to the building of the temple:

> I have taken great pains to provide for the temple of the LORD a hundred thousand talents of gold, a million talents of silver, quantities of bronze and iron too great to be weighed, and wood and stone. And you may add to them. You have many workers: stonecutters, masons, and carpenters, as well as those skilled in every kind of work in gold and silver, bronze and iron—craftsmen beyond number. Now begin the work, and the LORD be with you." (1 Chronicles 22:14–16)

It is worth pausing to consider the immensity of the treasures and human labor used in building the temple. King David alone provided one hundred thousand talents of gold (more than three thousand tons) and one million talents of silver (more than thirty thousand tons) to be used in the temple. The three thousand tons of gold used was the equivalent of the weight of up to one thousand elephants, or the weight of fifteen blue whales, more than thirty-five Boeing 737 airplanes, and more than all the gold produced each year around the world today (which is between twenty-five hundred and twenty-seven hundred tons).

32

Solomon's Temple

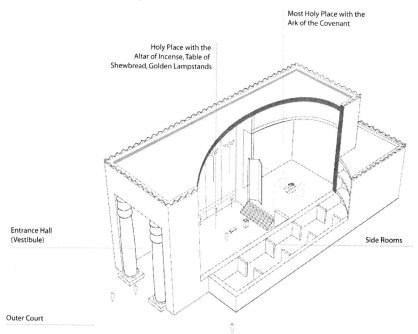

Figure C: Sketch of King Solomon's Temple. The two pillars were known as Jakin and Boaz.

Similarly, the thirty thousand tons of silver used was the weight of ten thousand elephants, or one hundred fifty blue whales, more than the weight of three hundred fifty Boeing 737 airplanes and more than the annual world production of silver today (which is about twenty thousand tons). This is in addition to quantities of iron, bronze, wood, and stone that could not be weighed. Furthermore, it took more than one hundred eighty thousand men just to procure the logs of cedar for the main building and to cut out the large blocks of stone used to build the foundation of the temple.[6] All the logs used were floated in on rafts from Lebanon and all the modeling work done on the blocks of stones used in the foundation was done at a quarry away from the temple site; there was to be no hammer, chisel, or any other iron tool used at the temple site![7]

You're God's most precious "commodity"

Here is another way of looking at the value of treasures used in the temple: in the year 2011, the cost of gold was about $1,500 per ounce and silver was $36 per ounce. One ton weighs the equivalent of 32,000 ounces. This means that the 2011 value of the gold alone used in the temple was about $144 billion (US) and the silver was worth about $35 billion. Thus, the total 2011 value of the gold and silver alone used in the temple, not counting the other metals or the cost of labor, was $179 billion.

If we factor in a modest $10 billion for all the other materials used, and conservatively estimate that the labor of the 180,000 workers was worth $15 per hour and they worked 2,080 hours per year over an average of three-and-a-half years, the value of the labor costs would be about another $20 billion. So we can conservatively assume that the 2011 value of the cost of the temple was $209 billion. This is more than the 2010 annual gross domestic product of half the states in the United States, more than the GDP of several nations, and more than the total combined net worth of the three richest men in the world (in 2011 they were Mexico's Carlos Slim Helu ($74 billion), Bill Gates of the United States ($56 billion); and Warren Buffet of the United States ($50 billion).[8]

You're Worth More to God Than Gold and All the Temple Treasures

The significance of the immensity of the value of the treasures dedicated to the building of the temple is that it gives us a small glimpse into the amount of honor, reverence, and respect King David and his son, King Solomon, had for God. They were the wealthiest kings of their era but devoted a substantial part of not only their own net worth but that of their nation to honor God. They also constantly sought after a close relationship with God, and He honored them in return. No wonder God called David "a man after my own heart."[9] Now consider this humbling notion: God, in choosing you as His desired place of dwelling over the Temple of Solomon, with all its riches, is indicating that you are worth a lot more to Him than all the gold and all the silver produced annually in the world today and much more the combined material value of the three richest men in the world! These are not just words. God proved how much He values you and His love for you by sending His only Son and most precious "commodity" Jesus Christ to die on a cross so that *your* life could be ransomed. "For God so loved the world that he gave His one and only Son, that whoever believes in Him shall not perish but have eternal life" (John 3:16).

"For you know that it was not with perishable things such as silver or gold that you were redeemed from the empty way of life handed down to you from your ancestors, but with the precious blood of Christ, a lamb without blemish or defect" (1 Peter 1:18–19, NIV 2011).

Pause and be amazed at this God who loves you so much that He would sacrifice His own perfect son for you and then tell you that He would rather come and live within you than in one of the most beautiful and expensive structures ever build by human hands! This may also explain how it is that some of the most breathtakingly beautiful and grand cathedrals and churches all over the world with exquisite designs and extraordinary adornment are sitting idle today. Without men and women with hearts dedicated to God, no manmade structure can entice God's permanent presence.

Use of Symmetry in the Design of the Temple

Just as in the Tabernacle, King Solomon's Temple's design consisted of the main building with two main rooms (the Holy Place and Most Holy Place) surrounded by a courtyard (the outer court), which was walled off by a large fence. The main building was about ninety feet long, thirty feet wide, and forty-five feet high. It was surrounded in front by a porch and all around by side rooms. Right in front of the temple were two large bronze pillars, twenty-seven feet high and six feet wide,[10] one on the right or south side (known as Jachin or Jakin) and the other one on the left or north side, known as Boaz. (Figure C) On top of these pillars was a "capital" of bronze adorned with a beautiful network of bronze pomegranates around the perimeter.

Symmetry reveals your need for God

"Hiram set up the pillars of the porch of the temple; he set up the right pillar and called its name Jachin [he will establish], and he set up the left pillar and called its name Boaz [in strength]" (1 Kings 7:21, Amplified). Hiram was a skilled bronze worker who was brought in from the kingdom of Tyre to work on all the bronze objects in the temple including the pillars of the porch.[11] Interestingly, the meaning of the names given by Hiram to the two symmetrical pillars taken in unison is, "He will establish in strength."

Thus, even this foreigner brought in to help build God's temple understood about the significance of what he was building and recognized that the pillars represented God's *promise* to establish those who come and worship at His temple in strength. Notice that the names of both pillars are needed to complete this message from God, reflecting God's nature of using symmetry, representing codependency and balance to complete His work. As a symmetrical creation of God with each side of your body complementary to the other analogous to Jachin and Boaz, you also are "established in strength." God designed you similar to the way He designed the temple and the Tabernacle to establish that even in your flesh, one side is not independent of the other, but the mirror image symmetry leads to your completion as a human being.

God also created you as His own mirror image, with the intention of your being dependent on Him to become complete. "So God created mankind in His own image, in the image of God He created them; male and female He created them" (Genesis 1:27, NIV 2011).

In essence, the whole purpose of symmetry in God's creation of the temple and Tabernacle and of your body is to remind you that even in your physical existence, one side depends on the other to be complete and you were also created to depend on Him to be complete. One hand cannot clap alone, and while one hand can lift, two hands can lift better than one. Two eyes can see better than one eye and two legs can move you around much easier than one leg can. "Two are better than one, because they have a good return for their labor: If either of them falls down, one can help the other up. But pity anyone who falls and has no one to help them up ... Though one may be overpowered, two can defend themselves. A cord of three strands is not quickly broken" (Ecclesiastes 4:9–10, 12; NIV 2011).

God created Adam (man) and Eve (woman) to depend upon each other. Jesus Christ was dependent on God the Father while on earth, and God the Father uses His Holy Spirit to reach billions of people around the world today. Similarly, He's calling you to relinquish control of your life and become dependent on Him so that you can become complete and He can rebuild you in strength and fully in His own image. Just as the names of the two pillars Jachin and Boaz are needed together to reflect God's promise to establish you in strength, you will see this promise of God will be fully fulfilled in you when you truly turn your temple over to Him to dwell.

The most reliable person for you, as His temple, to rely on is God Himself. However, He also calls upon you to be dependent on other members of His kingdom and to play a supportive role for Him in ruling over His creation: "Then God said, "Let us make mankind in our image, in our likeness, so that they may rule over the fish in the sea and the birds in the sky, over the livestock and all the wild animals, and over all the creatures that move along the ground" (Genesis 1:26, NIV 2011).

God created you to help Him rule over the rest of His creation. While the dominion God intended was lost by Adam, Jesus Christ reclaimed it for you when He died at Calvary and rose again to defeat death and its power forever. Unfortunately, many Christians have not chosen to regain this control because of failure to realize the power they possess by turning over control and tapping into the Holy Spirit deposited in them. Are you ready to relinquish control to God and to take *your* position of authority in His kingdom?

Pray This Prayer with Me:

Dear God my Father, I thank You for revealing to me how much You value me that You would forgo all the treasures of Your beautiful temple and choose instead to live inside of me. Help me grasp the full significance of this kind of love so I can open myself up to enable Your Holy Spirit to freely take residence within me. I recognize that Your plans for me are better than the best plans I may have for myself, and I am ready to relinquish control and take my position of authority on earth. Amen.

1. 2 Chronicles 3–6.
2. King Solomon's temple was destroyed in 586 BCE. It was ultimately replaced with a Second Temple between 516 BCE and 70 CE. In this latter temple, the Holy Place was separated from the Most Holy Place by a curtain (veil) instead of by a door.
3. Exodus 26.
4. Leviticus 16:15; Numbers 7:16, 22, 28, 34, 40, 46, 52, 58, 64, 70, 76, 82, 87.
5. Genesis 27:9, 30:25–43.
6. 1 Kings 5:13–18.
7. 1 Kings 6:7.
8. http://en.wikipedia.org/wiki/List_of_U.S._states_by_GDP, and http://en.wikipedia.org/wiki/Comparison_between_U.S._states_and_countries_by_GDP_(nominal) (last visited June 4, 2011).
9. 1 Samuel 13:14; Acts 13:22.
10. Jeremiah 52:21–22.
11. 1 Kings 7:13–14.

CHAPTER 5

The Outer Court, Part 1: Your Flesh

(Session 3a)

It is an undoubted truth that every doctrine that comes from God, leads to God; and that which doth not tend to promote holiness is not of God.—George Whitfield, English Anglican preacher (1714-1770).

Holiness is the very principle of eternal life, the very beginning of eternal life in the heart, and that which will certainly grow up to eternal life.—Jeremiah Burroughs, English Congregationalist and preacher (circa 1600-1646)

The outer court of the Tabernacle and temple was the part open to the outside world and was the place where all the Jewish people regularly gathered to worship God. It was the only visible part of these structures from the outside, illuminated by the rays of the sun during the day and the reflections of the moon at night.[1]

Contents of the Outer Court and Their Symbolism

The outer court of the Tabernacle and temple contained two main objects: the brazen altar (altar of burnt offering) and the brazen laver (the wash basin), plus the utensils used along with them (Figure D). The purpose of these items was to offer sacrifices to God and to cleanse the priests prior to their entry into the other two chambers of the Tabernacle and temple—the Holy Place and the Most Holy Place.

The Tabernacle

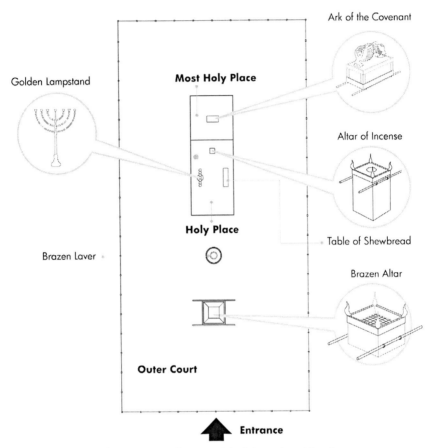

Figure D: Major Contents of the Tabernacle and temple

The Brazen Altar[2]: The brazen altar was a large (7.3 feet by 7.3 feet by 4.4 feet), hollow, square chest with four horns on its corners located near the Tabernacle or temple gate. It was on the brazen altar that the priests sacrificed and burned the animals brought to them by the Jewish people in place of their having to give their lives for the sins they had committed against God and also where the animals were sacrificed simply as an act of worship or offering to God. The fire on the brazen alter was kept continuously burning[3] as a reminder of the ongoing sinfulness of the people. Sacrifices of lamb were offered twice daily, during the morning and afternoon, thus keeping the focus and reverence constantly on God.

In essence, the brazen altar was a place of purification where animals were sacrificed to redeem the sinful lives of the Jews from destruction and where there was enablement of only God's perfection to be manifest in the priests prior to entry into the Holy Place and Most Holy Place.

The brazen altar was symbolic of the physical cross of Jesus Christ where He sacrificed His life "dying to His flesh" so that all believers in Him would never have to sacrifice animals for their sins and as a result may live forever.

Today there is no need for you to sacrifice animals in order to have forgiveness for your sins or draw near to God. Jesus Christ did all that work for you at the garden of Gethsemane when He became the final sacrifice so that you would never have to shed the blood of any animal in place of yours. However, in order to have a close relationship with God, Jesus Christ also said that *you* must take up His cross (your brazen altar) daily and follow Him. "Whoever wants to be my disciple must deny themselves and take up their cross and follow me" (Matthew 16:24, NIV 2011). This means you must continually remember the work Jesus did for you and learn to live a life that is glorifying to Him, even when it goes against what you would like to do in your flesh.

God wants you to be holy

We will learn later that God has given you more capacity to carry this cross than you ever imagined, and we will discuss the meaning of "dying to your flesh" in greater detail.

The Brazen Laver[4]: The brazen laver was a brass portal (dimensions unknown) that contained water with which the priests washed their hands and feet after offering sacrifices on the brazen altar and prior to entering the Tabernacle or temple. The Laver was located between the brazen altar and the entrance to the Tabernacle (Exodus 30:19–22) or temple. The act of washing in the brazen laver served two purposes. The first was for purification by removal of the contaminants or residue left over on the priests from the sacrifices made at the brazen altar. The second was as a constant reminder that entry into the two inner chambers of the tabernacle was entry into God's sacred chambers and thus a holy act and an act of reverence toward God that demanded cleansing.

The brazen laver was thus symbolic of your need for purity when approaching a pure God. While the act of washing was a physical one, the real intent was to focus the hearts of the priests on the purity of God and set the stage to observe God's holiness. As long as the priests utilized the brazen altar and the brazen laver in the outer court the way God intended—as utensils to serve Him, to atone for the sins of the people of Israel, and for cleansing—the atmosphere in the Holy Place was kept pure and God's presence dominated the whole Tabernacle or temple leading to blessings for the people of Israel.

Similarly, for you today when you purify your mind through what you let into your outer court prior to approaching God, you will be blessed with a much closer relationship and the light of His Spirit will shine through your soul and flesh.

You can accomplish this cleansing through regularly letting in (meditating on) His word as revealed in the Bible, and by praising and worshipping Him so you can focus on Him and on the aspects of His holiness that help you put into perspective how mighty and wonderful His gift of salvation and other numerous blessings are to you. You also accomplish this by keeping your flesh undefiled. No amount of reading God's word or praising Him will be rewarded by God if you turn around and consistently defile your flesh by what you watch, what you listen to, what substances you ingest, or how you use your body.

Your Flesh Is the Gateway

Just as with the outer court of the Tabernacle and temple, your own outer court (flesh) is susceptible to external influences, elements, longings, fantasies, ridicule or worship, and temptations. You cannot effectively hide your physical nature or hold in what's inside you for any period of time. As the outer court was the gateway into the Tabernacle and temple and the avenue of entry and exit for all persons and things that determined whether the activities inside were acceptable to God, so it is with your flesh as the gateway to your mind (soul) and spirit.

In the Tabernacle and temple outer courts, certain areas were restricted to the Jews only while nonbelievers (Gentiles) were allowed access as visitors to certain clearly delineated sections. Only priests were allowed from the outer court inside the Holy Place and Most Holy Place in order to maintain reverence. Similarly, God approves and disapproves of what you let into or do with your outer court (your flesh) and wants you to limit access to certain things that will have significant influence on what happens to your soul (your Holy Place) and your spirit.

"Flesh gives birth to flesh, but the Spirit gives birth to spirit" (John 3:6). As a believer, you are born again *of the spirit* (John 3:5). Your flesh is not born again and needs to be constantly influenced by your new spirit to attain the excellence God expects from it. What you let into yourself greatly influences what goes on in your soul (mind), which then influences your body further and ultimately the influence of God's Spirit within you and who you are. The way you dress, the music you listen to, the books you read, the images you look at, the shows you watch on TV or the Internet, the acts you engage your body in, and even the food you eat all influence your soul and will determine the quality of your relationship with God and your ability to have the dominion He intended for you to have in this world.

In the words of Jesus Christ: "Your eye is the lamp of your body. When your eyes are healthy, your whole body also is full of light. But when they are unhealthy, your body also is full of darkness. See to it, then, that the light within you is not darkness" Luke 11:34–35, NIV 2011). What Jesus means here is that your eyes especially are a primary gateway into your soul. If you let in unhealthy or dark things through your eyes, your mind will be unhealthy and full of darkness. There are many other verses in the Bible that exemplify the importance of the eyes in influencing our lives including the following:

Your eyes lead to your soul

"Turn my eyes away from worthless things; preserve my life according to your word" (Psalm 119:37); "I will set before my eyes no vile thing" (Psalm 101:3); "But they rebelled against me and would not listen to me; they did not get rid of the vile images they had set their eyes on" (Ezekiel 20:8a).

The Reverence You Show to Your Outer Court Determines the Degree of God's Relationship with You

In the Tabernacle and temple, the Holy Place was a strategically located crossroad between the outer court and the Most Holy Place. In the same way, your mind is at a strategic crossroad between your body and your spirit and can be influenced by both, depending on which you allow.

The activities in the outer court were crucial in determining the degree of holiness within the Holy Place,[5] which then created the conditions for how much the impact of God's Spirit resident in the Most Holy Place was felt.

When the Holy Place within Solomon's Temple became defiled because God's chosen people turned away from God and treated the outer court of His temple with contempt, God withdrew Himself, and His numerous blessings to them were lost. While the priests continued with the physical washing and the sacrifices, they had become mere rituals and had lost their intended purposes of focus on and showing reverence for God.

Similarly, when you stop washing at your brazen laver through a focus on God's holiness by reading His word, praising, worshipping, and thanksgiving, and by keeping your flesh pure, your temple will become contaminated and overwhelmed by the temptations and external challenges of this world. You will then have lost the benefits of a close relationship with God. God intends His temple within you to be sacred, and failure to recognize that God considers you sacred and constantly and deliberately bringing impure items into your temple will ultimately lead to your spiritual death. "If anyone destroys God's temple, God will destroy him; for God's temple is sacred, and you are that temple" (1 Corinthians 3:17).

Eli, Hophni, and Phinehas Disregarded the Outer Court

As an example, consider the story of Eli, one of Israel's last judges. Judges were priests who served as rulers of Israel before the people insisted on having kings like all the other nations around them. Judges lived in and cared for the Tabernacle and were responsible for the sacrifices and offerings that occurred in there. While Eli himself was dedicated to God, he had two wicked sons, Hophni and Phinehas, who had no regard or reverence for God. This was reflected in their behavior in the outer court of the Tabernacle. As priests under their father, Eli's sons were influential in what went on at the outer court. Rather than perform their duties with respect, they disregarded God's rules, keeping the best parts of the animals that were brought by the people to be sacrificed to God for themselves *before* the sacrifices were offered to God, and eating the meat before the fat was burned off on the altar against God's explicit commands.[6,7] In addition, they routinely slept with the women who served at the gate of the Tabernacle.

Yet their father, Eli, failed to strongly correct them or discipline them for their actions. As a result, God's presence in the Most Holy Place of the Tabernacle was stifled, and we are told in 1 Samuel 3:1b that "in those days the word of the Lord was rare; there were not many visions." Ultimately, the consequences of this disdain for God's outer court was severe, not only to both Hophni and Phinehas, who died suddenly on the same day, but also to Eli, who did not rein them in. All of Eli's descendants became cursed with early deaths and became beggars! (Read 1 Samuel 2:30–36 and 1 Samuel 4:11, 18.)

It is worthy to note that God's Spirit remained in the Tabernacle for quite a while, but He did not reveal Himself much to Eli and his children or show them or the nation of Israel visions as a result of their wickedness and blatant disregard for the activities in the outer court of the Tabernacle. Even though we have no evidence that the Holy Place or the Most Holy Place were defiled by Hophni and Phinehas, their behavior outside was enough to influence God's response inside.

God disciplines for your own good

Similarly, when you fail to honor your flesh the way God intended you to, even as a believer, you will effectively snuff out your ability to hear God's voice or to have the relationship He desires for you. Furthermore, there are consequences for this that often includes a shorter and more miserable life than God ever intended for you, and this may also have a negative impact on others around you.

By contrast, when the focus of the priests and people in the outer court was primarily on pleasing and showing reverence to God (by continuous acts of consecration, proper provision of burnt offerings of animals, and praise and worship that acknowledged His presence in the Most Holy Place), the Holy Place was itself kept totally pure because the atmosphere in it was not corrupted and was influenced more by God's presence in the Most Holy Place. Under these circumstances of total dedication to God, the people of Israel prospered physically and materially and their enemies were subdued and at peace with them. King Hezekiah was an example of a King of Israel who took God's word and care of the temple seriously and prospered as a result. "This is what Hezekiah did throughout Judah, doing what was good and right and faithful before the LORD his God. In everything that he undertook in the service of God's temple and in obedience to the law and the commands, he sought his God and worked wholeheartedly. And so he prospered" (2 Chronicles 31:20–21).

You will also prosper when you learn to dedicate your life to God and ensure that your body and everything you let into it is used primarily to honor Him, as you will enable the Holy Spirit within you freedom to become more active. As an example of how the conditions within the outer court influenced the whole Tabernacle and temple, two separate incidents illustrate how God's presence spilled over from the Most Holy Place into the whole Tabernacle and temple when they were first built because they had not yet been corrupted and subjected to the sinful behavior of the Jews. "Then Moses set up the courtyard around the tabernacle and altar and put up the curtain at the entrance to the courtyard. And so Moses finished the work. Then the cloud covered the Tent of Meeting, and the glory of the LORD *filled* the tabernacle" (Exodus 40:33–34; emphasis added).

"There was nothing in the ark except the two stone tablets that Moses had placed in it at Horeb, where the LORD made a covenant with the Israelites after they came out of Egypt. When the priests withdrew from the Holy Place, the cloud filled the temple of the LORD.[11] And the priests could not perform their service because of the cloud, for the glory of the LORD filled his temple" (1 Kings 8:9–11).

God's Rules Never Change

Both incidents occurred several generations apart, first with Moses in the Tabernacle and then with King Solomon in the temple that was built as a replacement for Moses' Tabernacle. After the temple was constructed, designated specially consecrated priests entered from the outer court into the Holy Place and the Most Holy Place to install all the articles that belonged in them before returning out through the same path. During this time of complete focus and dedication to God, we are told that God's glory (represented by a cloud) *filled* the whole temple, similar to the situation when Moses and Aaron had entered the Tabernacle.

These passages reinforce that the degree to which the presence of God was felt in the Holy Place and outer court—whether it was in the Tabernacle or the temple was determined by what the people focused on. As long as the focus was on God and His Most Holy Place, God's Holy presence was felt everywhere. God never changes, and the same conditions He expected during the times of the Tabernacle and the temple are the same conditions He expects today, and He will similarly reward your holiness.

When there is reverence of God, God's Spirit overflows from the Most Holy Place into the Holy Place, and all the way into the outer court. "Moses and Aaron then went into the Tent of Meeting. When they came out, they blessed the people; and the glory of the LORD appeared to all the people. Fire came out from the presence of the LORD and consumed the burnt offering and the fat portions on the altar. And when all the people saw it, they shouted for joy and fell facedown" (Leviticus 9:23–24).

In the above passage, the outer court was the place where the altar used for burnt offerings of the animals used in worshipping God and atoning for sins was located. Meanwhile, the location of the "presence of the Lord" and the "glory of the Lord" was the innermost room, the Most Holy Place. Because the conditions in the outer court and Holy Place were united on the focus on God (Moses had just come out of the tent where He had been worshipping God and had just finished blessing the people), God's presence was felt all the way out in the outer court in the form of fire. This fire came as an acknowledgment from God of acceptance of the offering due to the reverence of Moses and Aaron.

You are God's royal priest!

God honors those who revere Him and will honor you as well if you maintain respect and reverence for Him, and you will experience His Spirit flowing out of you such that those around you will know that there is something different about you.

Holiness and Priesthood

Since *you* are created as God's temple, you are God's royal priest, and your attitude toward God should also be one of reverence and holy fear. You can be direct with God and have a fun and loving relationship with Him, but you cannot take Him or His temple for granted.

During the times of the Tabernacle and temple, priests served as special intermediaries between the people and God, and as such they in particular needed to be holy in order to approach God. Prior to performing their duties of interceding for the Jews daily inside the Tabernacle and the temple, they needed to be specially consecrated by elaborate procedures that included the types of clothes they wore, sacrificing of animals, cleansing of their hands and feet, and anointing with olive oil.[8] "Anoint Aaron and his sons and consecrate them so they may serve me as priests. Say to the Israelites, 'This is to be my sacred anointing oil for the generations to come. Do not pour it on men's bodies and do not make any oil with the same formula. It is sacred, and you are to consider it sacred. Whoever makes perfume like it and whoever puts it on anyone other than a priest must be cut off from his people'" (Exodus 30:30–33).

Priestly Garments and Significance: Jewish priests wore special garments that were rich in their symbolic significance. These included long robes, turbans (cloths wrapped around their head), tunics (long items of clothing reaching from the shoulders to below the knees), sashes (belts made out of linen), and caps. Their robes were made entirely of blue cloth, with pomegranates of blue, purple, and scarlet yarn around the hem of the robe, and gold bells between them.[9] The blue, purple, and scarlet were the exact same colors that God chose for the curtain that separated His Most Holy Place from the Holy Place of the Tabernacle and the temple. As noted previously, they represented *royalty* (purple), *atonement for sins* (red), and *heavenly focus* (blue). The gold in the bells as well as the plate on the turban worn by the priests symbolized the *purity* and *holiness* of God. The turban itself symbolized the burden being carried by the priests as they temporarily bore the guilt involved in the sacred gifts consecrated and sacrificed daily by the Israelites for the forgiveness of sins. The tunics, sashes, and caps were items made of fine linen, intended to symbolize the *honor* associated with being a priest. All these items of clothing, colors, and activities of the priests were designed to keep the focus on God and His holiness during this time in their history.

Because of the work Jesus Christ did at Calvary, you do not have to be burdened by wearing all the items worn by the Jewish priests because Jesus removed the need for these. As a result, you have a direct Father-son relationship with God. However, as a keeper of God's temple, His requirement from you to respect your body as His dwelling place and what you do with it remains paramount if you want a close relationship with Him.

Ignoring God Has Consequences

After being chosen by God to represent Him, the Jewish nation soon started to turn away from God and chase after other gods. The conditions in the outer court of the temple changed from one of reverence to blatant disregard and even contempt of God's presence in the Most Holy Place. In ignoring the Creator of the universe who had set up residence with them to protect and bless them, the Holy Place became desecrated and was almost exclusively influenced by the ungodly atmosphere in the outer court. God's Spirit was stifled, the cover of His blessings was lost and the people of Israel ultimately suffered severe consequences including famine, exile, and slavery.[10]

Similarly, your decision to make either God or something else the focus of what you do will reveal the amount of reverence you have for God. This is demonstrated by what you do with your body (your outer court) and what you allow into your mind (your Holy Place). This will in turn determine the nature of the relationship you have with God and your ability to either make the most use of the full power of God within you to rule as a royal priest on earth or to live as a hopeless and fearful sinner.

An Encounter with Jesus Changes Everything

Kim (name changed to protect his real identity) was someone who had always lived in his outer court but was now at his wits' end. He had just been admitted to the hospital where he was to undergo detoxification for alcohol poisoning. As far as he was concerned, his life was at an end. As he recalled, "I was at the edge of the abyss, slipping away and watching my life disappear. I felt a deep emptiness and lack of purpose to my life." Kim had nothing to long for, no love, no joy, no desires, and worst of all, no hope. His childhood had been very difficult, having been raised from age two in a loveless home by his mother and a stepfather. As he recalled it, "I did not know love and I had very poor self-esteem." In order to protect his often broken heart, Kim sought to fill the void and obtain power by drinking, dating vulnerable women to "protect them," and avoiding commitment at all costs. Kim only knew and was controlled by the carnal nature of his outer court.

By age fourteen, Kim was drinking regularly. By sixteen he was staying out as long as he wanted with virtually no accountability to anyone. Kim recounted, "When I was with my friends I felt accepted, and alcohol was an important part of our relationship." His self-esteem virtually nonexistent, Kim sought to navigate life on his own terms and yielded control of his life toward gratification of his flesh. His thinly veiled world came crashing down the night he was admitted to the hospital. Faced with the grim reality of losing his wife and two children due to his drinking and self-destructive behavior, Kim was desperate. He had harbored a grudge against everyone in his life, including his mom, dad, stepfather, and even his wife for offences that he perceived were committed against him and which his memory relived every day.

In his darkest hour of need, Kim met staff member George in the emergency room on the night Kim was admitted. George told Kim about Jesus Christ and invited him to church. Something about George's testimony of Jesus gave Kim a hint of the hope he'd never had before. Having absolutely nothing to lose, he accepted George's invitation and attended church with him the next day. By the end of the service, Kim had given his life to Jesus Christ and received a life-transforming hope and joy that, "I had never experienced in my life." He soon received the gift of the Holy Spirit. His cravings for alcohol totally disappeared and he gave up drinking altogether. With his newfound relationship with God and infilling of the Holy Spirit, Kim started to cede control of his being from his outer court to his Most Holy Place. He renewed his fractured relationship with his wife and learned to forgive his perceived enemies. He vividly recalls the Holy Spirit telling him, "Forgive them. Your condemnation darkens the light I lit in you. You have received my love; now share it." Kim obeyed and altered his life and relationships. With the veil of darkness removed, Kim learned that God never viewed him the way he viewed himself all his life and that God loves and has always loved him exactly as he is. He recognized now that his feelings about himself were the lies of satan, who had total influence of him in his outer court and ultimately his Holy Place (his mind). He now no longer has to yield to his flesh but receives and takes guidance from the Holy Spirit in all his choices. He also now recognizes that there is nothing he can do to earn his salvation but that it is a gift from God.

Always seek to emulate Jesus

With regards to Jesus, Kim had this to say: "I realized His presence is freshness and cleanness. In Him, I was made new; all things are made new. In Him is life such as I never knew—He knows my state and still loves me. He freed me from the death that was in me. In Him is unity and oneness; I am no longer separated and alone. He is my champion and savior. I have never experienced love and mercy such as His. He is magnificent and wonderful!" The freedom Kim received is available to everyone who seeks

Christ, including you, if you choose to receive the free gift of salvation and release from bondage no matter how small or big.

Jesus Is the One to Emulate

Jesus Christ, who was perfect, showed us the way in His "dying" to His outer court so that His Holy Place could be fully yielded to His Most Holy Place.

Jesus is the one you are to emulate. He ignored what was happening to his body because His focus was on His Most Holy Place where God (the Shepherd and Overseer of our souls) had revealed His plan of salvation for mankind to Him. Jesus made this sacrifice so that you and I, both hopeless sinners "might die" to sins which come in through our outer courts and live for righteousness—which is accomplished through the grace of God who resides in our Most Holy Places. "He himself bore our sins" in his *body* on the cross, so that we might die to sins and live for righteousness; "by his wounds you have been healed." For "you were like sheep going astray," but now you have returned to the shepherd and overseer of your *souls* (1 Peter 2:24–25, NIV 2011, emphasis added).

You die to sins by recognizing that, as a Christian, you are no longer a slave to sin and can trust the Holy Spirit in you to guide you when sin beckons. You do not have to sin anymore because sin is no longer your master. Jesus, a sinless man, paid the price to free you from this burden by dying on the cross in your place, which is why *you* are now "dead" to sin. Dead men and women do not owe any debt to anyone and are not under the burden of any law. Similarly, since you are dead to sin, sin has no influence over you, except the influence you allow it to have. Since you are freed from serving sin, you can now focus your full attention on God, who will enable you to enjoy the joy and blessings of the gift of salvation that has been freely given to you. We will explore this concept in greater detail in chapter 13 when we talk about the school master and the school of life. May God release you from the heavy burdens of the yoke of sin into the freedom of a life guided by His Spirit!

Pray this Prayer with Me:

Dear Lord, I want my whole being to be dominated by Your Spirit. Please help me understand how to die to my outer court and burn away all the impurities that lie there so my mind can be fully focused on You and thus renewed daily. I willing release the burdens of my sins to Jesus Christ and trade them for the blessings of a close relationship with Him. Amen.

1. Exodus 27:9–17.
2. Exodus 27:1–8.
3. Leviticus 6:12–13.
4. Exodus 30:17–21; I Kings 7:23–26.
5. Exodus 29:1–46.
6. Leviticus 3:3–5.
7. 1 Samuel 2:22–30.
8. Exodus 29:1–44; 30:30–33.
9. Exodus 28:31–42.
10. 1 Samuel 2:12–17, 27–33, 3:1; Ezekiel 8–9.

CHAPTER 6

The Outer Courtyard, Part 2: Acacia Wood, Brass Coverings, and a Healthy Outer Court

(Session 3b)

Holy is the way God is. To be holy He does not conform to a standard. He is that standard. He is absolutely holy with an infinite, incomprehensible fullness of purity that is incapable of being other than it is. Because He is holy, all His attributes are holy; that is, whatever we think of as belonging to God must be thought of as holy.—A. W. Tozer, American Christian pastor and preacher (1897-1963).

Acacia Wood and Brass Coverings in Your Outer Court

Two other important aspects of the brazen altar and brazen laver relate to you as a person. The first aspect is that these two main objects of the outer court were similar to all the other objects contained within the Holy Place and Most Holy Place in that their core material was made from *acacia wood*. Acacia wood (also known as "monkeypod") is a beautiful, highly durable grain of wood found worldwide and known for its contrasting walnut brown to light tan colors. God's choice of acacia wood as the core wood for all the objects in the Outer Place, Holy Place, and the Most Holy Place has dual symbolic significance. The initial one is that in choosing acacia wood as the core material for His temple, God used one of His most durable and beautiful living plants. Just as He did in using acacia wood in the brazen alter and the brazen laver, God created all human beings including you and me with a beautiful and durable inner core treasure of acacia wood.

"But we have this treasure in jars of clay to show that this all-surpassing power is from God and not from us" (2 Corinthians 4:7). While your flesh is a "jar of clay" that may age and be corrupted by impurities that are visible for the world to see and susceptible to corruption, the material of your inner core consists of a treasure of a very beautiful material of durable quality that remains intact and incorruptible long after your surface beauty is gone. This treasure is the Spirit of God. The additional symbolism is that the contrasting walnut brown to light tan colors of acacia wood are a wonderful expression of God's love for all humanity, whether you are black, white, brown, yellow, or pink. "For God loved the world so much that He gave his one and only Son, so that *everyone* who believes in Him will not perish but have eternal life" (John 3:16, emphasis added).

You have a treasure in your jar of clay

"But there will be glory and honor and peace from God for *all* who do good—for the Jew first and also for the Gentile. For God does not show favoritism" (Romans 2:11, NLT, emphasis added). God is in effect saying, "within your core, I see all persons as the same and I love you as you are—you do not need to be a specific type of person." God loves you as much as He loves anyone you know, no matter what your current condition may be. His only request is that you believe in His Son and strive to be good,[1] just as His son, Jesus, was good.

Brass Coverings: In contrast to the coverings of all the contents within the Holy Place and the Most Holy Place of the Tabernacle and temple where everything was gold, all the items located in the outer court, including the brazen altar and the brazen laver were covered with brass. Brass is a metal made of copper and some other minerals such as zinc and which often contains other impurities such as arsenic, which make the brass harder. All the utensils, shovels, basins, cups, and vessels used by the priests in the outer court were also made of brass.[2] Thus, while the inner core of the brazen altar and brazen laver (contents of the outer court) were made of beautiful acacia wood, their outer covering was made of impure brass. This is very much analogous to your own human flesh. Your imperfect, impure "brazen" outer flesh covers a beautiful inner core of acacia wood and gold.

As you draw closer to God and you focus more on spiritual matters, you will soon find your impure brass focus transformed as the pure gold of God's Spirit within your gold saturated Most Holy Place shines through you, overshadowing all the impurities and imperfections of your flesh. This explains why persons filled with the Holy Spirit and who are walking close to God usually radiate an inner beauty that emanates from their Most Holy Place. It is noticeable to everyone near them because they take on the nature of the person they spend the most time with. Like an iron rod that is dipped into a hot furnace, you will begin to glow, taking on the nature of the fire within the furnace. This is God's desire for you, to take on His nature and to glow such that everywhere you are, you reflect His glory into your surroundings.

Significance of the Coverings of the Outer Court

Your flesh is symbolic of your outer court. Similar to the brass covering of all the materials within the outer court of the Tabernacle and temple, your imperfect flesh has many weaknesses and impurities and ages over time as a result of your sinful nature, genetic makeup and influence from the outside world. However, underlying this weak vessel is the durability and beauty of the "acacia wood" that is hidden within you but is covered by your impure "brass" flesh that everyone sees.

When you move to discover what it takes to move from your outer court and begin to live in your Holy Place and your Most Holy Place, where God's Spirit resides within you, God will in turn reward you by projecting a pure golden Spirit through your impure brass covering. You will become complete in being reshaped in God's image. However, the act of burning off your impure brass covering is one that needs your will and deliberate participation before you can enter deep into your Holy Place and Most Holy Place where God resides. You need to methodically sacrifice your outer court flesh so you can reflect the purity of your inner chambers.

When you start seeking to draw near to God who is perfect, He will show you the true condition of your heart and will reveal to you all the gods that are competing with Him for your attention and keeping you from having a full relationship with Him. This is the work of the Holy Spirit who resides in you. This does not mean God seeks to embarrass you by showing you your weaknesses and sinful tendencies—far from it. He simply seeks to show you that you can be much better than you currently are and to let you know He cannot be fully realized in you unless you seek to be more like Him daily.

God's goal is always to draw you nearer to Him, and if you drift away from His plan He seeks to convict you to get you back on track. God convicts to draw you back to Him while the devil condemns you to discourage you from drawing nearer to God. God can do a lot more through you if you are not contaminated by the baggage of persistent sinning for which you do not repent or confess or ask Him for forgiveness. Sin lodges in your mind and competes with your ability to focus on God.

Emptying Yourself of Contamination

As an illustration of decontaminating yourself of the baggage of sin, imagine going to your local grocery store and discovering a beautifully decorated decanter. You immediately picture this bottle on your dinner table as a wonderful addition for serving your guests olive oil to dip bread into. The only problem is that the decanter is presently filled with vinegar, which you have no use for. Your dilemma is clear—if you buy the decanter, and your intent is to serve olive oil from it, you would first have to empty it of the vinegar. The less vinegar left behind in the decanter, the more room you would have for pure olive oil. Any remaining vinegar would contaminate the olive oil and lead to an impure product to serve for dinner.

God convicts, while the devil condemns

Similarly, God wants to pour His pure "olive oil" (representing the Holy Spirit) to fill you up and awaken you, not just occupy a segment of your subconscious. He created you to be like Him. The more you empty yourself of your old self and your own "fleshly" desires, the more room there is for God to fill you with His Holy Spirit. Dying to your outer court (denying the cravings of your flesh) allows God's will to take over so you can fulfill His purpose for your life and be ready when He calls you home to heaven to spend eternity with Him. Notice though that when you do empty yourself of contamination, you have to refill the decanter with olive oil; otherwise, it will become contaminated again with things worse than the vinegar that will defeat the purpose of the initial purchase (read Matthew 12:43–45). You do this by ensuring your focus is on God's word and praise, and that you do everything, including your work, as unto God. God has given you all the tools to do this, and we will discuss in subsequent chapters how you make this happen.

A Healthy Outer Court

In addition to emptying yourself of contamination, it is important that you take good care of your outer court. God was so concerned about the maintenance of the Tabernacle and temple that He appointed a specific lineage of Jews (the Levites) exclusively for this purpose and gave detailed specific instructions for their activities.[3] He was showing them that how the outside of these houses of residence for Him were cared for impacted the reverence shown for Him on the inside.

Similarly, God is interested in your physical and spiritual well-being because how you treat your body impacts your whole being. What and how much you eat and drink; the substances you smoke, inhale, or consume; and what you watch and listen to and their nature impact your overall physical and spiritual health. They will ultimately determine not only your lifespan but the quality of the life you lead and the full extent of your relationship with God. When you have to focus on a body that is not working well, it can consume your attention, making it difficult for your focus to be fully dedicated to a strong relationship with God.

God cares about your body too

You cannot continually ignore the care of your temple and at the same time be praying to God to help you take care of the consequences of your neglect or personal choices. While God has a role to play in your overall health and is capable of healing you of all your diseases, you also have a role in ensuring that you do not contribute unnecessarily to the deterioration of your body. Just as the grace of forgiveness for your sins is not a license for you to continuing sinning (Romans 6:1–14), similarly, God's ability to heal is not a license to behave in ways that damage your body in the first place.

Let us consider obesity as an example. Failure to watch what we eat and to exercise has led to a historic epidemic of obesity in America and around the world.[4] More than one-third of all Americans are overweight and at least 20 percent, or one out of every five, are now considered obese. Obesity has been linked with higher rates of poor self-esteem, depression, diabetes, increased risk of strokes, heart disease, colon cancer, degenerative arthritis, and blood clots, among other problems. When you have to contend with these medical conditions, it is much harder to fully focus your mind on developing a close relationship with God. Obesity is now a major health concern confronting America and most of the world. This in turn siphons attention from God to your flesh.

Developing a Winning Strategy for Your Outer Court

In order to have a winning strategy to overcome challenges in your outer court, you need a vision of how God intended you to be. "When there is no vision (no redemptive revelation of God), the people perish; but he who keeps the law (of God, which includes that of man)—blessed (happy fortunate, and enviable) is he" (Proverbs 29:18, Amplified).

Whatever challenge you are facing that may impact or has already impacted your outer court, you need to first ask God to give you a vision of how He wants you to be or how He created you to be, so that you have a goal to reach for. You then have to pray to God to help you attain your vision and lead you to research how to combat the challenge. The research could involve talking to trusted friends for ideas, searching the Internet for credible sources of information, reading self-help books, or seeking help from your local pastor. For example, to personally combat obesity in your outer court, it is important to ask God to give you a vision of what type of body He intended for you and what normal weight would be like for you. This should then become your goal.

Next, you need to become familiar and alert to the various factors that have contributed to obesity in you so that you can develop your own strategy to either prevent it or to overcome it. These factors include a significant change in the eating habits of Americans with a lot more time being spent eating outside the home at fast food and other restaurants, which typically have larger portion sizes and empty calorie contents. In addition, there has been a substantial increase in the amount of sugar (and high fructose corn syrup) added by manufacturers into the foods and drinks we now consume, accompanied by a decline in our consumption of fruits and vegetables. We now also have a more sedentary lifestyle, with most people getting little exercise compared to past generations. More time is spent watching TV or playing video games, and there are fewer green or safe spaces within many neighborhoods for exercise.

In spite of this, our generation has been blessed by God to be living in an era of bountiful scientific information. It is important to take advantage of this information for limiting diseases such as obesity or other threats to your temple. While it is beyond the scope of this book to address all these issues, there is an abundance of resources available today for you and your family either online or elsewhere from credible organizations such as the American Heart Association,[5] American Academy of Pediatrics,[6] and the Centers for Disease Control and Prevention[7] to help guide you.

If you actually are already overweight or obese, I recommend you first pray for God's wisdom and help in combating it. The Holy Spirit that is deposited in you can be your daily guide in making the proper choices related to the health of your body. You should ask the Holy Spirit to give you the willpower to limit your food portion sizes as well as your fat and sugar intake, to eat a more balanced diet, which includes all the major food groups, and to ensure that you have the right balance of vitamins and nutrients in your system. Next, consult with your physician to help you determine what your ideal body weight should be and to guide you and monitor your health as you strive toward normal weight. Also seek advice from a nutritionist or credible nutrition source on starting to eat a balanced diet that includes all the right amounts of all the major food groups. You should aim to limit the junk foods you keep at home—if they are available and within reach, you will eat them. Use smaller plates when you eat. Drink more water instead of juices or sodas. Also, restrain the amount of time you spend watching TV or other media so you are less likely to be swayed by those tempting advertisements to buy all those high caloric foods and drinks. Try to eat more homemade foods, where you can control the calorie, fat, and sodium content of your meals. Avoid eating late at night. Breakfast is an especially important meal that has been linked to less obesity and greater alertness during the day. Finally, strive to exercise regularly (ideally one hour each day, but any exercise is better than none) so that you can burn off some of the calories you have taken in and keep your tissues and organs well tuned to doing what they were made to do. If you strive daily to do this, God will reward you with a healthier outer court.

The principles described here apply no matter what the challenge to your outer court may be—whether obesity, alcohol, drug or other addiction, or other seemingly minor temptation-related issues (lying, cursing, coveting, stealing, fornication, etc.) that are hard to break. Bringing toxic

Don't drown out the Holy Spirit's voice

substances such as drugs, tobacco, and other similar substances into your body will draw your focus away from God and impact your ability to have a close relationship with Him. Cocaine, heroin, methamphetamines, LSD, marijuana, and prescription pain medications are among substances that will give you momentary pleasures and seem initially beneficial in terms of altering your mood and giving you a high by making you feel good about yourself, but they will also encourage you to do things you would never do if you were in your conscious state without their influence.

As a result, these substances not only lead to decay of your temple but can alter your mood. They bring in other "voices" or ideas that drown out the voice of the Holy Spirit that is resident in you as a believer in Jesus Christ. Listening to or watching programs that are primarily depressing or that do not glorify God will also crowd out the voice of the Holy Spirit within you. Lying, cursing, and stealing will quash the voice of God within you. Once the voice of the Holy Spirit is drowned out, you are susceptible to the influence of your flesh and to the outside voices that will lead you to sin further and to ultimately harm yourself and others.

Five-Step Process for Breaking Decay in Your Outer Court

If you are currently struggling with a specific problem that is causing "decay" of your outer court, I recommend applying a five-step, "continuous loop" process of questions and actions to remedy the problem. Ask the following questions and act as suggested:

1. What is the impact of the current damage or neglect of my outer court on me and on others around me?
    a. Pray for God to reveal the impact of the issue affecting your outer court on your whole body, soul, and spirit and the impact of it on those around you—perhaps your family if you are married or others such as your coworkers if you are not. What is obesity doing to my body and how does it influence my spouse, children, siblings, and coworkers to react toward me? What is my excessive consumption of alcohol or my watching TV programs that always makes my blood boil doing to me or to others around me?
2. What are the factors contributing to your outer court being this way?
    a. Pray for God to give you a vision of the factors contributing to why you are the way you are in relation to the issue

you are dealing with. What is making me obese? What is making me drink or always want to watch pornographic images or listen to violent music? You may have to seek professional help from trained counselors in the area of your struggle to get insight into these issues. As God reveals the underlying factors to you, write down the factors and pray for God to reveal to you the ones that you can change and the ones you need Him to change. This is important because if you do not know what makes you as you are, it will be very difficult or impossible to change. If you do know what the contributing factors are, it will be less challenging to remove them.

3. How does God want me to be?
   a. Next pray for God to show you a vision of how you could be if these factors were not in your life. This is a very important step. If you are an alcoholic, ask for God to reveal to you how your family or your own life would look like without the violence, anger, or other erratic behaviors that go with drinking. If you are addicted to internet pornography, you should ask Him to show you what you would be like without the degradation of your body and soul. Regularly explore your Bible for a clear vision of how God wants you to be. This will give you a picture of what to aim for, especially during periods of your journey when you are facing discouragement.

4. How do I go from where I am to where or how God wants me to be?
   a. Take concrete steps to work on the things that cause you to be the way you are in advance of them occurring. For example, if you always get riled up or depressed when you watch a certain TV channel, then take concrete steps to avoid that channel or stop watching TV altogether. If you are unable to resist calorically dense and salty snacks that put you at risk of obesity, do not have them at home. If you are prone to watching images or movies that degrade your soul, cancel your cable or magazine subscription and avoid places where you are exposed to them. Most importantly, regularly fill yourself up with the word of God. Read God's word, which is full of very useful

instructions and information to keep your temple pure, and pray continually.

    b.   Seek counsel from trained experts and trusted friends who can guide you and who can hold you accountable. There is no shame in this; we all struggle with something for which we need help. Do not try to do this alone. Just as both of the Tabernacle pillars Jachin and Boaz were needed to complete God's desire to establish the Jews in strength, you also need others to help you succeed.

5.   Finally, take some time to reflect and to celebrate interval successes. Keep a diary of each stage along your journey to remind you where you came from. This step is important because your journey to where God wants you to be could be slower that you thought, perhaps even lifelong for some of you. Reflecting on how far you have come and the impact that has already had on you and others will help encourage you and help you maintain a positive attitude toward continuing the journey.

Remember that this will be a continuously looping process, meaning that you will have to continuously go through each of the steps to ensure ultimate and lasting success.

It's Never Too Late to Take Care of Your Temple

The good news is that it is *never too late* to gain some benefits by starting to take care of your outer court by exercising or eating healthy or purging yourself of damaging substances, behaviors, or images. If you are already caught up in an addiction, it may seem difficult to stop, especially if you are depending on your own strength. However, you can pray that God's Spirit will enable you to overcome this addiction and then seek help for it, ideally from organizations that have a strong biblical foundation. Confide in a strong Christian pastor or close friend who does not share your addiction and make yourself accountable to the person so he or she can help you in your path toward normalcy. As much as is possible for your situation, strive to avoid places where you will be in constant exposure to the substances that will tempt you. Seek to remind yourself each day that your body is not yours but belongs to God, and you will start to reap the benefit of seeing changes in your attitude toward it. All things are possible for you when you release them to the God inside you!

Pray This Prayer with Me:

Dear God, I thank You for this temporary body that You have given me and for the beautiful inner core of your Spirit that exists within me. I now humbly ask that You give me the wisdom and the willpower to maintain this body that is the only one I will have on earth in a way that is glorifying and honoring to You. Help me resist the temptation to defile my body with too much food, or with drugs, alcohol, or other addictive substances that can destroy me and instead to always remember that my body is Your temple and as such needs to be cared for by me. I desire to do this and ask these things in the name of my Lord and Savior Jesus Christ. Amen.

Questions to Ponder:

- What are the major threats in today's society to your outer court?
- Can you think of specific things in your life that are contaminating your outer court?
- Have you already experienced consequences of allowing these things in you? If so, what are they?
- Have you ever experienced success in getting rid of items that were contaminating you through your outer court? How did you do it? How did this make you feel?
- Do you have a vision for how to get rid of contamination through your outer court?

Pray for God to reveal the impact of any items contaminating your outer court on your whole body, soul, and spirit and the impact of it on those around you.

Pray for God to give you a vision of any factors contributing to why you are the way you are in relation to the issue you are dealing with.

Next pray for God to show you a vision of how you could be if these factors were not in your life.

Pray that God will enable you to take concrete steps today to start working on the things, before they occur, that cause you to be the way you are.

Pray for God to reveal to you the counsel of trained experts and trusted friends who can guide you and who can hold you accountable.

1. Micah 6:8.
2. Exodus 27:1–8.
3. Numbers 1:53b; 3:7–8, 20b–37.
4. Stein CJ, Colditz GA. The epidemic of obesity. Journal of Clinical Endocrinology and Metabolism 2004; 89 (6): 2522-2525
5. American Heart Association, Getting Healthy—Weight Management/ Obesity Information, http://www.heart.org/HEARTORG/GettingHealthy/ WeightManagement/Obesity/Obesity-Information_UCM_307908_Article.jsp (last visited May 3, 2011).
6. American Academy of Pediatrics—AAP Store—Patient Education Resources— Patient Education Online: http://www.aap.org/healthtopics/overweight.cfm (last visited May 3, 2011).
7. Centers for Disease Control and Prevention, http://www.cdc.gov/obesity/index. html (last visited May 3, 2011).

CHAPTER 7

The Holy Place and Your Soul, The Lamp of God

(Session 4a)

When your mind is focused on your flesh, your soul will be weighed down by all its corruption. When your mind is focused on "the good way" of God, you will discover joy and rest for your soul.

This is what the LORD says: "Stand at the crossroads and look; ask for the ancient paths, ask where the good way is, and walk in it, and you will find rest for your souls.—Jeremiah 6:16

The Holy Place Symbolizes Your Soul

The Holy Place of the Jewish temple and Tabernacle was strategically situated as a "crossroad" between the outer court and the Most Holy Place. It was the place where the Levite priests entered daily to perform specific functions that were critical for ongoing communication with and reverence of God. It was the "intellectual and emotional center" of the temple and Tabernacle.

In the context of your own body as God's temple, the Holy Place symbolically represents your soul.

Your soul is the combination of senses, including your mind, intellect, will, and emotions. It is the part of you that performs rational and intellectual functions. Similar to the middle nature of the Holy Place in the temple and Tabernacle, your soul is the middle ground (crossroads) between your flesh (outer court) and your spirit (Most Holy Place). Your flesh and your spirit both seek to have control and mastery over your soul and are at war with each other. A crossroads by definition is a place of decision where you have to choose between one or more routes. In the context of your temple, you get to choose between the crossroads of your mind yielding to your flesh or to God's Spirit within you. The one you yield to will determine who will have control of you.

"So I say, walk by the Spirit, and you will not gratify the desires of the flesh. For the flesh desires what is contrary to the Spirit, and the Spirit what is contrary to the flesh. They are in conflict with each other, so that you are not to do whatever you want" (Galatians 5:16–17). Understanding the Jewish Holy Place and the purpose of all the items that were contained in it can help prepare your own Holy Place to be what God intended it to be. God's Holy Spirit located within your Most Holy Place can then win over your flesh in the battle for your soul.

Contents of the Jewish Holy Place

The Holy Place in the temple and Tabernacle contained three objects of furniture and some associated accessories, all covered in pure gold. These objects consisted of the "golden candlestick" (menorah), the altar of incense and the table of showbread (bread of the presence) (Figure D, Chapter 5). Similar to the major objects in the outer court of the Tabernacle (the brazen altar and the brazen laver), the table of showbread and the altar of incense in the Holy Place were made of an inner core of acacia wood. However, in contrast to the outer court, where everything was covered in bronze, all the structures of the Holy Place as well as all the utensils within it including the bowls, dishes, and pitchers were either made entirely of or overlaid with pure gold (Exodus 25:23–30). This reflected the purity and perfection needed as a result of being right next door to the presence of God in the Most Holy Place. Similarly, God demands purity in your mind that is juxtaposed to His Spirit. In this chapter, we will examine the golden candlestick and its significance in detail while we will examine the table of showbread and the altar of incense in subsequent chapters.

The Golden Candlestick

The golden candlestick (menorah) was a lamp stand with a base and seven branches hammered out of pure gold that was used to worship God in the Tabernacle and the temple. Everything used in association with the menorah was made of gold, including its seven lamps, the snuffers, and fire holders (Exodus 25:31–40). The lamps were used to burn pure olive oil candles to provide light inside the Holy Place.

The menorah symbolized God's use of the nation of Israel as the means through which the world became enlightened. Each of its seven branches also represented each of the days of creation, including the seventh day of rest represented by the middle branch. Symbolically, all the side branches appear to be emerging from the middle one.

For Christians, the middle (central) branch represents Jesus Christ, who gives us rest and is the central focus of God's ultimate plan for emergence of light and salvation and rest for the world. "When Jesus spoke again to the people, he said, 'I am the light of the world. Whoever follows me will never walk in darkness but will have the light of life'" (John 8:12).

The Holy Spirit grants you peace

"I have come into the world as a light, so that no one who believes in me should stay in darkness" (John 12: 46). Jesus grants rest to all who are weary and burdened. "Come to me, all you who are weary and burdened, and I will give you rest. Take my yoke upon you and learn from me, for I am gentle and humble in heart, and you will find rest for your souls. For my yoke is easy and my burden is light" (Matthew 11:28–30).

As a child of God and believer in Jesus, you are like a branch of the menorah, emerging from but always connected to Him through the Holy Spirit. When your focus is on Jesus Christ, the Holy Spirit within your Most Holy Place is enabled to shine brightly through your mind and heart and soul. He (the Spirit) then helps in illuminating every area of your life including your flesh and helps you to obtain rest and peace for your soul and ultimately to cope with all the challenges you are guaranteed to face in your life. This is because all spirits bow to the person of the Jesus Christ who is in essence one with the Holy Spirit and have to flee in His presence.[1] For example, prior to meeting Jesus Christ, Mary Magdalene had seven evil spirits that tormented her mind (Luke 8:2). When she met Jesus, the demons were driven out of her, and she obtained peace and rest for her mind as she became a devout follower of Jesus.

Indeed, Jesus gave His disciples the ability to grant peace to people who welcomed Him or His disciples.[2] Today, Jesus Christ has guaranteed you peace which is a fruit[3] of the person of the Holy Spirit who is deposited into you. "But the Counselor, the Holy Spirit, whom the Father will send in my name, will teach you all things and will remind you of everything I have said to you. Peace I leave with you; my peace I give you. I do not give to you as the world gives. Do not let your hearts be troubled and do not be afraid" (John 14:26–27).

Use of Olive Oil in the Tabernacle and Temple

In the Tabernacle and temple days, olive oil was an important part of everyday worship by the Jewish priests who entered the Holy Place. In addition to being burned in the menorah to give light, olive oil was often mixed with incense in presenting sacrifices to God.[4] The use of olive oil has special significance, as olive oil has unique qualities. Olives have been an integral part of Mediterranean culture for millennia, and olive oil has often been referred to as "liquid gold" because of its color, consistent with the color of all the other items used in the Holy Place. The olive tree from which the olive fruit is derived is a hardy plant that is able to grow under relatively dry conditions by developing an extensive and deep root system. It is able to grow even in salty conditions near the sea where most other plants cannot grow. The oil from olives is actually a juice that is extracted by pressing the olive fruit. The resultant oil preserves the taste, smell, nutrients, and properties of the olive fruit and can be consumed fresh. Unlike most fruit juices, olive oil can be easily stored without refrigeration for up to a year without going bad if kept away from light and heat and is unaffected by humidity and insects or mold.

Olive oil has been part of a healthy Mediterranean diet for centuries and is famous for its healthy heart benefits—loaded in natural antioxidants and monounsaturated fats. It has also been in almost ubiquitous use for other purposes in the daily lives of the Middle Eastern people for the same period. It was applied in Ancient Greece by women to their skin and hair for protection against the elements of the weather and to give a pleasant aroma and was mixed with charcoal to produce eye shadow for beautification. The male Greek athletes rubbed olive oil on their skin to highlight the beauty of their bodies and combined it with sand to protect them from the sun and to regulate their body temperature. The oil has also been used to anoint dead bodies to mask their odor and to make soaps, medicines, and fuel for lamps. Indeed, possession of olives along with their oil has always been associated with great wealth. Olive oil remains an important part of the economic prosperity of countries such as Spain, Greece, and Italy.

Olive Oil and El Elyon

There is a symbolic spiritual connection with olive oil. The English etymology of the word "oil" actually originates from olive oil, which can be traced to the Latin word *oleum* (oil, olive oil) and the Greek word *elaion* (olive tree).[5] In turn, the word elaion appears to have been derived through trading networks from the Jewish Phoenician word *el'yon*, meaning "superior"—based on the known superiority of the oil compared to other vegetable oils of the time. The olive oil, with its superior and life-enhancing qualities, is the perfect symbolic oil for use in the worship of God.

Olive oil was a symbolic representation of the Holy Spirit within the Tabernacle and temple. Just as the Holy Spirit emanates from God and is a perfect representation of Him, preserving all the qualities of God, the olive juice that comes from olives preserves all the qualities of the original olive. Being gold in color, the use of olive oil in the Tabernacle and temple was consistent with God's perfect nature as were all the materials within the Holy Place. Its health and aesthetic benefits mirror the spiritual health benefits that result from a relationship with the Holy Spirit and from consuming a regular dose of the Word of God. The *wealth* derived from production of olive oil mirrors the "spiritual wealth" derived from cultivating a close relationship with God. Indeed, the origin and application of the word el'yon to olive oil has a direct connection to one of the key Jewish names of God, El Elyon, which means God Most High or Sovereign God. The olive oil thus represented a special daily anointing unto God recognizing His supremacy and sovereignty.

Olive oil symbolizes the Holy Spirit

Olive Oil: the Anointing and Consecrating Oil

Olive oil was also used for consecrating items as holy unto God[6] and for consecration of priests and royalty.[7] "Anoint Aaron and his sons and consecrate them so they may serve me as priests. Say to the Israelites, 'This is to be my sacred anointing oil for the generations to come. Do not pour it on anyone else's body and do not make any other oil using the same formula. It is sacred, and you are to consider it sacred'" (Exodus 30:30–32).

Anointing was used to set things or people apart for specific purposes. You are continuously anointed by the presence of the Holy Spirit within your Most Holy Place to set you apart to serve as a priest in the temple God has given you. Anointing with olive oil was associated with the presence or "pouring on" of the Holy Spirit. When David was anointed with oil by Samuel to become king of Israel, we are told that from that day on, the Holy Spirit came and dwelt in him: "So Samuel took the horn of oil and anointed him in the presence of his brothers, and from that day on the Spirit of the LORD came powerfully upon David" (1 Samuel 16:13).

Olive oil anointing was also associated with provisions, excellence, special blessings, and protection, all properties associated with the person of the Holy Spirit. "You prepare a table before me in the presence of my enemies. You anoint my head with oil; my cup overflows" (Psalm 23:5); "You are the most excellent of men and your lips have been anointed with grace, since God has blessed you forever" (Psalm 45:2); "Do not touch my anointed ones; do my prophets no harm" (Psalm 105:15).

Jesus was referred to as the Anointed One,[8] the ultimate ruler, and king. However, from the time of Jesus, the constant need for olive oil has been replaced by the direct presence of the Holy Spirit within your temple. Instead of using oil—which was purely a symbolic representation of the Holy Spirit—God directly anointed Jesus with the real person of the Holy Spirit. "How God *anointed* Jesus of Nazareth with the Holy Spirit and power, and how He went around doing good and healing all who were under the power of the devil because God was with Him" (Acts 10:38, emphasis added).

Similarly, as a believer and coheir with Jesus Christ, you have also been anointed with the Holy Spirit and with power. You also have the same authority Christ had. Because of the Holy Spirit in you, you do not need a daily dose of olive oil to confer you with authority. "Now it is God who makes both us and you stand firm in Christ. He *anointed us*, set His seal of ownership on us, and put His Spirit in our hearts as a deposit, guaranteeing what is to come" (2 Corinthians 1:21–22, emphasis added).

The Holy Spirit is the anointer and the anointing today, and He teaches you everything you need to know about God and how to live your life.[9] However, olive oil continues to play an important symbolic role in Christian worship, particularly in the healing ministry. Jesus' disciples still used oil to anoint and heal the sick everywhere they went.[10] We are also commanded by God through James that the sick within the church should be anointed with oil by the elders and prayed over in the name of Jesus to receive their healing.[11] I pray that you will receive the full anointing of the Holy Spirit today.

The Lamp and the Lamb of God

All the lamps of the menorah within the Tabernacle and temple were kept burning from evening till morning (Exodus 27:21). However, during the day, only the middle lamp, which symbolically was known as the "lamp of God," kept burning. "The lamp of God had not yet gone out, and Samuel was lying down in the house of the LORD, where the ark of God was" (1 Samuel 3:3).

Jesus is the light of the world

According to Jewish tradition, the middle "lamp of God" burned continuously all day even though it was usually the first to be kindled and had no more oil in it than the other lamps. This was considered an ongoing miracle during the original days of the temple built by King Solomon. However, about forty years before the destruction of this first temple in Jerusalem in 586 BCE, the sins of the Jewish people had become so great that this light was snuffed out and no longer burned continuously during the day.

Later, Jesus Christ came to the world as the Lamb of God who voluntarily died for our sins and the ultimate lamp of God who brought light into the world. "When Jesus spoke again to the people, he said, 'I am the light of the world. Whoever follows me will never walk in darkness but will have the light of life'" (John 8:12).

Similarly, God wants His light to continuously shine from within you. Your cooperation with Jesus Christ is determined by what you bring into your Holy Place through your eyes, ears and senses in your outer court to keep the light of the Holy Spirit within you from getting snuffed out. He needs your cooperation today.

What Type of Light Is in Your Soul?

The outer courts of the Tabernacle and temple were illuminated by natural light such as sunlight during the day and the moon at night. In contrast, the Holy Place had to be illuminated by light from the menorah using the special olive oil consecrated by God for such a purpose, which the priests lit daily to enable them to effectively perform their duties. The Holy Place was also periodically partially exposed to some natural light from the outer court. The use of olive oil was not only for illumination but also gave a strong symbolic connection to God in the person of the Holy Spirit. There was no way for the Holy Place to be lit if the priests did not focus on their duty to God and His commandments and go in daily to light the lamps. Neglect of their focus on God ultimately led to darkness within the Holy Place.

As with the Holy Place, the illumination of your soul is a direct result of the type of light you allow into it—either light focused on your flesh or light focused on God's Spirit within you. Your soul is alive and is a critical crossroads of your being and is influenced by the vitality of your intelligence, senses, understanding of the world around you, and your spiritual health. When you are a Christian whose focus is primarily on God's will for your life, the "lamp of God" shines within your soul and burns the pure olive oil of the Holy Spirit that will bless you and will be a blessing to the world.

"You are the light of the world. A town built on a hill cannot be hidden. Neither do people light a lamp and put it under a bowl. Instead they put it on its stand, and it gives light to everyone in the house. In the same way, let your light shine before others, that they may see your good deeds and glorify your Father in heaven" Matthew 5:13–16, NIV 2011). You have been created in God's image to let the light of the Holy Spirit within you shine brightly.

Your soul is the only part of you that will survive along with your spirit throughout eternity. God seeks to preserve it for eternal fellowship with Him in heaven, but satan would like to see it permanently destroyed in hell. It is not a coincidence that God intentionally excluded any imperfect materials from the Holy Place (in the temple and Tabernacle) because it was directly beside His resting place (the Most Holy Place).

Similarly, your soul in its natural state is the chamber closest to your spirit and has been created pure by God, and He intends it to be kept that way. However, the juxtaposition of your soul to your flesh (your outer place) also makes it vulnerable to allowing in impure and sinful elements that God never intended. Just as too much of the light from the outside can easily degrade pure olive oil and render it useless, constantly letting in sin and corruption through your flesh can degrade your mind and render the Holy Spirit within your heart useless. While your soul was created for perfection, you have free will and control over what you let into it. By allowing sin into your soul in the form of what you watch, consume, read, engage in, or listen to, you are contaminating and debasing the beautiful gift God has given you, which is akin to replacing the covering of pure gold within your mind with a covering of impure brass. When you sin, you effectively snuff out the "lamp of God" within you and your soul is left to fester in darkness, depriving you and the world of the blessings God has pre-ordained for you and through you. Alternatively, when the "lamp of God" that is Jesus Christ shines within you, there is no need to depend on natural light provided by the sun or moon from the outside to shine before others.

"The sun will no more be your light by day, nor will the brightness of the moon shine on you, for the LORD will be your everlasting light, and your God will be your glory. Your sun will never set again, and your moon will wane no more; the LORD will be your everlasting light, and your days of sorrow will end" (Isaiah 60:19–20). See to it then that the light within you is not darkness. "Therefore, if your whole body is full of light, and no part of it dark, it will be just as full of light as when a lamp shines its light on you" (Luke 11:35–36, NIV 2011).

I pray that you will always be full of light and your light will never be snuffed out. We will expand further on the significance of the light shining within you in chapter 14.

Pray This Prayer with Me:

Dear God Almighty, I thank You for giving me the Holy Spirit anointing that is the true representation of You to live within me. I pray that the pure olive oil burning within my soul and which represents Your "lamp" may never run out and indeed that it flows throughout my being in such a way that I can live the full measure of life that Jesus lived. As I carry Your lamp within me, may I shine brightly to the world, so that when people see me they will not see me but only see the light of Your presence within me, and I will be like a lighthouse that always draws people to You. Amen.

1. Philippians 2:10–11.
2. Matthew 10:12–13.
3. Galatians 5:22.
4. Leviticus 2:1–2, 4, 6:19–22, 8:12.
5. http://en.wikipedia.org/wiki/Olive_oil#cite_note-5.
6. Leviticus 8:11, 30; Numbers 7:10.
7. Exodus 29:5–7, 21; Exodus 30:30–32, 40:15; 1 Samuel 10:1; Judges 9:9; 1 Samuel 16:13; 1 Kings 1:34, 39, 19:16; 2 Kings 9:1–6.
8. Daniel 9:25–26; Acts 4:26, 27, 10:38.
9. 1 John 2:20, 27.
10. Mark 6:13.
11. James 5:14.

CHAPTER 8

The Holy Place and Your Soul: Bread of the Presence

(Session 4b)

The Bible is the bread of life, and it never becomes stale.—Our Daily Bread Campus Journal

Give us this day our daily bread.—Matthew 6:11, NASB

The Bread of the Presence

Adjacent to the right wall within the Holy Place of the Tabernacle and temple was a second object of furniture: the table of showbread (bread of the presence) (Figure D, Chapter 5). Twelve loaves of bread made from fine flour and consecrated to God were constantly placed on the table of showbread (Leviticus 24:5–9) and replaced every seven days on the Sabbath (holy day of rest). The bread of the presence symbolized the presence of God with each of the twelve tribes of Israel as well as their continual consecration to Him. During the Tabernacle days, only consecrated Levite priests could eat the bread of the presence.

In the new covenant between Jesus and believers in Christ, the bread of the presence symbolizes the Word of God that is available to all believers today. When you become a believer in Jesus Christ, you become one of God's "royal priests." "But you are a chosen people, a royal priesthood, a holy nation, God's special possession, that you may declare the praises of

Him who called you out of darkness into His wonderful light" (1 Peter 2:9, NIV 2011).

As a priest, your temple is your body that houses the Spirit of God, and you have access to a direct and daily relationship with God. The Word of God as found in the Holy Bible is your "bread of presence." It should be regularly ingested and digested by you in order for it to be influential in your Holy Place (your mind), just as the bread of the presence was continuously located in the Holy Place of the Tabernacle and temple. In the Bible, Jesus Christ is synonymous with the Word of God and was called the Word of God in the Gospel written by the apostle John. "In the beginning was the Word, and the Word was with God, and the Word was God" (John 1:1).

In addition to being the Word of God, Jesus also called Himself the "bread of life": "I am the bread of life. Your ancestors ate the manna in the wilderness, yet they died. But here is the bread that comes down from heaven, which anyone may eat and not die. I am the living bread that came down from heaven. Whoever eats this bread will live forever. This bread is My flesh, which I will give for the life of the world" (John 6:48–51, NIV 2011).

God's Word (in the Bible) is the bread of life

Since Jesus as the "Bread of Life" is the same person referred to as the "Word of God," as a believer in Christ whenever you are reading and meditating on His Word as written in the Bible, you are also imparting the "Bread of Life" Himself (Jesus Christ) within you. When Jesus talks about the "eating of the bread that comes down from heaven," He is referring to two things. The first is the sacrament of Holy Communion that we observe as Christians when we eat bread that represents His body that came down from heaven, which He broke for us. When we drink wine, it represents His blood that was shed for our sins on the cross at Calvary. "While they were eating, Jesus took bread, gave thanks and broke it, and gave it to His disciples, saying, 'Take and eat; this is My body.' Then He took the cup, gave thanks and offered it to them, saying, 'Drink from it, all of you. This is My blood of the covenant, which is poured out for many for the forgiveness of sins'" (Matthew 26:26–28).

Jesus—the Bread of Life and the Word of God—is also referring to the need for you to continuously ingest His words, which represent bread that gives life to your soul. Your focus cannot be on meeting your bodily needs alone but on taking in God's word daily. "Jesus answered, 'It is written: "Man shall not live on bread alone, but on every word that comes from the mouth of God"'" (Matthew 4:4, NIV 2011).

This truth is greatly exemplified by Job in the Old Testament, who upon losing everything important to him in his life—his family, his health, and his possessions—was kept whole by God and restored to a situation where he received double his previous blessings by relying more on God's words than on bread: "I have treasured the words of his mouth more than my daily bread" (Job 23:12b).

God can do the same for you when you treat His Word as more precious than bread.

Benefits of the Word of God

The Word of God has the power to give salvation and righteousness to everyone who believes. "I am not ashamed of the gospel because it is the power of God for the salvation of everyone who believes: first for the Jew, then for the Gentile. For in the gospel a righteousness from God is revealed, a righteousness that is by faith from first to last, just as it is written: 'The righteous will live by faith'" (Romans 1:16–17).

The Word of God helps to consecrate you and keep you from sinning: "I have hidden your word in my heart that I might not sin against you" (Psalm 119:11), and "How can a young man keep his way pure? By living according to your word" (Psalm 119:9).

The Word of God brings healing: "He sent forth his word and healed them; he rescued them from the grave" (Psalm 107:20) and "When evening came, many who were demon-possessed were brought to him, and he drove out the spirits with a word and healed all the sick" (Matthew 8:16).

The Word of God serves as a lamp that illuminates your temple and gives direction to your life: "Your word is a lamp to my feet and a light for my path" (Psalm 119:105).

The Word of God gives you wisdom: "The proverbs of Solomon son of David, king of Israel: for attaining wisdom and discipline; for understanding words of insight; for acquiring a disciplined and prudent life, doing what is right and just and fair" (Proverbs 1:1–3).

The Word of God blesses you as you obey its commands: "He replied, 'Blessed rather are those who hear the word of God and obey it'" (Luke 11:28). The Word of God contains promises to you that are certain and that you can hold on to: "As the rain and the snow come down from heaven, and do not return to it without watering the earth and making it bud and flourish, so that it yields seed for the sower and bread for the eater, so is my word that goes out from my mouth: It will not return to me empty, but will accomplish what I desire and achieve the purpose for which I sent it" (Isaiah 55:10–11).

The Word of God serves as a weapon against your enemies—the "Sword of the Spirit": "Take the helmet of salvation and the sword of the Spirit, which is the word of God" (Ephesians 6:17). When you regularly consume and meditate on God's word, it becomes a weapon that you can use to resist temptation and the attack of the enemy. It helps you tip the scale of balance in the battle for your soul between your Most Holy Place and your outer court in favor of your Most Holy Place.

Your hunger for God will always be rewarded

"For the word of God is living and active. Sharper than any double-edged sword, it penetrates even to dividing soul [psyche, Holy Place] and spirit [Most Holy Place], joints and marrow [body, outer court]; it judges the thoughts and attitudes of the heart" (Hebrews 4:12).

The Word of God helps keep your enemies at bay—particularly your most determined ones. Jesus regularly ate and digested the Word of God so much that it was a weapon He used to defuse all the attacks of satan upon His life.[1] When He was in the wilderness, being tempted by the devil, it was His knowledge of the word of God that Jesus used to refute all the attempts of satan to try to get Him to sin. Similarly, you must strongly hunger and thirst for and desire God to resist satan's attacks just like most of God's most ardent pursuers, such as King David of Israel, hungered and "thirsted" for Him.

King David, while being far from perfect, was known as a man "after God's heart" because of this constant longing and thirst for God. In return, God satisfied him and rewarded David with a close relationship, guiding him step by step into becoming one of the most famous and successful kings of Israel and a direct ancestor of the future Messiah, the Lord Jesus Christ. "As the deer pants for streams of water, so my soul pants for you, my God. My soul thirsts for God, for the living God. When can I go and meet with God?" (Psalm 42:1–2)

The Word of God teaches you to become the person God wants you to be and corrects you when you go off track: "All Scripture is God-breathed and is useful for teaching, rebuking, correcting and training in righteousness, so that the man of God may be thoroughly equipped for every good work" (2 Timothy 3:16–17). Additionally: "For these commands are a lamp, this teaching is a light, and the corrections of discipline are the way to life" (Proverbs 6:23).

The Word of God builds your faith: "Consequently, faith comes from hearing the message, and the message is heard through the word of Christ" (Romans 10:17).

The Word of God gives hope: "Do not snatch the word of truth from my mouth, for I have put my hope in your laws" (Psalm 119:43); "Remember your word to your servant, for you have given me hope" (Psalm 119:49); and "I wait for the LORD, my soul waits, and in His word I put my hope" (Psalm 130:5).

I pray you will also develop a constant hunger and thirst for God's Word in your life such that you can fully gain the benefits of a strong relationship with him throughout your life.

The Word of God Is the Seed for Your Life

Another illustration of the Word of God is that of a seed, which, when planted within your mind, has the ability to germinate, grow, and blossom into a powerful plant that bears fruit to feed your soul. We have already established earlier that Jesus is the Word of God[2] and the Bread of Life. However, Jesus is also referred to as the seed. The promises were spoken to Abraham and to his seed. Scripture does not say "and to seeds," meaning many people, but "and to your seed," meaning one person, who is Christ. Why then was the law given at all? It was added because of transgressions until the seed to whom the promise referred had come (see Galatians 3:16, 19, NIV 2011).

Jesus, who is described as the Word of God is also the seed, which when ingested blossoms and bears fruit that enables you to take on more of His nature in your daily life. After all, a seed can only develop into the type of plant for which it is programmed; an apple tree cannot grow oranges. However, the degree of bounty of the harvest to be gained in your mind when you deposit the seed of the "Word of God" depends on how well you cultivate and nurture your mind to receive the seed. If it is contaminated with so many other types of seed from your outer court, the seed will be snuffed out and will never yield good crops. However, when the seed of the Word of God is the primary seed in your soul, your harvest will be bountiful. In a parable taught by Jesus, He talked of a farmer who went to sow seed: "A farmer went out to sow his seed. As he was scattering the seed, some fell along the path; it was trampled on, and the birds ate it up. Some fell on rocky ground, and when it came up, the plants withered because they had no moisture. Other seed fell among thorns, which grew up with it and choked the plants. Still other seed fell on good soil. It came up and yielded a crop, a hundred times more than was sown" (Luke 8:5–8, NIV 2011).

Later Jesus explained to His disciples: "This is the meaning of the parable: The seed is the word of God" (Luke 8:11). The ground where the seed is deposited is your mind. Many people hear God's word, but they are quickly deceived to reject it or let it go because it falls on the path where it is trampled upon—other more persuasive ideas and distractive activities orchestrated by satan in their outer court are simply more powerful for them. Others read or hear the Word and gladly receive it, but their minds are "rocky"—too hardened by rocks of doubt to believe God is capable of doing what He said so there is no room for the roots of God's Word to spread. For some people, the value of the Word that you read, even after it has blossomed and borne fruit in you is ultimately crowded out or choked by all of life's worries, riches, and the pleasures that have made it to your mind from your flesh, and that you have become accustomed to having in your life, and the seed's products are rendered useless.

As a daily dose of vitamins for your body is God's word for your soul

You must aim to eat and digest the seed of God's Word every day to get the maximum benefit from it (the crop that yields a hundredfold more than you sow). Seek to know the Word of God intimately and ensure your mind is well cultivated to receive the Word, just as Jesus did when He walked on earth. This way it can spring up and be available to comfort and protect you when you need it for every situation you may encounter in your life. Knowing and constantly depositing and nurturing God's Word in your mind and following what it says makes you more like Jesus. It gives you the confidence to believe in God's promises to you and the freedom from behaving as the rest of the world is obligated to.[3] May God grant you a bounty of daily deposits of His word into your mind!

Pray This Prayer with Me:

Dear Lord, please let the seed of the bread of the presence, which is the Word of God, be constantly deposited and renewed in me daily and that it falls on good and fertile soil within my soul so that it can serve as a source of comfort and wisdom for every situation in my life. Amen.

Questions to Ponder:

- What does it mean to be "anointed" today?
- Do you believe Christians are anointed for specific purposes?
- Do you believe God has anointed you for any purpose? If yes, for what?
- Is there enough evidence in the church of the anointing of the body of Christ?
- Can anointing be sought after or is it something you either have or you do not?
- Review the described benefits of the Word of God from the last two chapters.
  - Have you experienced any of these benefits?
  - Describe your experience with one of these benefits.
- Do you think you know enough of what the Bible says to be able to fully benefit from it? If not, how can you increase your knowledge?

Prayer Points

- Pray for God to reveal to you what He has specially anointed you for today.
- Pray for God to increase your anointing in the areas for which He has called you to serve.
- Pray for God to increase the anointing of the Holy Spirit on the body of Christ at your local church and churches across America.
- Pray that God will show you and the other members of your group how to receive the full blessings from His written and spoken word.

1.   Matthew 4:1–11; Luke 4:1–13.
2.   John 1:1
3.   John 8:31–32.

CHAPTER 9

The Altar of Incense—
The Power of Praise and Prayer

(Session 5a)

Make an altar of acacia wood for burning incense ... "Aaron must burn fragrant incense on the altar every morning when he tends the lamps. He must burn incense again when he lights the lamps at twilight so incense will burn regularly before the LORD for the generations to come."—Exodus 30:1, 7–8

As we noted in chapter 5, there were two altars in the Jewish temple and the Tabernacle. The first was the brazen altar, located in the outer court which was used to offer the blood of animals sacrificed for the sins of the people in order to restore Holy relationships with God prior to contact with Him. The other temple altar was the golden altar, or altar of incense located within the Holy Place just in front of the veil separating the Holy Place from the Most Holy Place. The altar of incense was a place where God's priests continuously burned special incense as an offering of intercessory prayer to draw themselves close to God—"an aroma, pleasing to God" (Leviticus 2:2; 6:15). Each morning and evening, the priests offered this incense to God while tending to the light of the golden candlestick. In addition, once a year, on a day known as the Day of Atonement (Yom Kippur), selected animals were consecrated and sacrificed and their blood was sprinkled by the high priest on the horns of this altar for all the sins of the Israelites.

Your Daily Prayers Are like Incense to God

The incense offered in the temple and Tabernacle at the golden altar was symbolic of prayers of worship being offered up daily to God in heaven. The altar incense was made up of four ingredients: *stacte* (gum resin), *onycha*, *galbanum*, and frankincense (*olibanum*), all in equal parts.[1] Stacte, galbanum, and frankincense were all resins extracted from different trees and plants that were finely beaten and mixed with the shell of onycha,[2] an aromatic shellfish found in the Red Sea and Indian Ocean. Resins are secretions from plants that have the properties of repelling different kinds of insects, herbivores, and other predators that can harm the plant while attracting protective animals that can repel the herbivores that attack the plant. Frankincense in particular was regarded as a highly precious, sweet, and balsamic-smelling perfume originating from a hardy tree (*Boswellia*) that grows widely in India and North Africa, and is mentioned numerous times in the Bible.[3] It was often used alone in several Jewish rites and was one of the three gifts given by the wise men from the East who came to pay their respects to Jesus.[4] Together when burnt, these four components of incense produced a pleasant fragrance that was constantly released up to God in heaven from the Holy Place and their combination was strictly restricted for use in worshipping God.[5] This mixture of incense symbolized a formula for acceptable and pleasing prayer to God in both the Old and New Testaments of the Bible.

"And another angel came and stood at the altar, having a golden censer; and there was given unto him much incense, that he should offer it with the prayers of all saints upon the golden altar which was before the throne. And the smoke of the incense, which came with the prayers of the saints, ascended up before God out of the angel's hand" (Revelation 8:3-4, KJV). This passage in Revelation is referring to part of a vision of heaven seen by the apostle John. A censer is a vessel that is used to burn incense. Just as the golden altar in the Tabernacle and the temple was located in front of the Most Holy Place where God's mercy seat (representing His throne) was, God revealed to John that the original and permanent golden altar is also placed in front of God's throne in heaven. Furthermore, it is revealed that the incense represents or is closely associated with our prayers.

"And when he had taken it, the four living creatures and the twenty-four elders fell down before the Lamb. Each one had a harp and they were holding golden bowls full of incense, which are the prayers of God's people" Revelation 5:8, NIV 2011). The prayers that you offer to God with your own lips are like incense offered to God on your golden altar that rise and fill up golden bowls in heaven. "Let my prayer be set forth before thee as incense; and the lifting up of my hands as the evening sacrifice" (Psalm 141:2, KJV). These prayers, as with the incense offered to God when submitted regularly, are associated with blessings.

"He offers incense before you and whole burnt offerings on your altar. Bless all his skills, LORD, and be pleased with the work of his hands. Strike down those who rise against him, his foes till they rise no more" (Deuteronomy 33:10–11, NIV 2011). Just as the resins used in the golden altar incense enable protection for the trees and plants from which they are derived, the righteous prayers you offer up to God are "an aroma pleasing to God" that are also designed to protect you, repel your enemies and attract good virtues to you. The more you pray (communicate with God) the more your "golden bowl" in heaven is filled up. As with any bowl, the fuller it is, the more likely it is to spill over and has to be reckoned with. Your goal is to get your bowl overflowing so that God has to reckon with it.

Righteous prayers and praise are an aroma pleasing to God

As an illustration, consider the parable of the persistent widow told by Jesus. A widow who had been wronged kept going to a judge who "neither feared God nor cared what people thought."[6] The judge initially ignored her, but she persisted in going to him for justice. Eventually, the judge capitulated and gave her justice—not because he cared for her but because she kept coming back! "And the Lord said, 'Listen to what the unjust judge says. And will not God bring about justice for his chosen ones, who cry out to him day and night? Will he keep putting them off? I tell you, he will see that they get justice, and quickly'" (Luke 18:6–7). The widow kept "praying" until her prayer bowl overflowed. This is why you must continuously lift up your prayers to heaven, even when you do not seem to be getting results. You must never give up praying for issues that are important to you. God always hears you, but many people stop praying before their prayer bowl is even half full. Pray continuously until your prayer bowl is overflowing.

The Lord's Prayer: the Perfect Model to Build Your Relationship with God.

A thousand years after Solomon built the temple, Jesus taught His disciples the Lord's Prayer (Matthew 6:9–13, KJV) as a model of perfect *relationship building prayer* to God. Prayer is simply a means of communicating with God that enables you to be in touch with your heavenly Father and to continuously have the benefit of His wisdom. *There is no proper method of praying to God.* You can communicate with God in many different ways, depending on your situation. There are emergency prayers, raised in moments of desperation. There are intercessory prayers raised when the Holy Spirit moves you to pray specifically for someone or something. There are prayers that you pray just to say thank you to God, prayers in the Spirit[7] when you are uncertain how to pray, and so forth. All are important and can be effective. However, examining the structure of the Lord's Prayer gives a model of how to pray in most ordinary situations where your main goal is to dedicate time to building your relationship with God.

Just like the tabernacle incense had four components, the Lord's Prayer is also made up of four components.

The first component consists of *praise* (or adoration), occurring at the beginning and end of the prayer. Sandwiched in the middle of the praise are three requests. The second component (first request) is prayer to *increase the kingdom of God on Earth.* The third component consists of two *requests for specific needs* (daily bread and forgiveness). The final component is prayer for protection (such as *avoidance of temptation or deliverance from evil).*

Praise: The beginning and the end of the Lord's Prayer are comprised of praising God for who He is: "Our Father, which art in heaven, hallowed be thy name … for thine is the kingdom and the power and the glory for ever and ever. Amen" (Matthew 6: 9b, 13b, KJV).

Praising God is worshipping and adoring Him. To be "hallowed" is to be holy, venerated, or sanctified. It means holding God's name in the highest regard. There are three main reasons to praise God. The first is that you were created for this specific purpose (1 Peter 2:9). When you praise God, you clear the atmosphere for the full manifestation of His presence. There are several examples in the Bible of God's presence manifesting and victory being delivered as a result of the praise of His people.[8] When Paul and Silas, followers of Jesus, were unlawfully flogged and thrown into jail, instead of getting depressed and feeling sorry for themselves, they responded by praying and singing hymns of praise to God. As a result, a miracle occurred. "About midnight, Paul and Silas were *praying and singing hymns to God,* and the other prisoners were listening to them. Suddenly there was such a violent earthquake that the foundations of the prison were shaken. At once all the prison doors flew open, and everyone's chains came loose. The jailer woke up, and when he saw the prison doors open, he drew his sword and was about to kill himself because he thought the prisoners had escaped. But Paul shouted, 'Don't harm yourself! We are all here!'" (Acts 16:25–28, emphasis added). In the same manner, God wants you to praise Him, no matter what your circumstance in life may be. It is often in the midst of your praising Him in spite of your circumstances that miracles that will change your situation will occur.

Praise is designed to remind you of the full extent of who God is so your perspective of everything in your life changes. When you praise God, you are *Praise God to remind you who He is* reminded that He is the most powerful Being, the Creator and ruler of the whole universe, the one who is present everywhere, and yet spends intimate time with you, who is all-knowing and all wise and yet your most ardent lover and best friend. You are reminded that He is your divine healer, your divine lover, and your most vigilant defender. He is your miraculous provider and the only one who can grant you peace at the mention of a single word.

This is a lot wrapped up in one person! When you view God this way, your huge mountain of problems become insignificant in light of how great He is and His ability to help you overcome. It is no coincidence that the Lord's Prayer begins and ends with praise and why you should also always strive to begin and end your relationship-building prayers with praises and words or songs of worship to God. The praises will enable you to be encouraged about whom you are praying to, knowing that He is bigger than any circumstance you may be facing. If you do not yet know how to praise God or feel comfortable in praising Him, reading out the book of Psalms in the Old Testament (especially beginning from about Psalm 46 onward) is a great way to start.[9] King David, the author of much of the book of Psalms was devout at directing his soul (Holy Place) toward God through praise, and as a result was enabled to communicate regularly with God and gain all the benefits of a close relationship with Him.

David frequently praised God with all his soul: "Praise the LORD, my soul; all my inmost being, praise His holy name. Praise the LORD, my soul, and forget not all His benefits—who forgives all your sins and heals all your diseases, who redeems your life from the pit and crowns you with love and compassion, who satisfies your desires with good things so that your youth is renewed like the eagle's. ... Praise the LORD. Praise the LORD, my soul" (Psalm 103:1–5, 146:1, NIV 2011).

Praise is intended to remind you to thank God for all He has done for you. This is evident in David's psalms; he clearly knew and appreciated how much God had done for him. Giving thanks should also be a specific part of your praise time. Take time to thank Him for all He has done for you, and even though it is impossible to list them all, remember to specifically thank Him for what He has done for you recently. Even when things do not seem to be going well for you, thank Him anyway because He is still God and He knows what He is doing. "Rejoice always, pray continually, give thanks in all circumstances; for this is God's will for you in Christ Jesus" (1 Thessalonians 5:16–18, NIV 2011).

Your thankful praise will carry you through challenging periods because it will encourage you and ultimately you will look back and see that God was not only with you during these times, He also provided all you needed and always had a great plan for you.

Increasing God's Kingdom on Earth: The next component of the Lord's Prayer is increasing His kingdom on Earth. "Thy kingdom come, Thy will be done in earth, as it is in heaven" (Matthew 6:10 KJV).

This part of the Lord's Prayer is very easy to glaze over. However, it is not just a placeholder in the prayer but an equally important component to all the others. God wants you to pray for His kingdom to come on earth even *before* you pray for your own specific requests. This is because when you first take care of kingdom business, the King will take care of you. "But *seek ye first* the kingdom of God, and His righteousness; and all these things shall be added unto you" (Matthew 6:33, KJV, emphasis added).

This means you should be praying for and providing opportunities for God's love to be shown, and the gospel to be preached locally and globally for the salvation of everyone, including your loved ones, your coworkers, unsaved nations, and others ahead of your own needs! God promises that when you do this, He will in turn give you all you need.

The House of God Is a House of Prayer for the Nations

Tied to praying for God's kingdom to come, Jesus indicated that God's temple—now represented by you, is intended as a house of prayer for the nations. "Is it not written: 'My house will be called a house of prayer for all nations'? But you have made it 'a den of robbers'" (Mark 11:17).[10]

There are several implications to this statement. The first is that you as God's temple should be first and foremost a temple where you are in constant communication with God through prayer. Secondly, God in calling His house a "house of prayer for all nations" is stating that He wants you to pray not only for yourself but for people from all the nations. He wants people from all nations to be part of His house! His primary motivation is to bring all nations regardless of background to His saving grace and recognition of the hope of spending eternity in His presence. Indeed, Christ made it clear that we should hunger as believers to see people come to God. Why? Because God wants the whole world to have had the opportunity to hear the gospel before the end times come. "And this gospel of the kingdom will be preached in the whole world as a testimony to all nations, *and then* the end will come" (Matthew 24:14, emphasis added).

The gospel can only be preached by those who know Jesus which includes you and me. Beyond praying, Jesus commands us to make disciples of nations: "Therefore go and *make disciples* of all nations, baptizing them in the name of the Father and of the Son and of the Holy Spirit" (Matthew 28:19, emphasis added).

Everybody is part of a nation, which includes your neighborhood and your friends, as well as those far away from you. I pray that the Lord will instill in you the desire to pray for and materially support the local and global spreading of the gospel of Jesus. Whenever you can, remember to pray for people in other nations. You should also consider joining friends or others in praying for nations and peoples around the world either as part of a small prayer group or within your church.

Specific Requests: Daily Bread and Forgiveness

Daily Bread.

Sandwiched in the middle of the Lord's Prayer are your specific requests to God (supplication). The first request is for God to meet your daily physical needs: "Give us this day our daily bread" (Matthew 6:11, KJV). When you pray, it is important to recognize that the bread Jesus refers to is not only the food you eat each day. You are also asking God to give you more of Jesus (the Bread of Life) and a fresh deposit of His Word and His Holy Spirit each day. You are refreshing not only your body but your soul. When you have a fresh deposit of God's Spirit, He will always lead you to where you will get your daily bread or He will arrange for it to be delivered to you. Also note that Jesus said you should pray by asking God to "give *us* this day *our* daily bread" not "give *me* this day *my* daily bread." The use of plural is not a coincidence. God wants you to pray for the needs of others, not just your own. In requesting your daily bread, you should be praying for others to get their daily deposit to meet not only their physical but their spiritual and other needs and be constantly asking God for how you can contribute to the needs of others. When you pray for the needs of others and also seek to share what God has blessed you with, God will always reward you in turn.

God wants us to be rivers where His blessings constantly flow through us to others, and where there is abundance of life—not ponds that hold on to all we have been given and are not able to support others. Consider the richness of species that thrive on river beds compared with the relative lack of life in stagnant lakes. Life thrives when blessings are passed on. I pray God will give your life the richness of a river and not the stagnation of a stagnant lake.

When you pray for others, God remembers your own needs

As we discussed earlier, "daily bread" also refers to the Word of God as revealed in the Bible. An important part of relationship-building prayer is reading the Word of God regularly to get a dose of your daily bread, and spending some quiet time to hear what God is trying to reveal to you through His word and His Spirit.

Forgiveness.

The second request in the Lord's Prayer is asking God for forgiveness of your sins: "Forgive us our debts [or trespasses], as we also have forgiven our debtors" (Matthew 6:12). Confess to God directly any specific debts (sins) that you have committed and ask God to forgive you so that God will not only fully release you from them, but you will also be released from the burden of guilt. There is no unforgivable sin, nothing you have done that God cannot overlook if you come to Him with a penitent heart and are determined never to commit the same sin again. Nothing can separate you from the love of God.[11]

Christ died so that you can have direct access to God. As a result, you can make your confessions directly to God as an adopted member of His family. You no longer need any intermediary. However, when you ask God for forgiveness, you are also obligated to forgive those who have sinned against you. Since God gave up His only natural Son, Jesus Christ to die so that all your sins may be forgiven, your lack of forgiveness of others for sins committed against you is like slapping God in the face and you will forfeit the opportunity from God to be forgiven of your own sins: "For if you forgive other people when they sin against you, your heavenly Father will also forgive you. But if you do not forgive others their sins, your Father will not forgive your sins" (Matthew 6:14–15, NIV 2011).

Jesus warned Peter, one of His closest disciples, about the danger of unforgiveness through the parable of the unmerciful servant. In this parable, a king forgave his servant a debt worth the equivalent of ten thousand bags of gold. However, as soon as his own debt was forgiven, this servant refused to forgive or even have patience on a fellow servant who owed him the equivalent of only a hundred silver coins. When the king heard about this, he was outraged. "Then the master called the servant in. 'You wicked servant,' he said, 'I canceled all that debt of yours because you begged me to. Shouldn't you have had mercy on your fellow servant just as I had on you?' In anger his master handed him over to the jailers to be tortured, until he should pay back all he owed. 'This is how my heavenly Father will treat each of you unless you forgive your brother or sister from your heart'" (Matthew 18:32-35 NIV 2011).

Notice that Jesus was talking to one of His disciples who believed in Him, and yet He said, "This is how my heavenly father will treat each of you unless you forgive." This shows that even if you are saved, your lack of forgiveness of others can still put you in danger of eternal torture and condemnation. But God is always ready to forgive the penitent heart; it is never too late to forgive. Who are you still holding a grudge against and how can you forgive that person?

The Holy Spirit Helps You Forgive.

Forgiveness can be very difficult. You often cannot forgive on your own strength, especially when the perpetrator of the crime against you seems to be living a happy and apparently successful life, oblivious to the impact their act has had or is having on you or perhaps aware but unrepentant about it. You need the help of the Holy Spirit to forgive. Pray to God that you will receive a full measure of the Holy Spirit to help you forgive those who have hurt you. Even with repeated episodes, your failure to forgive impacts you more than it impacts the perpetrator. Lack of forgiveness opens the door of your mind to evil, especially to anger and rage that can derail your eternal destiny. "Do not be quickly provoked in your spirit, for anger resides in the lap of fools" (Ecclesiastes 7:9).

"My dear brothers and sisters, take note of this: Everyone should be quick to listen, slow to speak and slow to become angry, because human anger does not produce the righteousness that God desires" (James 1:19–20, NIV 2011). In fact, Paul teaches that unforgiveness and anger lead the Holy Spirit living within you to grieve. "And do not grieve the Holy Spirit of God, with whom you were sealed for the day of redemption. Get rid of all bitterness, rage and anger, brawling and slander, along with every form of malice. Be kind and compassionate to one another, forgiving each other, just as in Christ God forgave you" (Ephesians 4:30–32).

Forgiveness is refusing to drink your own poison

Failure to forgive is akin to grabbing hold of a grenade, pulling the pin, and hoping your enemy gets blown up by it. Chances are most of the time you are holding on to the source of your own destruction.

Forgiveness Does Not Mean Giving Up Justice.

God is the one who gives justice, and even though it may seem that the person is getting away with a crime, God sees all things and works all things for the good of those who love Him, for all who have been called according to His purpose—including you.[12] "Do not take revenge, my friends, but leave room for God's wrath, for it is written: 'It is mine to avenge; I will repay,' says the Lord" (Romans 12:19).

God wants you to forgive because even though it may not be that obvious to you, He has forgiven you a lot more for what you have done to Him than what has been done to you. God gave up His one and only precious Son to come to Earth, endure overwhelming suffering and torture, and die a horrible death on a cross for crimes He did not commit so that He could carry the burden of all your sins and my sins so that we would be forgiven and not have to suffer eternal condemnation.

As unfair as it may seem to you, the perpetrator of the crime against you is also God's child, and He wants him or her to have a chance to get to heaven, despite how evil and horrible that person may seem to you at the time.

Consider Jesus as your model. After He had been accused of things He did not do, was repeatedly and brutally beaten, and then nailed to the cross, He still had the grace to utter the words, "Father, *forgive them*, for they do not know what they are doing" (Luke 23:34, emphasis added). Jesus knew God could have sent His angels to destroy all those involved in causing the pain and suffering He had been put through for crimes He did not commit. He forgave in order to give all those involved in His suffering a chance at knowing about God's saving grace so they would still have the opportunity to make it to heaven. This is what you do when you forgive.

Forgiveness Does Not Mean Condoning Injustice or Sin.

Forgiving someone for what he or she has done to you does not mean you approve of it or that you will totally forget what was done. Neither does it mean there should be no consequences to the person responsible. What it does mean is that the Holy Spirit will enable you to personally move on each time you remember. Forgiveness also does not mean you should exhibit poor judgment and continue to allow an ongoing evil act to be perpetrated against you or others. If you are in this situation, you must act to remove yourself or the person involved.

Forgiveness is simply saying you will not allow the act committed against you to cause you to harbor bitterness and anger that consume your thoughts, ultimately leading to actions of revenge that will lead you to sin and could possibly lead to your own destruction. It also means the act committed against you should not stop you from showing kindness to the perpetrator of the crime if you are in a position to do so.

There are several amazing stories of courageous individuals who have forgiven others for horrible crimes committed against them and whose actions have resulted in the demonstration of the saving grace of the knowledge of Jesus Christ. In the book *Rachel's Tears*, written by Beth Nimmo and Darrell Scott in memory of their seventeen-year-old daughter, Rachel, who was the first victim killed in the 1999 Columbine High School massacre, Beth and Darrell describe why they forgave their daughter's killers. Here is an excerpt that cogently describes what forgiveness meant to them:

"Forgiving the Unforgivable"

People respond differently to tragedy when it strikes their lives. Some never get over it. Others become bitter and angry, and that is easily understandable. However, we are given the opportunity to experience a realm of grace that is incomprehensible to some when we choose to forgive. Were we angry when our daughter was killed? Yes! Were we sad? Beyond description! But are we forgiving? That is probably one of the most difficult issues to face when you have been so deeply wronged. Our understanding of God's heart left us only one choice, the decision to forgive. It was the choice of Jesus as He hung on a cross dying. He said in Matthew 5:43–44: "You have heard that it was said, 'Love your neighbor and hate your enemy.' But I tell you: Love your enemies and pray for those who persecute you." Forgiveness is not just for the offender. It is also for the one who is offended. If we do not forgive, we end up in perpetual anger and bitterness and eventually offend others with our words or actions. If we forgive, we experience a "letting go" or cleansing process that frees us from the offender. There is a great misunderstanding about forgiveness. Forgiveness is not pardon. Forgiveness is an attitude, while pardon is an action.... Such a thing is beyond human ability, but it is possible when we acknowledge our weakness and submit to God's grace."[13]

Forgiveness gives freedom to both you and your perpetrator

Similarly, Reverend Dale Lang chose forgiveness over anger and revenge when his teenage son was killed in Taber, Alberta, Canada, in a copycat shooting just eight days after the Columbine High School massacre. In an interview with the Ottawa *Citizen* newspaper, Reverend Lang noted

> If it wasn't for the grace of God in my life, I think I would be a very angry man. When I share my story, I talk about the initial anger—and the pain. But you don't have to live with

the anger. We prayed and we forgave the boy [who did the shooting]. That was very healing for our family.

More recently, following the killing of his 6-year-old daughter Emily Parker during the Sandy Hook Elementary School massacres in Newtown, Connecticut, her father Robbie Parker showed extraordinary grace and forgiveness in reaching out to her killer's family in love and prayers during a press conference even as his deep sense of loss was clearly visible.

Forgiveness is a powerful tool that God uses to release both the victim and the perpetrator from traps and to encourage repentance that will draw even His most wicked children back to Himself. In choosing forgiveness over revenge and hatred for three hundred years of oppressive, violent, and racist apartheid and the numerous heinous crimes committed to support it, Nelson Mandela and Desmond Tutu and others changed the future history of South Africa and prevented the inevitable and widely anticipated massive bloodshed. As noted by Mandela, "Men of peace must not think about retribution or recriminations. Courageous people do not fear forgiving, for the sake of peace." By contrast, in choosing hatred over forgiveness, up to a million Tutsis and moderate Hutus lost their lives in Rwanda's 1994 genocide and thousands in the "ethnic cleansing" and genocides that occurred in Srebrenica and all around Bosnia in the former Yugoslavia and the consequences are still being dealt with today. May God grant you the full grace to release any person you are still harboring anger against in your heart for a crime committed against you.

Pray for God to Forgive Those Who Have Sinned against You

Notice that in pluralizing the part of the Lord's prayer dealing with forgiveness: "forgive *us our* debts as we also have forgiven *our* debtors" (emphasis added), Jesus was effectively saying you should be praying not only for forgiveness of your own sins but for the sins of others, including those who have committed the crime against you. Praying for someone who has done you injustice is a powerful method of coming to a point of forgiveness and is actually commanded by Jesus.

"But to you who are listening I say: Love your enemies, do good to those who hate you, bless those who curse you, pray for those who mistreat you" (Luke 6: 27–28, NIV 2011). Try praying for forgiveness for your enemies and you will be amazed at how God will transform your demeanor toward them and enable you to start to view them differently than you currently do. This may be difficult at first, but ask God to grant you the grace to carry it through, and you are promised by Jesus that, "Then your reward will be great, and you will be children of the Most High, because He is kind to the ungrateful and wicked" (Luke 6:35, NIV 2011).

Avoidance of Temptation and Deliverance from Evil:

The final part in the Lord's Prayer is the request for deliverance from satan's schemes for your life: "And lead us not into temptation, but deliver us from evil" (Matthew 6:13, KJV). Notice that Jesus says you should pray that you are not led into temptation, not that you should seek temptation first as many people do and then ask for deliverance afterward. You should refrain from things and places you know will be cause for you to want to sin. When you pray, you should make your requests for protection or other needs to God specific so God can answer them specifically. You should mention what your areas of temptation are—such as gambling, drinking, drugs, pornography, sex, pride, or greed—and ask God daily to keep you away from them. You then need to plan ahead to avoid these situations or it will be too late if you try to resist when you are suddenly exposed to your weakness.

Avoidance of temptation is always better than escape

Billy Graham, while far from perfect, is considered one of the world's greatest evangelists. He has preached the gospel during a career that spanned more than 6 decades to billions of people, including more than 215 million people in person and 1.5 billion worldwide on the same day on April 14, 1995.[14] Millions of people can credit Graham for leading them to Christ. In spite of these extraordinary accomplishments, perhaps the most remarkable aspect of his career is that there has never been a hint of the scandal that has plagued the careers of several other leading evangelists associated with Graham. Why? Because in 1948, while in Modesto, California, Graham, along with his close friends and ministry partners George Beverly Shea, Grady Wilson, and Cliff Barrows made a concerted decision early in their career to avoid the three major areas that they concluded were associated with temptation and with giving evangelism a bad reputation: sexual immorality, pride, and greed. As a result, Graham has never entered a hotel room without an aide first checking to ensure nobody was there. He has never traveled or been alone in private with a woman who is not his wife or relative. In relation to pride, he practiced modesty and honesty in reporting, never exaggerating or arguing with the media about how many people attended his huge crusades, and always cooperating with local churches. To avoid appearance of financial abuse and greed, he put himself on a salary and banned "love offerings" from being collected for him during his crusades. He also does not accept speaking fees or honoraria for his engagements because he is aware of the danger of greed. Graham and his friends truly took Jesus' words "lead us not into temptation" seriously and honored God with their lives. Similarly, you should ask God to reveal your own areas of temptation and seek to protect yourself ahead of time.

As noted earlier, Jesus accused those who were using God's temple for purposes other than for praying and worshipping God as turning it into a den of robbers.[15] This suggests that when you choose to disregard your temple as a house of prayer where you develop a close relationship with God, and instead choose to focus on other things, you are robbing God. In allowing things into your temple that do not honor God, you are not only robbing God of His desired relationship with you but are robbing yourself of a wonderful relationship with Him. We all have a choice with our temples, either to make them into houses of prayer or dens of robbers; may yours always be a house of prayer. I pray that God reveals to you a perfect formula that works for your own prayer life and enables you to be blessed by a close relationship with Him.

Pray this Prayer with Me:

Dear Lord, I pray that You open my eyes to see how glorious and majestic You are so that my praise, prayer, and fasting life are enhanced. May they be like holy incense, an aroma pleasing to You, and may the perfect conditions be set up within my Holy Place to benefit maximally from a deeper relationship with You. Keep out of me anything that will rob me of a great relationship with You. Amen.

1. Exodus 30:34–38.
2. Some experts dispute whether onycha could have been a component of incense due to its strong smell and origin from a sea snail that would have been considered unclean in Biblical days.
3. Song of Songs 3:6, 4:6, 14; Leviticus 2:1–2, 15–16, 6:15, 24:7; Numbers 5:15; Nehemiah 13:5, 9 (Hebrew *lĕbownah*, meaning frankincense, Strongs Heb. #3828). See also Matthew 2:11; Revelation 18:13 (Greek *libanos*, meaning frankincense, Strong's Gk. #3030) (all these passages translate these words *frankincense* in the KJV, and *incense* in NIV).
4. Matthew 2:11.
5. Exodus 30:34–38.
6. Luke 18:2.
7. Ephesians 6:18; Romans 8:26.
8. 2 Chronicles 5:13–14; 20:22–25;
9. 2 Chronicles 29:30
10. Isaiah 56:7.
11. Romans 8:38–39.
12. Romans 8:28.
13. Beth Nimmo and Darrell Scott with Steve Rabey. *Rachel's Tears: The Spiritual Journey of Columbine Martyr Rachel Scott*, Thomas Nelson, 2000.
14. http://www.liferocklin.com/Pastors/ModestoManif.htm; http://www.midtod.com/9612/billygraham.phtml; http://en.wikipedia.org/wiki/Billy_Graham#cite_note-12; http://www2.wheaton.edu/bgc/archives/faq/4.htm; accessed October 1, 2011.
15. Mark 11:17.

CHAPTER 10

Your Holy Place and Fasting

(Session 5b)

Bear up the hands that hang down, by faith and prayer; support the tottering knees. Have you any days of fasting and prayer? Storm the throne of grace and persevere therein, and mercy will come down.— John Wesley, British Anglican evangelist and theologian (1703-1791).

Dying to Your Flesh

In order for the Jewish people to fully receive forgiveness and ongoing blessings by God, He instructed the priests to regularly sacrifice animals to atone for their own sins and the sins of their people. These sacrifices took place on the brazen altar of the outer court of the temple and Tabernacle. The regular sacrifice of animals and shedding of their blood was a necessary part of approaching a holy God. Following sacrifices, the priests then had to purify themselves by washing their hands and feet in the brazen laver prior to entering the Holy Place. These rituals were part of the first covenant that God made with the Jews. Through Jesus Christ, God provided a new way and a new covenant. Jesus Christ, in shedding His own blood once and for all, made it unnecessary for anyone who believes in Him to ever have the blood of animals shed on his or her behalf. However, Jesus' sacrifice was not intended as a means for believers to do as we wish. Jesus talked about the need for self-denial and personal sacrifice in order to follow Him.

111

"Then Jesus said to his disciples, 'Whoever wants to be My disciple must deny themselves and take up their cross and follow Me. For whoever wants to save their life will lose it, but whoever loses their life for me will find it. What good will it be for someone to gain the whole world, yet forfeit their soul? Or what can anyone give in exchange for their soul?'" (Matthew 16:24–26, NIV 2011). This means that for you to fully enter your Holy Place, enjoy closeness to God, receive His blessings, and have a fruitful relationship with Him, you have to learn to "deny yourself and take up your cross," which is dying to yourself or your flesh. Dying to your flesh means that you should be willing to submit the will and desires of your flesh to God's will, so that you are more alert and sensitive to the desires of the Spirit within you. This requires courage, but know that God's plans for you are better than the plans you have for yourself.

Self-denial honors God

"'For I know the plans I have for you,' declares the LORD, 'plans to prosper you and not to harm you, plans to give you hope and a future'" (Jeremiah 29:11). Dying to your flesh effectively means active self-denial to things that do not honor God. It means learning to resist the cravings and temptations of your flesh that lure you to engage in practices that can desecrate you as the temple of the living God. When you are tempted to engage in practices that are questionable, a good question to ask is, "How does this glorify God?" It means that you need to filter through the eyes of Jesus all the junk that wants to come into you—what you listen to, what you let into your eyes, and what you do with your body. What will He see or hear if it were Him in this situation? Remember, "You are not your own; you were bought at a price."[1]

But there is more to dying to your flesh.

Cleansing Yourself on Your Brazen Laver

In addition to denying your flesh of things that will dishonor God, in dying to your flesh you also need to wash out or cleanse yourself of the things that are already inside your temple that could cause you to sin. The most effective way of doing this is by filling yourself up with things that glorify Him, such as reading His Word as contained in the Bible or listening to praise music and to programs that glorify Him. This then makes your communication with God (through prayer) a lot more rewarding as you will be totally unimpeded from hearing the voice of God within your soul.

The altar on the outside of the Tabernacle (brazen altar) was covered with imperfect bronze while the one on the inside (golden altar) was covered with pure gold. When you learn to sacrifice or die on the brazen altar of your flesh you no longer allow its imperfections and temptations to influence or dominate you. You can then enter into the golden altar of the Holy Place of your mind as you enter into a personal relationship with God that is dominated by the nearness of the Holy Spirit and where you are constantly purified by Him. Just as the impure rod of iron takes on the brilliant nature of the furnace's fire after a long enough time, so constant immersion in the presence of God will make you more like Him.

Fasting As a Method of Dying to Your Flesh

One of the most effective ways of learning to die to your flesh as a believer is through the discipline of regular fasting. Fasting is a means of denying your body of food and sometimes water or other liquids while fully focusing your attention on God. The primary purpose of fasting is to sharpen your awareness of the voice of the Holy Spirit within you so you can draw nearer to God.

Fasting sharpens your spiritual awareness

Fasting is also an effective means to call God's attention to a situation in your life or the life of others so He can intervene on your behalf. Fasting as a discipline aids and hastens the effects of your prayer life and must *always* be combined with prayer. It may involve not eating any food for several days while continuing to consume liquids, or it may mean denying your body of a certain number of meals each day. The method used depends on the reason you are fasting and what you feel God is calling you to do. The limit of going without water for the human body is about three days while it can be denied food for up to about forty days. Fasting is not the same as dieting and should never be used as a means of losing weight.

Fasting has been used by several great men and women of God to intervene in ways that often changed the course of their lives and the lives of those for whom they were interceding. When King Jehoshaphat and his kingdom of Judah were under attack from a vast army against which he had no defense, he responded by turning to God and proclaiming a fast for all Judah (2 Chronicles 20:1–4). The three days of fasting was combined with praying and worshipping God, and as a result Judah was miraculously delivered from much more powerful enemies without having to lift a finger. "Alarmed, Jehoshaphat resolved to inquire of the LORD, and he proclaimed a fast for all Judah. As they began to sing and praise, the LORD set ambushes against the men of Ammon and Moab and Mount Seir who were invading Judah, and they were defeated. The Ammonites and Moabites rose up against the men from Mount Seir to destroy and annihilate them. After they finished slaughtering the men from Seir, they helped destroy one another" (2 Chronicles 20:3, 22–23, NIV 2011).

Notice that the deliverance came specifically at a time when the people of Judah were singing and praising God.

Fasting Sharpens Your Spiritual Senses and God's Urgency

There are several other great stories in the Bible of the use of fasting by God's people to sharpen their spiritual senses and to either draw nearer to God or to get His attention. Ezra, one of the great Jewish leaders, led his people in fasting and praying for protection prior to going on a perilous but ultimately successful journey with several families to resettle Jerusalem after several decades in exile in Persia.[2] Queen Esther, the Jewish wife of King Xerxes of Persia ordered a three-day fast when Haman, the king's proud deputy and an enemy of the Jews, sought to annihilate all the Jews, and God granted Esther courage and favor with the king that led to the Jews lives being spared.[3] Daniel, a great Jewish prophet and leader who was captured and exiled to Babylon in 606 BCE learned of a prophecy by the prophet Jeremiah that the exile of the people of Judah and the desolation of Jerusalem would last seventy years. As the seventy years were about to be up, Daniel prayed and fasted, petitioning God for forgiveness and favor that the promised return of the exiles would occur on time.[4] As a result, God sent the angel Gabriel to show Daniel a vision of the future rebuilding of Jerusalem; and as a bonus He gave Daniel a vision of the coming of Jesus Christ as the Messiah and of the end times.

Fasting literally enables you to turn around from facing your outer court to face God's mercy seat in your Most Holy Place where you can hear, feel, and be directed by God. I have found that when I fast, my senses are sharpened. I am more discerning and spiritually alert and I am more effective in my service to God. I have seen several miracles occur during fasts. In turn, it is through the power of the Holy Spirit that I am enabled to effectively fast. Jesus Christ Himself, under the power of the Holy Spirit, embarked upon a fast that lasted forty days and nights. "Then Jesus was led by the Spirit into the wilderness to be tempted by the devil. After fasting forty days and forty nights, he was hungry" (Matthew 4:1–2).

As a result of this prolonged fast, Jesus' spiritual senses were so sharpened that He was able to resist all attempts of satan to persuade Him to sin (Matthew 4:3–11). Similarly, when you fast, you have a leg up on the devil in his attempts to tempt you because you have effectively shut out one of his most powerful methods of getting at you—your flesh.

Fast to Reach God, Not to Impress Man

When you fast, you are not supposed to make it obvious to everyone that you are doing so,[5] unless of course in a situation of corporate fasting when you are joining with a group of other believers to petition God for a specific request. Since you have jointly decided you will fast and will probably be joining others to pray, you cannot hide the fact that you are fasting. Fasting also calls you to be humble, generous, and kind to others, actions that may be hard to do when your focus is on your flesh but which the Holy Spirit can help you accomplish. God, through the prophet Isaiah, details the conditions under which you should fast and the main reasons for fasting:

> Is not this the kind of fasting I have chosen: to *loose the chains of injustice* and *untie the cords of the yoke,* to *set the oppressed free and break every yoke?* Is it not to *share your food with the hungry* and to *provide the poor wanderer with shelter*—when you see the *naked, to clothe them,* and *not to turn away from your own flesh and blood?* Then your light will break forth like the dawn, and your healing will quickly appear; then your righteousness will go before you, and the glory of the LORD will be your rear guard. Then you will call, and the LORD will answer; you will cry for help, and he will say: Here am I. If you do away with the yoke of oppression, with the pointing finger and malicious talk, and if you spend yourselves in behalf of the hungry and satisfy the needs of the oppressed, then your light will rise in the darkness, and your night will become like the noonday. The LORD will guide you always; he will satisfy your needs in a sun-scorched land and will strengthen your

frame. You will be like a well-watered garden, like a spring whose waters never fail. Your people will rebuild the ancient ruins and will raise up the age-old foundations; you will be called Repairer of Broken Walls, Restorer of Streets with Dwellings. (Isaiah 58:6–12, NIV 2011, emphasis added)

So, fasting has both obligations and blessings. The main obligation is to be holy, just as God is holy, and to show your love for God. A yoke is a wooden beam typically attached to the head or neck of pairs of oxen or other animals while they are pulling a load. It also sometimes refers to an arched device formerly laid on the neck of a defeated person.[6] It has a connotation of oppression or subservience. The passage suggests that God expects you not to be oppressing others while petitioning Him in a fast. He wants you to be especially fair, kind, and considerate to others while you are fasting, not imposing your will on them or ignoring their needs and then expecting God to respond to yours. In return, you will receive blessings in the form of guidance and provisions from the Most High God, as well as His mercy if the situation you are fasting for calls for it.

Your Complete Holy Place

In summary, the contents of the Holy Place of the Jewish temple and Tabernacle symbolize how God wants you to prepare your own Holy Place in order to have a close relationship with him. After you receive Jesus Christ, the *Lamb* of God, as your personal savior, He becomes the *lamp* of God within your Most Holy Place through the person of the Holy Spirit and lights up your soul. However, this lamp is easily snuffed out by the things you allow to enter into your mind. You can keep this lamp burning forever by continuously presenting and eating God's bread of presence through reading His Word and by continuously offering an aroma of incense pleasing to Him, through your continuous time of prayer and fasting with Him. Even if you are not seen or do not consider yourself to be the most beautiful physical specimen by human judgment, when you are under the authority of the Holy Spirit, there is an inner light that shines and radiates about you and sets you apart from the rest of the crowd and draws others to His light in you. When you cede

Your flesh corrupts, but the Holy Spirit perfects

control to your flesh, your Holy Place is corrupted by outward impurities as symbolized by the brass in the brazen altar. By contrast, when you cede control to the Holy Spirit,[7] it is ruled by perfection as symbolized by pure gold.

"In a large house there are articles not only of gold and silver, but also of wood and clay; some are for special purposes and some for common use. Those who cleanse themselves from the latter will be instruments for special purposes, made holy, useful to the Master and prepared to do any good work. Flee the evil desires of youth and pursue righteousness, faith, love and peace, along with those who call on the Lord out of a pure heart" (2 Timothy 2:20–22, NIV 2011).

"Therefore, with minds that are alert and fully sober, set your hope on the grace to be brought to you when Jesus Christ is revealed at his coming. As obedient children, do not conform to the evil desires you had when you lived in ignorance. But just as He who called you is holy, so be holy in all you do; for it is written: 'Be holy, because I am holy'" (1 Peter 1:13–16, NIV 2011).

When you fully cede control to your Most Holy Place (the Holy Spirit), you will have accomplished something few Christians ever do, and God will reward you with an extraordinary life that will confound the wisdom of everyone around you. I pray that this is your portion in life.

Pray This Prayer with Me:

Dear God, Thank You for the spiritual discipline of fasting. Help me to develop this discipline to the fullest and to understand the conditions under which my fasting can be effective, so that I can sharpen my spiritual senses and experience the fullest impact of Your mercy and grace upon my life and be truly extraordinary. In Jesus' name, I pray. Amen.

Questions to Ponder:

- The book of Revelation describes golden bowls full of prayers of God's people.
  - Is your "prayer bowl" overflowing, generally full, half full, or empty?
  - What determines how full your bowl is?
  - Why is it important to have a full prayer bowl?
- How often have you used praise as part of your prayer life, and how has it helped you?
- How often have you used fasting as part of your prayer life and how has it helped you?
- What does it mean to seek first God's kingdom before your own needs?
- Is there anyone you are harboring unforgiveness toward?
  - How often do you think of this person?
  - How do you feel when you think of this person?
  - How often do you think this person thinks of you?
  - Who do you think is suffering more as a result of your unforgiveness?

Prayer Points

- Pray for God to give you a strategy to always keep your prayer bowl filled.
- Pray for God to give you a heart of continuous praise for Him.
- Pray for God to give you the discipline to develop an Isaiah 58:6–12 fasting lifestyle.
- Pray for God to reveal which nations to specifically target as part of your routine prayers.
- Choose one nation to pray for, asking God to bring forth the light of His kingdom.
- Ask God to teach you how to always seek first His kingdom.
- Pray for God to forgive you of your unforgiveness.
- Pray for daily grace from the Holy Spirit to help you release everyone you are holding captive in your mind because of your unforgiveness.

1. 1 Corinthians 6:19b–20a.
2. Ezra 8:21–23.
3. Esther 4–8.
4. Daniel 9:1–26.
5. Matthew 6:16–18.
6. Merriam-Webster dictionary, http://www.merriam-webster.com/dictionary/yoke?show=0&t=1308385592 (last visited June 18, 2011).
7. Beware: you can also cede control of your spirit to evil spirits. See I John 4:1–6.

CHAPTER 11

The Most Holy Place—1

(Session 6a)

And there I will meet with thee, and I will commune with thee from above the mercy seat, from between the two cherubim which are upon the ark of the testimony, of all things which I will give thee in commandment unto the children of Israel.—Exodus 25:22 (KJV)

The Contents of the Most Holy Place and Their Significance to Your Being

The Most Holy Place was the "heart" and most sacred part of the temple and Tabernacle, a structure measuring a perfect cube of fifteen feet in length, width, and height. It was separated, or "veiled," from the Holy Place by a curtain in the Tabernacle as well the temple, which also had a door. The veil signified the importance of the holiness and reverence needed to approach the room where God's Spirit resided. The Most Holy Place contained only two objects in the Tabernacle (the ark of the covenant and the mercy seat) and three objects in the temple (large sculptures of golden cherubim, along with the ark and the mercy seat). In the temple were sculptures of a pair of mighty angels (cherubim) made of olive wood overlaid with pure gold with a combined wingspan of thirty feet,[1] They stood on their feet facing the main hall (toward the Holy Place) with one wing of each angel touching the other angel's wing, while the other wing of each touched the opposing walls.[2] Under the middle wings of these cherubs were the other two objects of the Most Holy Place: the ark of the covenant and the mercy seat. The ark of the covenant was a chest that represented one of the most revered objects in the Bible (Figures D {Chapter 5} and E). It had an atonement cover (mercy seat) overlaying it, representing God's throne in heaven. It was on the mercy seat that "God's presence" in the temple resided. On the edges of the mercy seat were sculpted two identical statues of beautiful golden angels facing each other and looking down toward the cover. The ark and mercy seat were the same in the Tabernacle.

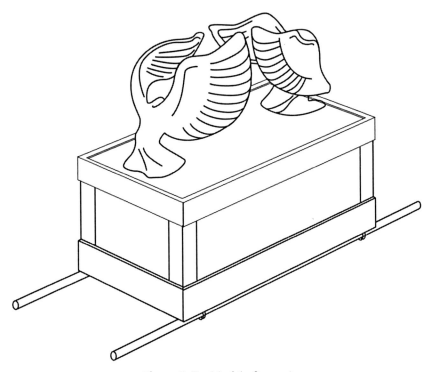

Figure E: The Ark of the Covenant

God's Mighty Angels Watching over You: Significance of the Cherubim

Cherubim were important symbols displayed throughout the Most Holy Place. In addition to the ones standing in the Most Holy Place overshadowing the ark and the mercy seat, there were two sculpted facing each other on the mercy seat. Cherubim were also carved into the two olive wood doors leading to the Most Holy Place of the First temple, along with palm trees and open flowers completely overlaid with hammered gold.[3] In both the Tabernacle and the temple, cherubs were woven into the curtain separating the Holy Place from the Most Holy Place and into the fabric of the first layer of the roof of the Tabernacle.

Cherubim are symbolic of God's angels. Angels are God's helpers (ministering spirits) who worship and serve Him and help protect His kingdom, and who are also dispatched to serve His people on earth, serve as His messengers, or help to administer justice.[4] "For He will command His angels concerning you to guard you in all your ways; they will lift you up in their hands, so that you will not strike your foot against a stone" (Psalm 91:11–12).

"Are not all angels ministering spirits sent to serve those who will inherit salvation?" (Hebrews 1: 14). Angels attended to Jesus during His ministry on earth, especially after the strong but futile efforts by the devil to tempt Him in the wilderness.[5] Similar to the Jewish temple, you are the temple of God, and you have the power of God's mighty angels ministering to you and protecting you alongside the supreme power of His Holy Spirit.

Whereas the Holy Spirit is inside you to interact with you and guide you, God's angels are outside to serve you even when you may not recognize they are doing so. They get all their instructions from God and are continuously seeing God's face[6] and worshipping Him in heaven,[7] as symbolized by the way the cherubim on the atonement cover (the lid for the ark) faced the mercy seat upon which God's Spirit resided.

God's angels actually form a camp around you when you fear God (respect Him, hold Him in awe), and they are used by Him to deliver you from trouble[8] and to guard and strengthen you.[9] "The angel of the LORD encamps around those who fear Him, and He delivers them" (Psalm 34:7).

As an example, God used an angel to lead the procession of Israelites on their journey out of slavery in Egypt and to bring darkness to the Egyptian soldiers who were pursuing them. "Then the angel of God, who had been traveling in front of Israel's army, withdrew and went behind them. The pillar of cloud also moved from in front and stood behind them, coming between the armies of Egypt and Israel. Throughout the night the cloud brought darkness to the one side and light to the other side; so neither went near the other all night long" (Exodus 14:19–20).

Angels are not always creatures with wings. Sometimes angels appear in human form, as we will later discuss in the story of Lot. Angels are sent to serve humans and humans are distinct beings from angels.

However, at times God uses ordinary human beings to bless others in miraculous ways similar to the way He uses angels, as He has done for me on many occasions. Here's an example.

On January 24, 2002, while living in Canada, my family and I had an angel-like encounter. We had set out on a trip from the city of Calgary to Edmonton (about three hours' drive) to attend a "breakthrough" Christian worship conference. Prior to leaving, we committed our trip to the Lord in prayer as is our usual manner and put the journey under the covering of the atoning and protective blood of Jesus Christ. It was a clear beautiful evening under the big blue skies of Calgary with the temperature hovering around 50° Fahrenheit when we left. As we were just about sixty miles into our trip and were approaching the town of Red Deer, snowflakes started to slowly drift down, initially appearing as small dust-sized particles. Within a few minutes the weather changed so dramatically we were enveloped in a cloud of snow and fog so dense we could barely see up to eight feet ahead of us. This coupled with the sudden emergence of the darkness without a hint of moonlight quickly led to extremely dangerous driving conditions. The visibility was so poor that I had no idea which lane we were in or if anyone was beside, behind, or in front of us. This was on a major highway with several lanes each direction!

It was an extremely eerie feeling, especially having my wife, mother, and infant son all buckled in with me. I instinctively prayed under my breath, "Lord, we did cover this trip with the blood of Jesus prior to leaving. Now I cannot tell where a lane begins or ends, or who is ahead or behind of me. You are going to have to lead my family and me out of this storm." Having said this prayer, I felt a surreal calmness, confident of the guiding hand of the Lord in the midst of the storm. By now, I had slowed down to about twenty miles per hour on a highway designed for speeds of up to seventy miles per hour. For a brief period I had to turn off the road and stop due to the poor visibility, a real act of faith as I had no idea if or where the real shoulder was. I recognized this was also a dangerous place to be since other cars would not be able to know we were there if they were struggling to find their way.

Suddenly, seemingly right out of the fog, a truck showed up, followed by a car with hazard lights flashing, and slowly passed us. I felt a strong sense of the Holy Spirit telling me these were His angels sent to lead us out of the storm. Instinctively, I obeyed and followed this convoy, quite certain of their role. As we drove, I literally would have followed them into a ditch if they went into one, as the flashing taillights of the car in front of us became our beacon of hope. After about one hour of being led through this unflinching stormy weather, the convoy of truck and sedan suddenly disappeared. Almost immediately, another large sedan appeared out of the blue to take over the guidance until we reached the edge of the city of Edmonton. As we approached Edmonton, the fog gradually lifted and the streetlights beamed as a very welcome guide.

As soon as we reached our hotel destination in Edmonton, we knelt and gave thanks and glory to God for sending his guardian angels to watch over us and for providing our security and protection, literally in the midst of this storm. At this time, I discovered I was not the only one who had been praying, but my wife and mother had also been deep in intercessory prayer for the situation. On our return trip home the following day, we saw several cars that had indeed fallen off the highway on that fateful night, confirming our conviction of the protection we had received from God.

God Uses Angels and Uses His People!

God had revealed Himself fully to me on numerous other occasions as a God who can and will lead us through any storm that may come at us as we go through life. He has often sent one guardian angel after another to guide me through challenging situations and has often used me to provide support for other people through the movement of the Holy Spirit in a manner that is similar to what His angels do. God does not prevent the storms of life from occurring, but He allows them to happen so we can grow spiritually and increase our faith and hope in Him.[10] He has gifted us today as believers with His Holy Spirit and occasionally with His angels to guide us through these trials. God always looks after His own people, even at times when it is not obvious that He is doing so.

There are angels assigned to watch over you

In the Bible there are several examples of people who were guided by angels during times of trials. For example, God allowed Peter, one of Jesus' apostles, to be arrested and put in jail by King Herod for a crime he did not commit because Herod wanted to please and improve his popularity with the Jews.[11] However, while in jail, God miraculously used an angel to lead Peter out of the cell and into the city despite being guarded by four squads of four guards each, in two different sections of the jail who remained totally oblivious to what was going on.[12] There is no question that this experience expanded Peter's faith tremendously, even though he would probably have preferred not to have gone to jail.

Similarly, when Daniel, a Jewish exile who had risen to become a governor of Persia refused to stop praying to God against the command of the king, the king ordered he be thrown into a den of lions. God allowed Daniel to be thrown into the den, but He then sent an angel to miraculously shut the mouth of the lions so they could not devour Daniel.[13] Allowing Daniel to go through the turmoil of the lion's den was important for building Daniel's faith and for allowing God's name to be glorified with the king and people of Persia and generations of Bible readers to follow.

God can do the same for you as you go through the storms of your life, and He is totally faithful to keep His promise to protect you if you enable Him to do so by learning how to honor His temple within you.[14] His ultimate goal is to help you understand that there is no storm too big in your life that He cannot handle, and in allowing you to go through the storm, He is also building up your character and teaching you how to learn to trust Him.

Angels as Messengers of God

God also often uses His angels to deliver messages to those He wants to communicate with in some fashion. The Bible is full of several examples of people who had encounters with God's angels bringing messages from God in both the Old and New Testaments, including several of the prophets and of course, the Lord Jesus Christ.[15] In one of the most famous descriptions, God used the angel named Gabriel to deliver the good news to Mary the mother of Jesus that she would be the one to give birth to the long-awaited Savior.

> In the sixth month of Elizabeth's pregnancy, God sent the angel Gabriel to Nazareth, a town in Galilee, to a virgin pledged to be married to a man named Joseph, a descendant of David. The virgin's name was Mary. The angel went to her and said, "Greetings, you who are highly favored! The Lord is with you."

Mary was greatly troubled at his words and wondered what kind of greeting this might be. But the angel said to her, "Do not be afraid, Mary; you have found favor with God. You will conceive and give birth to a son, and you are to call Him Jesus. He will be great and will be called the Son of the Most High. The Lord God will give Him the throne of His father, David, and He will reign over Jacob's descendants forever; His kingdom will never end." (Luke 1:26–33)

Similarly, God used angels to deliver messages to numerous other people in the Bible: Hagar; Lot; Jacob; Balaam; the nation of Israel; Gideon; Samson's mother; Elijah; David; Daniel; Zechariah, the prophet to the Jews in exile; Zechariah, the father of John the Baptist; his wife, Elizabeth; Mary, the mother of Jesus; shepherds watching their flocks at night; Mary Magdalene; Joanna; Mary, the Mother of James; Philip; Cornelius; and the apostle John.[16]

Strangers Could Be Angels Sent by God

Since angels are spirits sent by God to minister to you, it is important to recognize that they can appear any time disguised as strangers and in strange ways. This is why God calls you to show love and hospitality to strangers, since in doing so you may be showing hospitality to angels without being aware of it.

"Keep on loving one another as brothers and sisters. Do not forget to show hospitality to strangers, for by so doing some people have shown hospitality to angels without knowing it" (Hebrews 13:1–2, NIV 2011). Showing hospitality to people is showing hospitality to God. Human beings are not angels; angels are separate beings sent to serve us. However, the Holy Spirit moving within you will often stir you to play a role similar to angels and respond to the needs of others, and you will be blessed for it. On more than one occasion, I have been blessed by taking time out to help someone only to discover that God was using me as His instrument to reach out to this person at a very critical junction in that person's life. I have been moved by the Holy Spirit to pick up the phone and encourage someone; to invite someone over or take him or her out for lunch; or to give specific amount of money or a specific item only to hear the person declare in a stunned way that this was a specific need for which they had been praying to God at the time.

When you respond to an urge of the Holy Spirit, it means you are allowing God to use you as His representative to those He has sent you to. The wonderful part of this arrangement is that you will always be blessed when you recognize God has included you in His plans to help someone who has prayed to Him for a specific need. Often you will find that God will use the experience to bless you in unexpected ways. including sometimes the provision of some helpful information you would not otherwise have known, helping build your faith, or just giving you joy in the knowledge that you have done God's will and are feeling His pleasure. When you allow God to move in you in this way, you are playing a role similar to His angels in heaven.

Hospitality to Angels Saved Lot's Family

Sodom and Gomorrah were two cities in which the inhabitants were known for their extreme acts of wickedness. God revealed to Abraham, His friend, that "The outcry against Sodom and Gomorrah is so great and their sin so grievous" (Genesis 18:20) that He needed to judge the people and destroy the cities in order to stop the sinful behavior from carrying on to the next generation. The nature of their sins was so pervasive that just about everyone in these cities was constantly thinking about evil, a situation that mandated eternal condemnation to hell not only for them but for the generations to come who had no hope of knowing there was a different way to live. Allowing the sin to continue would have caused more people than necessary from suffering the eternal torment of an eternity in hell.

Abraham tried to intercede for the cities, asking God to spare them if there were even ten people present living there who were righteous. Unfortunately, ten righteous people could not be found. However, Lot, Abraham's nephew, was one of the few righteous men who lived in Sodom, and his hospitality toward God's angels who appeared in human form as strangers to him saved his family from certain destruction along with all the other inhabitants of the city. Lot met these two angels who had been sent by God to execute justice at the gateway of Sodom. Without knowing who they were, he offered to wash their feet and invited them into his home to rest for the evening (Genesis 19). (We will discuss the importance of feet washing as a common biblical gesture of kindness and humility later in chapter 19.)

Even though they initially refused to go into his home, Lot insisted and the angels ultimately went with him, where Lot prepared a meal and a room for them. However, the wicked men of Sodom soon found out there were strangers in Lot's house and took an opposite approach, surrounding Lot's home and insisting Lot release them so they could have sex with the angels. It was only following an unsuccessful attempt by Lot to negotiate with the Sodomites that the angels revealed their identity to him. They then blinded the wicked men who were outside so they could not find their way into the house and urgently pulled Lot, his wife, and their two daughters out of the house.

Unfortunately, Lot's two sons-in-law were too attached to their lives in Sodom and did not heed the advice to leave. As a result, they were left behind to be destroyed along with all the other evil inhabitants of Sodom and Gomorrah by a storm of burning sulfur. Lot's wife also disobeyed a command not to look back to see what was going on, and she also was also destroyed, being turned into a pillar of salt. (We will expand upon the importance of obedience to God in chapter 20.) This incident involving Lot and his daughters illustrates that you may actually be blessing yourself when you show kindness to strangers. In addition to the principle of exhibiting kindness to strangers as an act of compassion and love toward God, when you practice hospitality you are reflecting His character because God is the embodiment of love. "God is love. Whoever lives in love lives in God, and God in them" (1 John 4:16b, NIV 2011).

Later we will discuss how your temple as the house of God is intended to be a house of love. The story of Lot also reveals another characteristic of angels—they are agents used by God to execute judgment against wickedness.[17] Indeed, Jesus taught that during the end times, angels will be used by God for the final judgment, to separate sinners from the righteous in preparation for their eternal destination. "The Son of Man will send out his angels, and they will weed out of His kingdom everything that causes sin and all who do evil. They will throw them into the blazing furnace, where there will be weeping and gnashing of teeth. Then the righteous will shine like the sun in the kingdom of their Father" (Matthew 13:41-42, NIV 2011).

Angels are not gods and must never be worshipped

Finally, note that angels are not gods and must never be worshipped. They are servants of God who were created to do His will, to worship

Him, and to serve His people on earth, including you. Only God the Father and His son, Jesus Christ, who is superior to all the angels and the Holy Spirit have earned the right to be worshipped.[18] "The Son is the radiance of God's glory and the exact representation of His being, sustaining all things by His powerful word. After He had provided purification for sins, He sat down at the right hand of the majesty in heaven. So He became as much superior to the angels as the name He has inherited is superior to theirs" (Hebrews 1:3–4).

Pray This Prayer with Me:

Dear Lord, I thank You that You do not simply stop me from experiencing the storms of life but that You are always by my side as I go through them. I am grateful to You for sending Your guardian angels to watch over me, so that I do not strike my foot against a stone or drown in the storms of life. I recognize that going through the storms makes me a stronger Christian, builds my faith, and enables me to understand more clearly the full extent of Your dominion. Help to recognize when You have sent Your angels to me in the form of strangers and to always practice hospitality. Amen.

1. 1 Kings 6:23–28.
2. 2 Chronicles 3:10–13.
3. The original Temple of King Solomon had a door separating it from the Holy Place. After it was destroyed, the temple that was built to replace it instead had a curtain (veil).
4. Hebrews 1:7, 14.
5. Matthew 4:11; Luke 22:43.
6. Matthew 18:10.
7. Revelation 7:11.
8. Psalm 34:7.
9. Psalm 91:11; Luke 22:43.
10. Romans 5:1–4.
11. Acts 12:1–4.
12. Acts 12:5–11.
13. Daniel 6:22.
14. Psalm 91:11–12.
15. Genesis 18:1–2; 2 Kings 1:3, 15; Matthew 4:11.
16. Genesis 16:7, 19:1, 31:11, 32:1–2; Numbers 22:35; Judges 2:1, 6:11–20, 13:3; 2 Kings 1:15; 1 Chronicles 21:16; Daniel 6:22; Zechariah 1:9; Luke 1:13–19, 26–38, 2:8–12, 24:1–10; Acts 8:26, 10:3–4; Revelation 1:1.
17. 2 Samuel 24:15–17; 2 Kings 19:35; 1 Chronicles 21:15;.
18. Hebrews 1.

CHAPTER 12

The Most Holy Place 2— The Ark of the Covenant and God's Mercy Seat

(Session 6b)

*Approach, my soul, the mercy seat, where Jesus answers prayer;
there humbly fall before His feet, for none can perish there.*—John
Newton, Olney Hymns (London: W. Oliver, 1779)

The Ark of the Covenant and Its Contents

Underneath the outstretched wings of the cherubim sculptures in the Most
Holy Place of the original Jewish temple was the second object in the Most
Holy Place—the ark of the covenant. A covenant is a sacred agreement
between God and man. The ark of the covenant was a chest built from
instructions given by God to house the terms of a sacred agreement (the
Ten Commandments) made between God and the Israelites, in which God
promised to protect and bless the Jews in return for their obedience to the
commandments. The ark was a rectangular chest three and three-quarters
feet long, two and a quarter feet wide and high, carved out of acacia wood,
and completely overlaid with pure gold on the inside and outside.[1] A gold
molding decorated it, and it was lifted up on four gold-covered carrying
poles. Four gold rings were attached to each foot of the ark, into which
were inserted the four carrying poles. On top of the ark was a golden
cover (the mercy seat), with two golden cherubim molded onto it. The
ark contained two stone slabs (tablets) on which were written the Ten
Commandments of the laws God gave Moses to pass on to the Israelites

(Jews). In addition, it contained the staff (or rod) God used to perform miracles through Moses' brother, Aaron, during the plagues God used to deliver the Israelites from slavery in Egypt. Elsewhere in the Bible,[2] the ark was also said to have contained a golden jar of the manna (bread that fell from heaven) that God used to provide food for the Israelites while they were wandering through the desert. The symbolic importance of each of these objects is described below.

The Sacredness of the Ark

The ark of the covenant represented the most sacred portion of the Most Holy Place of the Jewish temple where God resided. The ark and its contents represented an exclusive agreement between God and the Israelites of His presence with them and a pledge to always watch over them and protect them from all their enemies, as long as they also kept their part of the bargain—obeying His commands.[3] The ark was recognized by the Israelites and all their neighbors as an object that conferred great powers and blessings.[4]

Because it was created with specific instructions from God and God "resided" on the mercy seat covering the ark, it had to be treated with utmost respect. The ark itself was never to be directly touched, with the risk of death, but was always carried by the poles holding it.[5] When it was being carried, it was always covered by a veil, so that it was concealed from the eyes of the people. When not being carried, it had to remain in the Tabernacle or later in the temple, concealed by a curtain or door separating the Holy Place from the Most Holy Place. During the exodus of the Israelites in the desert from Egypt and on their way to Canaan, the land God promised them, the ark was always separated and carried three thousand feet ahead of the people and their army to pave the way for a successful and safe journey.[6]

As an example of the miraculous powers present in the ark as a result of the presence of God's Spirit, when the priests carrying the ark stepped into the edge of the river Jordan, the waters parted and enabled all the Jewish people entry into Canaan. "Now the Jordan is at flood stage all during harvest. Yet as soon as the priests who carried the ark reached the Jordan and their feet touched the water's edge, the water from upstream stopped flowing. It piled up in a heap a great distance away, at a town called Adam in the vicinity of Zarethan, while the water flowing down to the Sea of the Arabah (that is, the Dead Sea) was completely cut off. So the people crossed over opposite Jericho" (Joshua 3:15–16, NIV 2011).

Similarly, on instructions from God, the ark was carried around the city of Jericho as the Jewish people marched around it daily for six days and seven times on the seventh day, behind armed men and seven priests blowing trumpets made from the horns of rams. Following the seventh march around the city on the seventh day, the people let out a great shout and the walls of Jericho came tumbling down, enabling the Israelites to capture Jericho (Joshua 6:4–20).

The ark is represented in you as a believer as your heart where the Holy Spirit resides. With the Holy Spirit resident in your heart, you are guaranteed blessings and the ability to accomplish miraculously great things in your life, outside the scope of your own ability—conditional on how highly you regard the God who now resides in you and how much respect you show to your temple daily.

The Stone Tablets of the Ten Commandments

The stone tablets within the ark were the written reminder of the first covenant God made with the Israelites. The Ten Commandments contained on the tablets represented the moral law of God[7] (Exodus 20). Through the law, the Jews (and subsequently all humanity) were reminded of our sinful nature and the need for ongoing sacrifice (through the blood of animals) to make us worthy of a perfect and sinless God and to keep us from dying.

As a believer, God's laws are written on your heart

Today, if you are a believer in Jesus Christ, you are the temple of God and your heart represents the Most Holy Place containing the ark of the *new* covenant. His laws are automatically written on the "tablets" of your heart. You instinctively know when you have grieved God by violating one of His laws. The more you make His Word part of you and develop a close relationship with Him, the more you lose any desire to break His laws as your whole soul cries out and is alienated when you do so.

One of the most incredible surprises is that when you develop yourself as God's temple, it will no longer be a chore to keep His commandments. As a believer, you no longer bear the burden of condemnation of trying to gain salvation through the laws of the Ten Commandments and constant sacrifices of the blood of animals. Instead, your heart has been purified by a new covenant in which the blood of Jesus was shed as a permanent atonement for all your sins—every one that you have ever committed or that you will ever commit. The act of Holy Communion,[8] in which Jesus commanded all believers in Him during His last supper on earth to regularly drink his "blood" (represented by wine) and eat his "flesh" (represented by bread) is intended as an ongoing reminder of this permanent sacrifice He made on your behalf, leading to the gift of salvation, which is given freely but which came at a great price.

Importance of the New Covenant

While salvation through Jesus is a free and unconditional gift from God, your ability to experience the full impact of a close relationship with God remains conditional. Jesus' part of the new covenant is that He shed His blood for you so that when you accept Him as your Lord and Savior, you will spend all of eternity in heaven. Your part of the covenant demands obedience to Jesus Christ. While this may appear to be burdensome, you will soon learn that it is actually much easier and much more rewarding than the alternative, especially if you allow the Holy Spirit to teach you and help you. God has made two profound differences in His covenant with you through Jesus Christ compared to the first covenant He made with the Jews through Abraham and ultimately Moses.

Ten Commandments Simplified: The first difference in the new covenant is that Jesus simplified all of the Ten Commandments into two principles rooted in His great love for you. "Love the Lord your God with all your heart and with all your soul and with all your strength and with all your mind"; and "Love your neighbor as yourself" (Luke 10:26–27).

When God gave the Ten Commandments to Moses, they were intended to convict men and women (you and me) of our sins and to make us understand the condemnation that comes from breaking the law. The simplification of the law with the new covenant of Jesus is to remind us that the underpinning purpose of the Ten Commandments was always to draw us closer to a loving God, not to condemn us. Jesus is simply telling you that all of God's laws are boiled down to loving God and your neighbor, and when God asks you to love Him, always remember that He loved you first. "For God so loved the world that he gave his one and only Son, that whoever believes in Him shall not perish but have eternal life. For God did not send His Son into the world to condemn the world, but to save the world through Him" (John 3:16–17).

When you truly love God with all your heart, soul, strength, and mind, you will be transformed by the Holy Spirit into viewing the Ten Commandments differently than you ever did before. If you view the Ten Commandments through the lens of Jesus, they will no longer be a series of rules that make it difficult for you to live. Instead, they become a series of promises God has made to you to give you the full freedom you need to live a life free of negative consequences and to have a close relationship with Him. We will explore this concept in great detail in chapter 20.

The Holy Spirit as a Guide: The second difference in the new covenant compared with the first one was in something that was accomplished after Jesus' resurrection. Jesus sent the Holy Spirit to come and live within everyone who accepts Jesus as his or her personal savior, making it much easier to have a close relationship with God. The Holy Spirit is exactly the same in nature with Jesus and with God and He is here as your counselor, your personal guide, and your direct line to God. He knows God better than anybody since He is part of God. You no longer need to live in darkness wondering what God wants from you or how to reach God—you can communicate with Him directly! If you seek God and love Him with all your heart, He will not only reside in a part of you but will spread out to all your chambers and fulfill all your longings to know Him. You are God's preferred temple over any manmade building or sculpture no matter how beautiful these structures may appear to you. He is knocking on the door of your heart and wants to come in and have a close loving relationship with you.

"Here I am! I stand at the door and knock. If anyone hears my voice and opens the door, I will come in and eat with him, and he with me" (Revelation 3:20). Is He in you? If not, what is keeping you from letting Him in?

Significance of Aaron's Staff (Rod)— Authority and Miraculous Power

The second object within the ark was Aaron's rod, which budded. Aaron's rod was used by God to perform great miracles, first in Egypt, when Aaron and Moses were confronting Pharaoh to deliver the Israelites from slavery, and then later during their exodus through the dessert to the Promised Land of Canaan.

Aaron's rod symbolized the authority and discipline of God, as well as His miracle performing nature. In Jewish culture, the rod was a symbol of authority, which was often associated with the staff used by shepherds to guide and keep their sheep safe and for discipline when they went astray.[9] Moses had a staff in his hand when God first appeared to him while he was tending to sheep belonging to the flock of Jethro his father-in-law at Mount Horeb.[10] Both Moses and Aaron's rods are mentioned repeatedly in connection with the great miracles God performed in front of Pharaoh, including changing into a snake when put on the ground and bringing on plague after plague on the Egyptians as a result of Pharaoh's obstinacy in refusing to release the Israelites from slavery.[11]

In the most dramatic example of the rod representing both authority and God's miraculous powers, Aaron's rod is put in the spotlight in the book of Numbers. In this story, while the Israelites were wandering in the wilderness, God commanded Moses to consecrate Aaron and his children to serve as His priests. Korah, Dathan, and Abiram, along with 250 other well-known community leaders, became offended and felt slighted at this command and challenged Moses and Aaron and ultimately God's authority to confer this honor on Aaron.[12] As a result of this open rebellion against God, God separated the whole community from the three leaders, and the ground split open and swallowed them alive along with their households and all their possessions. In addition, all of the 250 men who were part of the rebellion were consumed by fire. Instead of humbling themselves before God, the remaining Israelites were incensed at God, Moses, and Aaron and grumbled against them.[13] This led to even greater catastrophe as a plague sent by God consumed 14,700 of the people. Finally, God sought to put an end to the grumbling and asked each of the leaders of the twelve ancestral tribes of Israel to produce a staff and to write their name on it and place it in the Tabernacle. God promised that the staff belonging to the man He chooses to be His priest would miraculously sprout by the next day.

> The next day Moses entered the tent and saw that Aaron's staff, which represented the tribe of Levi, had not only sprouted but had budded, blossomed and produced almonds. Then Moses brought out all the staffs from the LORD's presence to all the Israelites. They looked at them, and each of the leaders took

his own staff. The LORD said to Moses, "Put back Aaron's staff in front of the ark of the covenant law, to be kept as a sign to the rebellious. This will put an end to their grumbling against Me, so that they will not die." (Numbers 17:8–10)

This event established several lessons to the Israelites that are germane to you as a temple of God today.

Lessons from the Budding of Aaron's Rod

The first lesson is this: God is the supreme authority of the whole universe. When you challenge His authority, you are putting your life and your destiny in grave danger. Satan, a spiritual being created by God was kicked out of heaven for challenging God's authority[14]—the same reaction can occur to you. Rebellion sets you up as being equal to God but without the knowledge or power He possesses. God cannot tolerate this situation because it will allow you to lead not only yourself but others of His beloved creation into deception and ultimately into eternal ruin as they follow you. If people start to look at you in your rebellious state as a savior instead of God, they will fall since you have no real ability to make the type of changes in anyone's life that God can.[15] This lesson should apply to all those in authority over you.[16] Open rebellion is considered one of the most grievous sins against God. "For rebellion is like the sin of divination, and arrogance like the evil of idolatry" (1 Samuel 5:23a).

God is the supreme authority in all the universe

Consider this as a warning when you seek to overthrow the person in authority over you. Even if you are under the authority of a wicked ruler, God should always be the one to fight your battles for you. Saul, the first king of Israel persistently sought to kill David because David had become too popular and a threat to his kingdom. In spite of this, when David had the opportunity to kill Saul, he refused to do so because he recognized Saul's authority.[17] As a result, God rewarded David with the crown, and he became one of the most successful kings of Israel as well as an ancestor of the Lord Jesus Christ. Similarly, both Daniel and Joseph were young Jewish boys in exile at separate times in history who became very highly placed in positions of authority under the command of foreign kings, often wicked, who did not know or worship God.[18] In spite of the wickedness of the rulers over them, both men served their kings with diligence and honor, and in Daniel's case we are told he actually prayed for the kings he served.[19] However, while committed to serving their kings, neither Daniel nor Joseph forsook or compromised their relationships with God.

Similarly, God wants you to serve those in authority over you, even if they are evil, but without ever compromising your relationship with Him. If this is your situation, you will need to spend a lot of time praying that God will give you wisdom in how to deal with this person in a way that is loyal but in which you do not violate your personal beliefs. You can be totally confident that God will make a way for you even under these trying circumstances, and He will make it clear to you if and when it is time to move on.

God has not changed, He still does miracles today

The second lesson from Aaron's rod that sprouted and budded was that it established without a shadow of doubt that Aaron and his family were God's chosen ones to be His priests. Similarly, since you are now the temple of God and carry God's Most Holy Place with the ark written on your heart, you are established as part of God's royal priesthood. We will expand on this in greater depth in chapter 13.

Finally, the same God who caused Aaron and Moses' rods to perform numerous miracles can still perform miracles in your life. Some people, including Christians, believe miracles no longer occur today, and yet miracles are happening every day in the lives of those who put their faith in God. I have personally been witness to numerous miracles in my own life and the lives of others around me, especially when a group of believers gather together in one mind to pray and petition God. Following prayer, men and women with aggressive cancers who have been given little hope by physicians have remained cancer free several years after their diagnosis. A man with multi-organ failure in the intensive care unit who had been proclaimed unable to recover by his physicians, to the point of turning off all life support, walked out of the ICU following intensive prayers by believers. A woman who needed to buy a building to provide medical care for the poor was initially turned down by the banks when she offered a six-digit figure. A year later, the same bank called to ask her to make any offer on the building and she got it for a five-digit figure.

Miracles of timely provision, of improbable deliverance from catastrophic accidents, of victory when defeat was all but assured—I have seen them all and they continue to occur today. All these examples are just snippets of what God has done and is still doing today and can do in your life.

However, the most amazing miracles God performs today are the miracles of changed lives. Men and women whose lives were on the path of destruction from self-hatred, rage, alcoholism, drugs, and addictions of various kinds have been transformed by the miraculous touch of the knowledge and power of God and of His Son, Jesus Christ, and the Holy Spirit in their lives. God is able to do the same and more in your life if you accept His rod of authority and believe in the power of the Spirit He has deposited within you.

The Atonement Cover (Mercy Seat)

Within the Most Holy Place, the ark of the covenant was covered with an "atonement cover," or mercy seat, carved out of pure gold with two cherubs whose wings were spread upward overshadowing the cover and facing each other, looking toward the cover.[20] God's Spirit resided on this mercy seat. "When Moses entered the tent of meeting to speak with the LORD, he heard the voice speaking to him from between the two cherubim above the atonement cover on the *ark* of the covenant law. In this way the LORD spoke to him" (Numbers 7:89, NIV 2011, emphasis added).

Significance of the Mercy Seat (Atonement Cover)

This atonement cover had huge spiritual significance. God, as we have noted earlier, is pure and without sin. Sin separates man from God. The consequences of sin should be death, but God in His infinite love and mercy chooses to spare His people in the hope that we will all ultimately come to Him in repentance of our own free will. In choosing to spare sinners, God still demands that blood be shed as the price for the remission of sins. In the days of the Tabernacle and the temple, the blood of bulls was shed once a year on the brazen altar in the outer court and then brought into the Most Holy Place to be sprinkled over the atonement cover, as an act of atonement or sacrifice in place of human blood for the remission of the sins of the Jewish people. Only a meticulously consecrated high priest could enter the Most Holy place to sprinkle this blood of the sacrificed animal to make amends for the sins of his people.

"[The high priest] shall then slaughter the goat for the sin offering for the people and take its blood behind the curtain and do with it as he did with the bull's blood: He shall sprinkle it on the atonement cover and in front of it" (Leviticus 16:15). God specifically said He would meet with the high priest over the atonement cover between the two cherubim that were over the ark of the covenant.

"There, above the cover between the two cherubim that are over the ark of the Testimony, I will meet with you and give you all my commands for the Israelites" (Exodus 25:22). Since the atonement cover was the meeting place between God and man, man's sin would have caused him to die immediately upon contact with a perfect God. However, in His mercy and love, God did not want any of His children to die. This made it necessary to shed the blood of animals in place of human blood, hence the meaning of the name "mercy seat" as a place where God's mercy was shown. God later performed His ultimate act of mercy when He sent His one and only Son to become the sacrificial lamb, shedding his blood once and for all for all sinners so that there would no longer be any need for sacrificing animals. "God presented Him as a sacrifice of atonement, through faith in His blood. He did this to demonstrate His justice, because in His forbearance He had left the sins committed beforehand unpunished—He did it to demonstrate His justice at the present time, so as to be just and the one who justifies those who have faith in Jesus" (Romans 3:25–26).

If you have accepted Jesus Christ as your savior, then you have accepted his shed blood as the atonement for your sins—forever. No more bloodshed is needed. He has left you with an atonement cover within your heart where God lives and meets with you. More significantly, your interaction with God can now be continuous twenty-four hours a day and 365 days a year and it needs no intermediary priest. If you have never had this interaction with God and would like it, I encourage you to pray the following prayer.

Pray This Prayer with Me:

Dear Lord, I acknowledge that I am a sinner, and I understand that the wages of my sin is death. I also understand that in Your mercy, You sent Your one and only Son, Jesus Christ, to shed His blood as atonement for my sins and that because of His death, I can live forever. I ask that You forgive me of all my sins and cleanse me of all unrighteousness. I welcome Jesus Christ into my heart to be my Lord and Savior. Thank You very much for Your great love for me and for Your daily provision of manna for me in the meeting of both my physical and spiritual needs. Amen.

If by chance you prayed this prayer for the very first time, well done! You have said the most important prayer and made the most important decision you will ever make in your lifetime. I strongly encourage you to find and start attending a local Bible-believing church where you can be under the anointing of a godly pastor so you can grow spiritually and enjoy the blessing of the fellowship that comes from knowing other believers. Congratulations on welcoming Jesus into your heart and receiving His free gift! However, remember one very important point. When you become born again, it is only your spirit that becomes born again. "Jesus answered, 'I tell you the truth, no one can enter the kingdom of God unless he is *born* of water and the *Spirit*'" (John 3:5, emphasis added).

Your mind is not born again and still has to be uncluttered from the longstanding influence your flesh has had on it all its life. Know that for some of you, this "uncluttering" will be instantaneous and you will no longer have any further desire to serve your flesh. However, for others, this will require a concerted effort to work with the Holy Spirit through immersion in Him and a very conscious effort to "die to your flesh." Just because you are born again does not mean your struggles will go away. It does mean you will have supernatural power to deal with these struggles if you allow the Holy Spirit to take control.

The Golden Jar that Contained Manna

The final content of the ark was a golden jar that contained manna. Manna was special food God provided to the Israelites during their forty-year journey through the wilderness on the way to the Promised Land of Canaan following their time of slavery in Egypt. The manna fell daily from heaven like dew around the place where they camped.

> The people of Israel called the bread manna. It was white like coriander seed and tasted like wafers made with honey. Moses said, "This is what the LORD has commanded: 'Take an omer of manna and keep it for the generations to come, so they can see the bread I gave you to eat in the wilderness when I brought you out of Egypt.'" So Moses said to Aaron,

"Take a jar and put an omer of manna in it. Then place it before the LORD to be kept for the generations to come." As the LORD commanded Moses, Aaron put the manna with the tablets of the covenant law, so that it might be preserved. (Exodus: 16:31–34, NIV 2011.)

The stored manna was a reminder of God's ability to provide for His people daily and under every circumstance, even in the tough environment of the wilderness.

In the same way, God is able to meet all your daily needs, and often He will do so using methods that seem strange and unexpected to you. You just have to believe in Him and trust that He is able to keep you through feast and famine, and always keep open the lines of communication with Him. May God instill in you a complete trust in Him for the provision of your daily needs, amen.

Questions to Ponder:

- Do you have any experiences of an encounter with angels? If so, describe one such experience.
- Why does God want us to show hospitality to others?
  - What does hospitality mean to you?
  - Have you benefited from the hospitality of others? If so how?
  - Have you benefited from showing hospitality? If so, how?
- Have you witnessed any miracles in your life or the lives of those close to you?
  - Under what circumstances do most of God's miracles occur?
- In what ways has God shown you mercy in your life?
  - What should your response be as a result of the mercy He has shown you?
- Why does God hate rebellion?
  - How have you ever rebelled against those in authority over you?
    - Were there any consequences?
  - Does respect for authority mean you should obey when your personal beliefs are challenged?
    - Are the two principles (respect for authority and having core Christian values) incompatible?

Prayer Points

- Pray for God to expand the contingent of angels He has dispatched to watch over you and to fight on your behalf.
- Pray for God to give you a continuous heart for hospitality toward strangers.
- Pray for God to enable you to show mercy to others and for you to always be shown mercy.
- Pray for God to squash the spirit of rebellion within you, and that He should instead instill a trust in His ability to fight on your behalf.
- Pray that you will never violate God's laws in deference to man's authority.
- Pray for all those in authority over you, starting with your pastors, church leaders, boss(es) at work, and your civic and governmental leaders.

1. Exodus 25:10.
2. Hebrews 9:3–5; Exodus 16:33–34.
3. Numbers 10:33–35.
4. 2 Samuel 6:11; 1 Samuel 4:5–8; 1 Samuel 5:1–4, 6–12.
5. 1 Chronicles 13:9–10.
6. Numbers 4:5–6.
7. See the description of the school master in Chapter 13.
8. 1 Corinthians 11:23–25.
9. Psalm 23:4; Leviticus 27:32; 2 Samuel 7:14; Psalm 89:32; Proverbs 10:13, 13:24, Isaiah 9:4; Micah 6:9; 1 Corinthians 4:21.
10. Exodus 3:1–2; 4:1–2.
11. Aaron's rod: Exodus 7:8–13, 19–21; 8:5–6, 16–17; Moses' rod: Exodus 4:2–9; 9:23–26; 10:12–15; 14:15–28.
12. Numbers 16.
13. Numbers 16:41–50.
14. Isaiah 14:12–14.
15. Ezekiel 28:11–19.
16. Hebrews 13:17.
17. 1 Samuel 24:8–15.
18. Daniel 2:48.
19. Daniel 4:19, 27; 5:21.
20. Exodus 37:6–9.

CHAPTER 13

The Most Holy Place 3— The Importance of the Veil

(Session 7a)

God is always previous, God is always there first, and if you have any desire for God, and for the things of God, it is God himself who put it there.—A. W. Tozer

The curtain will separate the Holy Place from the Most Holy Place.—Exodus 26:33b

The Tabernacle and Temple Veil

Both the Tabernacle and the temple[1] had an impressive veil separating their Holy Place from the Most Holy Place.[2] The temple veil in particular was an elaborate and beautifully embroidered curtain made of purple, crimson (or scarlet), and blue yarn with immaculate angels woven into it. It measured thirty feet wide, sixty feet high, and has been estimated in Hebraic literature to have been one hand breadth or about three inches thick.[3] This veil symbolized the separation of humanity from our perfect God due to our sinful nature. Only one person, the Jewish high priest, could enter behind the veil once a year into the Most Holy Place, during a time known as Yom Kippur, to offer atonement for the sins of all the people of Israel.[4]

The temple during the time of Jesus was a different temple from the one built by King Solomon. The first temple had been destroyed in

586 BCE during the destruction of Jerusalem and exile of its people to Babylon. It was rebuilt in 516 BCE when Cyrus the Great became the ruler of Persia which had conquered Babylon. Cyrus and a subsequent leader, Darius, allowed waves of Jews to return to Jerusalem which set the stage for the building of the second temple.[5] This temple was further expanded by King Herod around 19 BCE and retained a massive three-inch veil separating the Most Holy Place from the Holy Place. However, this temple was distinct in that it not have a door between the two rooms, nor did it have the ark of the covenant or any of its contents. It was this temple veil that was ripped into two following the crucifixion of Jesus. "And when Jesus had cried out again in a loud voice, he gave up His Spirit. At that moment the curtain of the temple was torn in two from top to bottom. The earth shook, the rocks split, and the tombs broke open" (Matthew 27:50–52a, NIV 2011).

The significance of this amazing event was huge. By spontaneously tearing up a curtain that was three-inches thick and sixty feet high, God was declaring that as a result of His Son Jesus' sacrifice on the cross, and the shedding of His own blood, the Most Holy Place was now open for entry to anyone who is willing to accept Jesus Christ's sacrifice. Notice that this offer is for everyone, not a specific group of people. Christianity is not exclusive.

The veil separating you from God has been ripped apart

This is the importance of the veil for your own temple today: before you gave your life to Christ and invited Him to reside in you, your soul chamber (Holy Place) was separated from your spirit chamber (Most Holy Place) by a veil because of sin. You could not have a relationship with God. If God tried to advise or caution you, it was impossible for you to respond; you could not perceive Him because of the veil that kept Him hidden from you. This separation was because God, who is perfect, could not live directly with someone who is imperfect and sinful.

However, when you accepted Christ as your personal savior, the Holy Spirit took residence in you and the veil was ripped into two removing the barrier between your soul and God's Spirit now residing in your Most Holy Place! There is no longer a separation between your spirit chamber and your mind chamber because your acceptance of Christ makes it possible for God to view you through the lens of Christ who was without sin, allowing

Him to take up permanent residence in you. Even though you did not become perfect when you gave your life to Christ, God now sees you as perfect as long as you strive to remain obedient to Christ! You no longer need to go through special rituals just to interact with God and hear His voice; He is always with you.

The Colors of the Veil

Interestingly, the colors of the veil: purple, scarlet, and blue, were exactly the same colors that God chose for the robes worn by Aaron and the Levites whom He chose to serve as His priests prior to their entering the Tabernacle as we described in Chapter 5 (Exodus 28:31-34). As with everything God does, there was special meaning to the colors He chose for the veil and the priestly garments, symbolizing His intent. Let us examine the significance of these colors chosen by God.

The Color Purple

The color purple in the veil symbolized the authority or kingship of God. Every kingdom usually has a king and a royal family. Of course Jesus Christ is the firstborn (prince) among God's royalty. He declared during His time on earth that He had brought with Him the kingdom of God, and taught and told several parables that involved the kingdom.[6] In fact, there are over eighty references to the kingdom of God in the New Testament, including over fifty in the gospels alone. "After this, Jesus traveled about from one town and village to another, proclaiming the good news of the kingdom of God" (Luke 8:1).

Everyone who has given their life to Jesus Christ is an adopted son or daughter of this kingdom by virtue of being born again into His kingdom. Adoption confers all the rights and privileges of being a member of the adopted family. Since you are adopted into the kingdom of God, it means that you also are part of the royal family. "But you are a chosen people, a royal priesthood, a holy nation, God's special possession, that you may declare the praises of him who called you out of darkness into His wonderful light" (1 Peter 2:9, NIV 2011).

You are a royal priest because as a result of giving your life to Jesus Christ, you now have a deposit of God's Spirit living within your heart, and you can interact with Him continuously, just as Jesus did, without the need for an intermediary. This is one of the most precious and freely given gifts of God and should be one of your most highly motivating factors in terms of where your mind is focused.

As a royal prince or princess and priest, you become an ambassador for the kingdom to which you belong. As a member of the kingdom of God, you are an alien in this world, and even though you are living here, your native home country is now heaven. You are thus an ambassador of God on Earth. Your behavior as a Christian will be watched by others seeking to determine what Christianity and God's kingdom is all about. For this reason, your behavior should reflect the kingdom to which you belong. An ambassador should represent the views and behaviors of the country that he or she represents. "You, my brothers and sisters, were called to be free. But do not use your freedom to indulge the flesh; rather, serve one another humbly in love. For the entire law is fulfilled in keeping this one command: "Love your neighbor as yourself." If you bite and devour each other, watch out or you will be destroyed by each other" (Galatians 5:13-15, NIV 2011).

As an adopted child of God, you have full inheritance rights

While this has almost become a cliché, it is very important to ask the Holy Spirit who is resident in you in every situation whether in your privacy or in public, "What would Jesus do?" An ambassador for any nation would always seek the opinion of his or her native country's government through direct instructions or consulting rulebooks prior to making pronouncements involving their relationship with the nation in which he or she is serving. Similarly, you should regularly and prayerfully seek consultation from your native country for every situation in your life. And who knows more about heaven than the Holy Spirit who is one with God, and which guidebook can help you more than the inspired Word of God, the Holy Bible?

"In the same way, the Spirit helps us in our weakness. We do not know what we ought to pray for, but the Spirit himself intercedes for us through wordless groans. And He who searches our hearts knows the mind of the Spirit, because the Spirit intercedes for God's people in accordance with the will of God" (Romans 8:26–27, NIV 2011).

The Color Scarlet

The color scarlet symbolized blood. It represented the price that was needed by sinful men and women to be paid in order to be able to approach a perfect God. God wants to have a relationship with *all* members of His creation, but He is perfect and our sin has separated mankind from Him, since darkness and light cannot coexist.

"For all have sinned and fall short of the glory of God" (Romans 3:23). Since sinful man could not approach God and deserved death, God needed a new arrangement to be able to have the relationship He desires with us. In the special agreement (covenant) between God and the people He chose—the Jewish people—to ultimately redevelop His relationship with humanity, God chose to exchange the blood (lives) of animals as atonement for the sins of men and women. In the shedding of animal blood the peoples' sins were wiped out, so that God saw those for whom the blood was shed as being perfect and He was able to have a relationship with them. Since their sin was continuous, the blood needed to be continuously shed.

> This is why even the first covenant was not put into effect without blood. When Moses had proclaimed every command of the law to all the people, he took the blood of calves, together with water, scarlet wool and branches of hyssop, and sprinkled the scroll and all the people. He said, "This is the blood of the covenant, which God has commanded you to keep." In the same way, he sprinkled with the blood both the tabernacle and everything used in its ceremonies. In fact, the law requires that nearly everything be cleansed with blood, and without the shedding of blood there is no forgiveness. (Hebrews 9:18–22)

The continuous shedding of animal blood during the temple days was thus as a "cleanser" to purify the "dirt of sin" from every man and woman so they could approach a perfect God. As Christians, our focal point is now the blood of Jesus, which was shed once and for all to replace the need for shedding of animal blood and has cleansed us from the dirt of our own sins. To illustrate this point further, I would like to introduce the concept of the school master.

The School Master and the Need for Blood

The Ten Commandments (Exodus 20) were laws given to Moses by God to be followed in order for the children of Israel, and through them the rest of the world, to be able to draw near to Him in this world and the next. Sin did not suddenly come into play as a result of the Ten Commandments; it has existed since the time of Adam and Eve (Genesis 3:1–19). All the rules in the Ten Commandments already existed before Moses came along, but God gave them to Moses so the Israelites would recognize their desperate need to draw near to Him. In a sense, the written law represented a "school master," whose job was to lead mankind to a realization of the impossibility of keeping the laws on our own due to our naturally sinful nature, and thus helping us to seek someone else who can help us keep them—that is God.

In this analogy, consider that you are in an architectural school known as the school of life. The sole purpose of this school is to learn how to build a physical bridge to use both while you are alive and after you die to connect you directly to the kingdom of God in heaven. The bridge must be perfectly designed to withstand all the challenging elements that can threaten it such as water, wind, fire, snow, ice, earthquakes, and tsunamis and it must be long enough to reach the final destination you desire (heaven) or you will end up in a wrong place (hell). The bridge is exclusive; you must build your own bridge, you will have full ownership of it, and you will have to use what you build. No one else can use your bridge and you cannot use someone else's. For obvious reasons, in the school of life, the passing grade is 100 percent. Even if you are the smartest person in your class and you were to get 99 percent, it would not be good enough to pass because the bridge would not work for you at 99 percent accuracy. The tests you receive are fair because the information on them truly reflect what it will take to build your own successful bridge in order to make it, but the volume and complexity of information on these tests are impossible for you or any single human being to know on your own.

Not surprisingly, many students in the school of life protest and quit the school, noting that it is unfair, arrogant, and conceited of the school master to think that His particular method of building a bridge is the only one that will get then to heaven. Realizing the impossibility of the task at hand, many others quit because they do not believe they need any bridge to get to heaven. Others still do not believe there is a heaven, so why should they be bothered to waste time that could be spent having fun on earth on a futile project that has no value? As a student in the school of life, it is easy for you to get depressed because even when you have tried your best, stayed up late for several nights, shown your teacher that you are a more dedicated and hardworking student than your peers, you are still failing to make the grade. Many of the students in the school who have quit have written letters of condemnation about the school master and His cruelty for making the program so hard and the tests so impossible.

Meanwhile, outside the impossible school of life there are literally thousands of other schools that proclaim they can accomplish building you a bridge that will get you to heaven but who demand much less of your time, energy, or resources. Their tests are much easier to pass than the school of life with its 100 percent requirement. When you check out these schools, they have many more students enrolled in them and many seem to be thriving without making all the sacrifices being demanded in the school of life and its tough school master. In fact, no other school demands a 100 percent pass rate. All the other schools simply compare how you have done in relation to the other students or whether the design of your bridge has more strengths than flaws in determining if the bridge would be sufficient to get you a passing grade which they claim would suffice to get you into heaven. Since there is no way of knowing for sure if the bridge you get to design and build in the school of life is any better that any of the bridges from the other schools until you have died, why waste all your energies on the complicated system of the school of life?

Meanwhile, the school master in the school of life is adamant that the consequences of anything short of 100 percent pass rate is a flawed bridge that will not work but will lead you to fall off the end into a place of eternal condemnation. In fact, one of the basic rules of the school of life is a law called the law of flaw and death. The law is simple: if your bridge has a single flaw, it will fail you and you will die. Any single flaw on the bridge you design will lead to failure in life with the consequence of death. This is clearly not the best way to advertise for a school hoping to attract the most or best and brightest students. Is this a school you would like to attend? Obviously no one in his right mind would want to attend this school—unless of course the claims of the school master happen to be true and unless there really is a hope of getting through with 100 percent success.

Three conditions will have to be met for anyone to enroll in the school of life. The first condition is that somehow in your consciousness you would need to truly believe there is a place called heaven. The second condition is that once you have visited the school of life and met with the school master, you would have to believe, based on all the evidence presented to you, that only the bridge designed and built at His school will have the blueprint to get you into heaven. The final condition is that you would have to know there is a solution that enables you to get 100 percent on the tests so you can actually build the bridge that will get you to heaven. Since it has already been established that you cannot get 100 percent on your own, there would need to be another way that involves help from another source. The amazing thing is that all these conditions are fully met by the school for those who take the time to discover them.

The "school of life" is real, and the school master is God. The bridge is the means by which you can erase the separation between you and Him due to your sins and get to heaven. The school of life bears the principle from God that you are a sinner, and there is no way you can approach God on your own, no matter how "good" a person you are and how hard you try.

Jesus is the bridge that gets you to heaven

If you break one of God's laws, what you deserve is eternal condemnation because those are the rules. The tests at the school are the Ten Commandments given by God to Moses (Exodus 20). God already knows that on your own accord you will fail the tests, but that does not mean He is going to change the requirements of the tests. The reason He gives the hard tests are not to make you look stupid or feel condemned but because they contain the real requirements for what is needed to build the perfect bridge to the specifications that will get you to Him. Many human beings have condemned God because of the impossibility of keeping His commandments. They believe they are too restrictive, too grave, too difficult to follow; that they are unfair, unkind, unjust, etc. They instead choose other ways and faiths that are more permissive and which all claim to give the same results without the burden of full obedience to the laws of Moses.

The irony is that God has met the three conditions for attending His school of life, which actually makes it much easier than all the other schools to make heaven.

First of all, He has given you overwhelming evidence with numerous references in His inspired book—the Holy Bible—that there is a place called heaven.[7]

Secondly, he has made it abundantly clear that there is indeed a law that states that *any* sin leads to death. "For the wages of sin is death, but the gift of God is eternal life in Christ Jesus our Lord" (Romans 6:23). Leading a "good life" in which you have done more good than bad or in which you have behaved better than others is not enough to make it to heaven; you will never make the grade alone.

Finally, He has provided an alternative method for His people, first the Jews and then followers of Jesus Christ to "purchase"—for free—the perfect bridge that will get us to heaven. He has not only paid your school fees to the school of life, He has freely given you the blueprint for your own bridge to heaven. While the gift is free, it was not without cost to God.

The price for your perfect bridge had to be paid with blood, since the law of flaw and death says your failure has to lead to death. Since you have no chance of passing, God had to substitute someone else who was flawless to provide the solution for you who could enable you to pass with 100 percent scores. Before the arrival of Jesus, God provided the escape mechanism for the Jews who had sinned to "purchase" their bridges in the form of the continuous sacrifice of the blood of animals in place of having to give their own blood. This was only a temporary plan that He had in place until the permanent solution came into being. Later on, of course, God paid the price for your bridge Himself, giving you the perfect and most precious gift you will ever have so that you would no longer have to toil in the school of life. This gift came in the form of His one and only Son, Jesus Christ, who shed his own blood once and for all to pay the price so that you and everyone who accepts the tenets of the school of life can receive the perfect bridge to get into heaven.

My prayer for you is that you will truly accept and embrace and treasure this free gift.

The Blood of Jesus and the Gift of Salvation

Jesus Christ is the only person who has ever lived who was perfect and without sin. He is the only one who has scored 100 percent on the test in the school of life. He is thus the only person possible who could approach God and whose bridge design for you can get you into the presence of God. In dying on the cross, Jesus made the ultimate sacrifice in shedding His own blood once and for all to spare you from the need for continuous animal sacrifices for your sin in order to enter your Most Holy Place to have a relationship with God. In this new agreement or covenant with God, God promises to bless you with an ongoing relationship and to give you eternal life, but you have to accept the free gift of the blood of Jesus as atonement for your sins.

When Christ came as high priest of the good things that are already here, He went through the greater and more perfect tabernacle that is not manmade, that is to say, not a part of this creation. He did not enter by means of the blood of goats and calves; but He entered the Most Holy Place once for all by His own blood, having obtained eternal redemption. The blood of goats and bulls and the ashes of a heifer sprinkled on those who are ceremonially unclean sanctify them so that they are outwardly clean. How much more, then, will the blood of Christ, who through the eternal Spirit offered Himself unblemished to God, cleanse our consciences from acts that lead to death, so that we may serve the living God!

For this reason Christ is the mediator of a new covenant, that those who are called may receive the promised eternal inheritance—now that He has died as a ransom to set them free from the sins committed under the first covenant. (Hebrews 9:11–16)

Here is the most important part of the gift of the Blood of Jesus. When you receive it, you now have the Holy Spirit who has the blue print for the school of life deposited within you. Since the Holy Spirit and God are one, the Holy Spirit knows all the answers to the tests in the school of life. When you look at the Ten Commandments or any of God's laws, they are no longer a burden because the Holy Spirit within you guarantees that He has the solution for all of them and you will be able to keep the Commandments, if you enable Him to act within you! The same tests that you struggled with before you accepted the gift in the school of life are now possible to pass with a 100 percent score because the author of the tests lives with you and can give you all the solutions to them. God will now enable you to look afresh at the Ten Commandments with joy in the recognition that they are not a burden for you because you have the Spirit of God living within you who has promised to help you keep them all. I urge you to meditate on each of the commandments regularly and ask the Holy Spirit to reveal to you that they are promises to you that none of them will ever again need to be broken in your lifetime.

The Holy Spirit holds the blue print for success in your life

The Color Blue

The color blue was chosen in the temple curtain to focus attention on God's heavenly abode, being the color of the sky when there are no clouds present to obscure it. "Moses and Aaron, Nadab, and Abihu, and the seventy elders of Israel went up and saw the God of Israel. Under his feet was something like a pavement made of lapis lazuli, as bright blue as the sky" (Exodus 24:9-10, NIV 2011).

Seeing the color blue regularly was a reminder to the priests to maintain a heavenly focus. Blue was also mixed into the veil colors to serve as a reminder that the Jewish Tabernacle and temple were simply replicas of the most perfect tabernacle, the one in heaven.

> Now the main point of what we are saying is this: We do have such a high priest, who sat down at the right hand of the throne of the Majesty in heaven, and who serves in the sanctuary, the true tabernacle set up by the Lord, not by a mere human being.
>
> Every high priest is appointed to offer both gifts and sacrifices, and so it was necessary for this one also to have something to offer. If He were on earth, He would not be a priest, for there are already priests who offer the gifts prescribed by the law. They serve at a sanctuary that is a copy and shadow of what is in heaven. This is why Moses was warned when he was about to build the tabernacle: "See to it that you make everything according to the pattern shown you on the mountain." But in fact the ministry Jesus has received is as superior to theirs as the covenant of which He is mediator is superior to the old one, since the new covenant is established on better promises. (Hebrews 8:1–6)

We will discuss in chapter 23 how the beauty of heaven makes everything on earth shabby in comparison and why it is important for Christians to remember that our time on earth is only a momentary part of eternity where we will spend forever in the presence of God.

Summary of the Veil Colors and the Bridge of the School of Life

All the colors of the veil were pointing to Jesus Christ, who at the time of the temple was still the coming Messiah but today is the life-giving, ever-present Savior who has already paid the price as the sacrificial lamb for your sin and mine, permanently removing the need for a veil between us and God (Matthew 27:50–51). God was never pleased with the separation by a veil from His people. That is why He sent Jesus Christ to earth as a perfect human being to live a life of total obedience culminating in His crucifixion and resurrection to bridge the gap between God and us. Christ defeated death and ripped apart the curtain that separated man from God, making it possible for God and man to be reconciled. God has thus established this "new covenant," in which anyone who accepts Jesus Christ as his or her savior is no longer subject to condemnation and eternal separation from God. That includes you, and I encourage you to receive this gift with joy!

Pray This Prayer with Me:

Dear God, I thank You for being such a wonderful school master and that You have given me the most precious gift I could ever possess in my school of life, the gift of my Lord and Savior Jesus Christ. I pray that You grant me the wisdom to always accept this gift freely and to recognize that Your Ten Commandments were not given to condemn me but to make me aware of the impossibility of my keeping them without the help of your Holy Spirit. Thank You for this wonderful insight and for putting Your love within my heart through Your Spirit. Amen.

1. The first (King Solomon's) Temple had a door separating the Most Holy Place from the Holy Place. After this temple was destroyed, the temple that replaced it had a veil instead of a door.

2. Exodus 26:31–33; 2 Chronicles 3:14.

3. Maurice Henry Harris. *Hebraic Literature: Translations from the Talmud, Midrashim and Kabbala*, M. Walter Dunne, 1901, 195–96. http://books.google.com/books?id=qU hk0UUgrAkC&printsec=frontcover&dq=Hebraic+Literature;+Translations+fro m+the+Talmud,+Midrashim+and+Kabbala,&cd=1#v=onepage&q&f=false (last visited April 28, 2011).

4. Exodus 30:10; Hebrews 9:7.

5. Ezra 1:1–4, Ezra 4, 5; 2 Chronicles 36:22–23.

6. Matthew 19:24, 21:31, 43; Mark 1:15; 4:11, 26, 30, 9:1, 47, 10:14–17, 23–25, 14:25, 15:43; Luke 4:43, 6:20, 7:28, 8:1, 10, 9:2, 11, 27, 60, 62, 10:9, 11, 11:20, 13:18–20, 13:28–29, 14:15, 17:20–21, 18:16–18, 25, 29, 19:11, 21:31, 22:18, 23:51, John 3:3, 5.

7. Genesis 1:1, 14:19, 22:11; Exodus 16:4; Deuteronomy 2:25; 1 Chronicles 29:11; Isaiah 55:10; Daniel 7–9; Matthew 5–7; John 1:51; Acts 7:55; Revelation 13, 14.

CHAPTER 14

The Most Holy Place 4—
The Light That Shines within You

(Session 7b)

A holy life will make the deepest impression. Lighthouses blow no horns, they just shine.—Dwight L. Moody, American evangelist and publisher (1837-1899).

A Need for Holiness

We have already established that the priests ministering in the Jewish Tabernacle and temple needed to consecrate themselves prior to entering the Holy Place, symbolic of the needed purity associated with anyone who is to approach God. However, entering the Most Holy Place where God's presence was required a much more stringent level of purification. The only time God allowed anyone to enter the Most Holy Place was once a year, during the Day of Atonement (Yom Kippur) when the high priest went in to offer atonement for the sins of all the Jews. The daily offerings occurring in the Holy Place required immersion by the officiating priests in the bath and washing of their hands and feet prior to entry. By contrast, the high priest preparing for Yom Kippur had to go through five different immersions and four changes of clothes. He then had to separate himself for seven days from all the people, during which time he underwent further purification rites including being sprinkled with water containing the ashes of a sacrificial cow (a red heifer without spot) and going over the procedures for the ceremony with experts of temple worship prior to entering the Most Holy Place. There was always a back-up high priest in case the chosen one did not make the cut for any reason.

All this effort reflected the extraordinary effort that was demanded of the high priest in relation to his Holiness in preparation to meeting with God. This is because God is pure and perfect and demands perfection in order for imperfect and sinful man to come into contact with Him. Unfortunately, since the fall of Adam and Eve, perfection is not possible for any human being working on their own efforts. The good news for you as we previously noted is that God has already paid the price for your sins through the sacrifice of His perfect son Jesus Christ who died in place of you.

If you come to Him with a truly repentant and humble heart, you can always "come boldly to His throne of grace, [so you] may obtain mercy and find grace to help [you] in your time of need" Hebrews 4:16. You are now free to approach God as the new covenant high priest at every waking moment of your life and have a close and personal relationship with Him without having to undergo the complex purification acts of the Old Covenant high priest. However, as we will see later on, God still demands Holiness in *you* as His preferred temple.

No Light Needed in the Most Holy Place

In contrast to the outer court and the Holy Place, the Most Holy Place was a room with no natural or artificial illumination. This is because God's Spirit resided there and His presence was enough to give supernatural lighting. When the Tabernacle was replaced by the temple in Jerusalem during the time of King Solomon, the Most Holy Place was built as beautiful a room as human hands have ever made. For a room that was only thirty square feet, entering it inspired the reverent fear of God in anyone who dared to venture inwards. The walls and ceiling glittered with the luminescence of the pure gold in which they were overlaid. Indeed, every single object in the Most Holy Place glittered in gold, reflecting the purity of God and the need for any place of His abode to be pure.

Significance: the Most Holy Place was the structural equivalent of your heart, where God's Spirit resides today if you have given your life to Christ. When God is present in you, and you allow Him to influence you, your whole Spirit becomes supernaturally illuminated, and the light in your spirit dominates the outside light that is competing to influence your soul. Even though your mortal flesh is perishable, when you have the Holy Spirit residing within you, your inner being is pure, inlaid with pure gold, incorruptible, imperishable, and impervious to decay. You are more radiant than the midday sun and you have an inner beauty that is inexplicably attractive to those around you. While clouds, fogs, storms and other events can dim the natural light in your outer court, they can never influence God's supernatural light in your Most Holy Place, which never wanes. If your soul is dependent on outside light, the clouds, fogs, and storms of life will lead you to a gloomy and very rocky life. On the other hand, if your soul is dependent on the Holy Spirit for its light, it never has to worry about the constancy of the source. This means that your soul is always refreshed and glowing, even when external circumstances are dire and dull. It does not mean you will not face storms; it only means that the light within you will overwhelm and guide you through any storm that may come.

Indeed, before the Lord Jesus Christ (the Redeemer) came to Earth, the Prophet Isaiah in prophesying about His coming seven hundred years earlier linked His coming to the outpouring of the Holy Spirit on those who repent of their sins (Isaiah 59:19–20). Isaiah then links this outpouring of the Holy Spirit in the very next chapter and verses with the presence of a light that would shine through in those on whom He is present in a very powerful way.

Light from the Holy Spirit never fades

"'The Redeemer will come to Zion, to those in Jacob who repent of their sins,' declares the LORD. 'As for me, this is my covenant with them,' says the LORD. 'My Spirit, who is on you, will not depart from you, and my words that I have put in your mouth will always be on your lips, on the lips of your children and on the lips of their descendants—from this time on and forever,' says the LORD" (Isaiah 59:20–21, NIV 2011).

"Arise, shine, for your light has come, and the glory of the LORD rises upon you. See, darkness covers the earth and thick darkness is over the peoples, but the LORD rises upon you and His glory appears over you. Nations will come to your light, and kings to the brightness of your dawn" (Isaiah 60:1–3).

"The sun will no more be your light by day, nor will the brightness of the moon shine on you, for the LORD will be your everlasting light, and your God will be your glory. Your sun will never set again, and your moon will wane no more; the LORD will be your everlasting light, and your days of sorrow will end" (Isaiah 60:19–20).

Isaiah gives us a powerful illustration of the significance of the Holy Spirit living within your Most Holy Place as a source of light and of ability to take on the qualities of God, including the ability to overcome the burden of the laws of Moses. This light will overcome the darkness of the world and will be attractive to people around you, including nations and kings. Indeed, in the vision God gave to the apostle John of a future New Jerusalem in the book of Revelation of the Bible, we are told there will be no need for sun or moon because of God's presence there.

> I did not see a temple in the city, because the Lord God Almighty and the Lamb are its temple. The city does not need the sun or the moon to shine on it, for the glory of God gives it light, and the Lamb is its lamp. The nations will walk by its light, and the kings of the earth will bring their splendor into it. On no day will its gates ever be shut, for there will be no night there. The glory and honor of the nations will be brought into it. (Revelation 21:22–26)

When you allow God's Spirit not only to reside within you but you also respond to Him, you will experience this supernatural light that comes from the living God and the extraordinary blessings that flow with walking with Him. Indeed, you take on the qualities of the company you keep. When you keep God's company, you will radiate His characteristics. There are two clear glimpses of this supernatural light from the two principal leaders of the Bible: Moses in the Old Testament, who presented the laws of God to mankind, and Jesus, the Son of God, who presented the grace of God to mankind. When both had finished spending substantial amounts of time with God during their lives on Earth, they shined so brightly and their faces became so radiant, it was difficult for their followers to look directly at them.

> When Moses came down from Mount Sinai with the two tablets of the Testimony in his hands, he was not aware that his face was radiant because he had spoken with the LORD. When Aaron and all the Israelites saw Moses, his face was radiant, and they were afraid to come near him. But Moses called to them; so Aaron and all the leaders of the community came back to him, and he spoke to them. Afterward all the Israelites came near him, and he gave them

all the commands the LORD had given him on Mount Sinai. When Moses finished speaking to them, he put a veil over his face. But whenever he entered the LORD's presence to speak with him, he removed the veil until he came out. And when he came out and told the Israelites what he had been commanded, they saw that his face was radiant. Then Moses would put the veil back over his face until he went in to speak with the LORD. (Exodus 34:29–34)

"After six days, Jesus took with him Peter, James, and John, the brother of James, and led them up a high mountain by themselves. There he was transfigured before them. His face shone like the sun, and his clothes became as white as the light. Just then there appeared before them Moses and Elijah, talking with Jesus" (Matthew 17:1–3). The radiance of Moses and Jesus is a glimpse into how everyone who makes it to heaven will look when we are constantly in the presence of God. In the same way, when you spend time in this life in your Most Holy Place, developing and fostering a relationship with your Creator, you will radiate an inner beauty and light so bright that people cannot fail to notice the God in you.

Consider yourself as an iron rod and God a blazing hot fire. Spending time with God (reading and meditating on His word, praying and praising Him, attending church with other believers) is equivalent to being dipped into the blazing hot fire. The longer it spends, and the more often it is put back to get dipped into the fire, the longer the iron rod will remain hot and red and take on all the properties of the fire. The rod will glow and be able to burn just like the fire as long as it is dipped often and long enough into it. However, remove the rod for any length of time, and it will still be a rod, but it will be powerless to take on the nature of the fire. It will not be able to burn anything. In fact, it will be very cold. Not filling up with the Holy Spirit is akin to being a cold iron rod. You will be powerless and will not be able to influence anyone for Christ. I pray that the rod of your life will always blaze with the flames of the Holy Spirit within you.

Significance of the Holy Spirit within Your Holy of Holies

Your Most Holy Place (Holy of Holies) represents the location of your spirit (*pneuma* in the Greek), that part of you that interacts with and houses the Spirit of God if you are a Christian. Unfortunately in many people, it has not been turned over to Christ and as such is a place that houses other spirits.[1] Your Holy of Holies is the deepest part of you—closely related to "your heart," which is hidden from your soul by a veil while you have not had the experience of Christian rebirth.

The original Greek word for the Holy Spirit was pneuma. It is what "pneumatic" originated from, a word related to "air" or "breathing." Your spirit, like the air from which it is derived, is thus an invisible organ that has been given to you by God to interact with His Spirit, to discern and reflect the unseen influence of the Holy Spirit. God's Holy Spirit is the limitless extension of Himself and He is able to pour Him on every one who desires to have Him. The Holy Spirit is unseen because He resides in the hidden compartment of your being—your Holy of Holies. Just as with the Holy of Holies in the Jewish temple, your Most Holy Place by nature of its being hidden is "dark." When the Holy Spirit takes up residence in it though, your Holy of Holies receives a different kind of illumination. It is this type of light that we noted earlier as coming from Moses and Jesus when they had face-to-face encounters with God.[2]

Constant training helps you to recognize the promptings of the Holy Spirit

Although it is the most hidden part of your being, your spirit is very much alive and active; since it cannot be seen it requires an element known as faith. Its influence on you, on the other hand, is totally dependent upon you.

"The wind [pneuma] blows wherever it pleases. You hear its sound, but you cannot tell where it comes from or where it is going. So it is with everyone born of the Spirit [pneuma]" (John 3:8). Your rational mind cannot figure out where the wind is coming from or going, you either rely upon your "intuition" or you need this to be revealed to you! Billions of dollars are spent on special equipment every year to try and understand the movements of the winds, and in doing so, to predict the weather and give man some semblance of control. In spite of this, there is a lot of uncertainty about true weather patterns. Invisible currents cannot be easily traced and predicted, although doing so would allow planning that could influence our human behavior. If the tsunamis that occurred on December 26, 2004, in Asia could have been predicted and the people alerted, one of the biggest tragedies in human history that cost more than two hundred thousand lives could have been averted.

This is also true of the Holy Spirit. Investing the time to learn how to interact with the Holy Spirit and responding to His non-verbal promptings could help avert unnecessary misery and tragedy in your life.

The Holy Spirit and Intuition

What so many people call "intuition" is a prompting from their spirit. Intuition involves making a choice without any physical or logical reason to do so. Intuition usually makes no sense and cannot be explained. Similarly, learning about the Holy Spirit and recognizing and differentiating His promptings from other spirits could lead to making sense of what is currently seen as intuition.

On a Tuesday afternoon in February 2005, a powerful explosion rocked an apartment building in Lansing, Michigan. A twenty-six-year-old man had driven his car into the side of the building, causing leakage in a gas pipeline. Fortunately, the building had been evacuated by firefighters just one minute prior to the explosion. Fire Engine 46 was parked about twenty yards away from the building. Moments before the explosion, two firefighters, both Christians, sensed an urging to move to the opposite side of Engine 46, facing away from the building. They obeyed this instinct. There was no rational reason for this decision. It was not a conscious action based on a logical rationing that they could explain. It was what ordinary people call intuition. This action saved their lives. The explosion was severe enough to shatter the driver's side as windows ripped out the gauges on the pump panel of the truck. Had they remained on the side of the truck facing the building, they would have been severely maimed if not killed. One of the firefighters recounted the episode a week later at a church service in Lansing, Michigan. "I am convinced this was the work of the Holy Spirit residing within me, as I have no other logical reason as to why we moved over to the other side to talk that afternoon."

The Holy Spirit has similarly instructed me on countless occasions and saved me from untold tragedy. As an example, on one occasion I was in the garage of our home getting ready to proceed on a trip to a restaurant. I had my (at the time two) children strapped into their seat belts in our minivan (which at the time did not have any rearview camera). Ordinarily I would reverse the car so that the front door was adjacent to the door leading inside the house and wait patiently for my wife to come in directly into the front seat, saving minute fragments of time on our journey. On this occasion, although my body was ready to reverse the car, I felt a strong movement of the Holy Spirit to stay where I was until I established where my wife was. I asked my boys, "Where is Mommy?" Almost immediately, I heard my wife's voice reply, "I'm right here." I looked in my rear-view mirror. My wife had been bent over, looking for something in the trunk of the car in a position in which the rear seats concealed her. I had not seen her come out of the house or approach the trunk. Although the trunk was open, there was enough space between it and the ceiling that I could have reversed the few yards out of the garage. Responding to this whisper of the Spirit saved my family potential tragedy that evening.

We all have this ability to be in tune with the Holy Spirit and respond to Him as He nudges us. Many Christians have ignored this prompting so much that they are no longer even sensitive to it. Rediscovering this relationship is not only possible, it should be a vital part of every man and woman's desire for the rest of your life. The nudging could be a sense that you should take a different route to work than you normally do, or to pick up the phone and call a friend you have not spoken to in years, or to stop someone on the road and ask if they need help.

The Holy Spirit will never ask you to contradict God's Word

It could also be something bigger that could change the course of your life. In this situation, you will have to confirm the urging through prayer, God's Word in the Bible, and sometimes through the counsel of strong Christians that you have a good relationship with. Hearing God's voice requires that you learn to listen to the small still voice within you. Of course, whatever the nudging is must be totally consistent with the Word of God as written in the Bible.

The Holy Spirit will *never* ask you to contradict God's Word. If the voice you are hearing is asking you to do harm to someone or something or to disobey one of God's commands, this cannot possibly be from God—it is the influence of your own mind or other spirits, since God does not lie. "[In] the hope of eternal life, which *God, who does not lie*, promised before the beginning of time" (Titus 1:2, emphasis added).

"Because God wanted to make the unchanging nature of His purpose very clear to the heirs of what was promised, He confirmed it with an oath. God did this so that, by two unchangeable things in which *it is impossible for God to lie*, we who have fled to take hold of the hope set before us may be greatly encouraged" (Hebrews 6:17–18, emphasis added).

If the voice you are hearing is a persistent one that is contrary to God's Word and causing you or others distress, you may need to seek medical help to rule out organic causes that are amenable to treatment or spiritual help. As you learn to hear and recognize God's voice within you, you will experience the supernatural power of God as He leads you along paths that will lift you to a higher realm of spirituality and makes the lamp within you shine bright. May this be your destiny for the rest of your life!

Pray This Prayer with Me:

Dear Lord, I need the supernatural light of the Holy Spirit to shine brightly within each of my chambers every waking moment of my life. Help me to remain embedded in You at all times, so that I may be filled up with the power of Your light, which will not only guide me moment by moment each day through what the world calls "intuition" but will help me to be Your guide to others. Help me learn to clearly recognize Your voice and to learn how to obey it. Amen.

Questions to Ponder:

- The Bible describes you as a royal priest in the kingdom of God, and God's ambassador.
  - What does it mean to be a priest in God's kingdom?
  - What are the implications to your day to day living to be an ambassador of God's kingdom to others here in the kingdom of Earth?
- What does it mean when the Bible says that the Spirit intercedes for you in accordance to the will of God (Romans 8:26–27)?
  - How do you enable to Spirit to intercede for you?
- Is it helpful to you to view the Ten Commandments as promises from God instead of burdensome rules?
  - If so how is this helpful?
- Have you met anyone who just seems to glow from the presence of the Holy Spirit?
  - What is it about them that makes him or her this way?
  - Do you desire to also have the radiance of Jesus shine out of you?
  - If so, how will you get it?
- Have you ever felt the Holy Spirit nudge you to do something out of the ordinary?
  - Describe one such occasion and what happened as a result.
  - How do you know if the voice you are hearing is from God?
  - What are some clues that a voice you hear is not from God?

Prayer Points

- Pray that God will teach you to truly be the priest He has called you to be in His kingdom, and to be the best possible ambassador for Him to those around you.
- Pray that you will always enable the Holy Spirit to intercede for you in accordance to the will of God through your total surrendering of your words, thoughts, and actions to Him.
- Pray that God will always remind you that you can resist through the power of the Holy Spirit within you whatever temptation you have to break one of His Ten Commandments.
- Pray for such a powerful presence of the Holy Spirit within you at all times and for God to help keep you embedded in Him so that you will always have His glow.
- Pray that God will give you the ability to hear and respond whenever the Holy Spirit nudges you to do something out of the ordinary, and to also give you a spirit of discernment to know when the voice is not from God.

1. 1 John 4:1–3.
2. Exodus 34:29–34; Matthew 17:1–3.

CHAPTER 15

You Are a Three-Part Being— Carnal, Natural, and Spiritual

(Session 8a)

People who are crucified with Christ have three distinct marks: they are facing only one direction, they can never turn back, and they no longer have plans of their own.—A. W. Tozer

Carnal, Natural, and Spiritual Beings

The separation of body, soul, and spirit makes it difficult for many people including Christians to truly know or fully interact with God. God being Spirit cannot be seen and as a result will only interact with the hidden part of your temple—your spirit—not directly with your body or soul unless specific conditions are met. The implication of the division is that there are three types of human beings, depending on which part of your temple has the major influence over you.

The Carnal Person

The first type of person is one who is controlled by and whose prime goal is to satisfy his or her carnal (*sarkikos,* or "fleshly" in Greek) needs. Sarkikos is defined as "being under the control of the animal appetites governed by mere human nature, not by the Spirit of God."[1]

The carnal person lives mostly in and is influenced primarily by his or her outer court. For such people, there is no influence of the Holy Spirit whatsoever on their mind. They do as they please with themselves, in the process, subjecting themselves to all kinds of bondages. They have no "willpower" and give their bodies over to promiscuity, drugs, addictions, or different kinds of perversion or plainly denigrate their bodies in other ways. Indeed, they may initially have equated or still equate their behavior with freedom—freedom from God's rules, but in reality they are in bondage to satan. They cannot choose to stop this behavior on their own accord without paying a big price: strong cravings, withdrawals, rejection by their peers, or experiencing depression. If this is you, you need help from Jesus Christ who is the person fully able to help you break away from this bondage.

If you have not already given your life over to Him, this is as good a time as any to do so in order to be set free. All you have to do is open your mouth and tell Him that you want Him to be your Savior, and seek to follow Him and obey Him, and He does the rest! "This is what the Lord says—your Redeemer, the holy one of Israel: 'I am the Lord your God, who teaches you what is best for you, who directs you in the way you should go. If only you had paid attention to my commands, your peace would have been like a river, your righteousness like the waves of the sea'" (Isaiah 48:17–18).

The carnal person focuses primarily on their flesh

It is never too late. God still seeks to give you this peace but it will require your cooperation. In later chapters, we will discuss how you can move from this type of person to the spiritual being God created you to be.

The Natural (Logical Person)

The second type of person is the *natural* (Greek: *psychikos*,[2] or "man of the soul") person. A natural person is the type who rationalizes everything and needs logical evidence before believing God is at work.

These people live mostly in their Holy Place (soul, mind). If this is you, you are a logical person. Logic is an excellent trait and is often a blessing that can help you accomplish a lot in life and shield you from bad decisions. However, your logical mind can also be a major stumbling block that prevents you from having a close relationship with God. Although you are not necessarily carnal, your need for physical proof can keep you veiled from acknowledging or believing the presence and power of God. You will likely question the truthfulness of any miracle of God, and will not accept that God can do anything your mind cannot conceive. Indeed, even as a Christian with the presence of the Holy Spirit living within you, it is very easy to turn your back on His promptings and His desire to influence you for your own benefit because His promptings do not always make logical sense.

A villager who only knows the streams in his village cannot believe vast oceans exist.— African Proverb

The logical person rationalizes everything

You may believe in God, but it is hard for your logical mind to believe His written word or that His supernatural ways apply to you. Although you can control many influences of your outer court, you are living based on your natural intelligence, while discounting the supernatural light coming from your Most Holy Place (the supernatural intelligence of God in the person of the Holy Spirit). You are thus missing out on the greatest blessing God has given you while you are on this earth—an opportunity to have a direct relationship with Him and be blessed through interacting with His Holy Spirit. This will often mean learning to discern the moments when you should let go of your logic and enable the Holy Spirit to direct you in ways that you had not thought possible.

Consider Zipporah, a Cameroonian professional living in Lansing, Michigan. She was on the second day of a three-day fast while she was watching a Christian program at her local library. During the program, the bishop conducting the service was instructing his congregation to praise God, pray, and repeat certain confessions of faith. Even though she was in a public place, Zipporah faithfully followed along, raising her hands to worship God and murmuring the words required by the bishop, even while recognizing that her behavior would seem odd and illogical to those around her.

As she was continuing, the bishop asked everyone to pray for their own healing. Zipporah prayed avidly for healing of her vision, which has been deteriorating for the past several years such that she needed to bring books close to her eyes to be able to see even with her prescription glasses. Indeed, during the program, she had been unable to read messages and everything had been blurry for her, including the screen she was watching. Following the prayer, the bishop asked the congregants to examine themselves to see if there had been any healing. Immediately, Zipporah obeyed and noticed to her amazement that she could see the TV screen brilliantly without her glasses. Initially, she was afraid that this was a temporary effect and continued to use her glasses to read. By the following week, it was pretty clear that her vision was now perfect. During her attendance at the prayer meeting fellowship Zipporah was a member of, she recounted her miraculous testimony and took the final act of faith, breaking her glasses in front of the whole group. Her vision has remained excellent since then. Zipporah did not rely on logic to believe she would get her healing, and she was healed as a result. God wants to do the same with you, but your logical mind can get in the way of His supernatural ways.

God Does Not Think the Way You Think

God does not always use logical thinking to accomplish His purposes. When more than a million Israelites were stopped by the Red Sea in front of them and Pharaoh's army behind them as they tried to escape Egypt, the last thought that occurred to them was that God would separate the waters in a wall on either side to enable them to cross (Exodus 14). Similarly, when they were in the desert and became hungry, their logical minds could not have conceived that the food would be provided the same way rain came, from above in the form of manna (Exodus 16).

None of the miracles Jesus Christ performed were logical. Water was turned into wine.[3] Shriveled limbs were instantly restored.[4] The sight of the blind was restored and the deaf heard.[5] Raging storms were calmed with a few words.[6] A dead girl, man, and boy were brought back to life again.[7] Five thousand men, women, and children were fed with five loaves of bread and two fish.[8] There is often no logic to God except for the logic of trusting Him. "For my thoughts are not your thoughts, neither are your ways my ways, declares the Lord. As the Heavens are higher than the earth, so are my ways higher than your ways and my thoughts than your thoughts" (Isaiah 55:8–9).

God's miracles continue today and are experienced by those who are able to allow for the fact that He is sovereign and His realm of knowledge and capacity is vastly outside that of man's. It requires faith. "And without faith it is impossible to please God, because anyone who comes to Him must believe that He exists and that He rewards those who earnestly seek Him" (Hebrews 11:6).

If you are a "logical" person, this is a wonderful trait, but I pray for you that the Lord will release you from the trap of relying on a logical mind when you are faced with spiritual issues. Once you do this, you will see God start to move in new ways in your life.

The Spiritual Person

Spiritual persons are sensitive to promptings of the Holy Spirit

The third type of person is the spiritual (Greek: *pneumatikos,*[9] or "man of the wind or breath," or "one aided by the Holy Spirit"). Spiritual persons are sensitive to the promptings of the Holy Spirit and enjoy the benefits of a close relationship with God. If this is you, you strive to know God through constant prayer, delving into and memorizing His Word as divine food and source of power, and you have control over the promptings of your flesh. Your control over your outer court is not because of any special effort on your part, it is because of the dominance of the Holy Spirit in your life. You are logical, but you also often do things and act in ways that make no sense to the rest of the world simply because this is how the Holy Spirit has prompted you to act. You do not rely solely on the logic emanating from your Holy Place but the spillover of supernatural light from your Most Holy Place. Persons who consider themselves Christians should be either natural or spiritual, although there are some carnal people who think they are Christian.

God wants all Christians to be spiritual Christians. When you are a spiritual Christian, the light emanating from the Holy Spirit within your Most Holy Place is the dominant light within you. Since this light is constant, you are not given to the ups and downs of the natural light that dominates your flesh, which can be blackened out by the storms of life so that you stumble in the resultant darkness. You are not dominated by the light in your Holy Place that can be snuffed out by events that do not make logical sense. A spiritual Christian stands on the word of God, follows His precepts, and obeys His commands, knowing that not to do so is opening themselves up to dire consequences, especially a fractured relationship with God. In contrast, believing in God opens you up to a life of miracles and power.

What type of a Christian are you? Who has control of your soul? Are you content to continue living in your outer court with its natural light that is easily clouded by the storms of life? Perhaps you prefer to live in your

Holy Place with its artificial light that can be snuffed out when your logic fails you? God has prepared an inner room of pure gold with supernatural light that cannot fade for you! Are you as Kim was (in chapter 5), living in and controlled by your outer court, facing an empty life and an eternity separated from God? Or are you like Zipporah, who ignored logic and as a result got her vision back? Are you content to continue living as you are or are you ready to move on to the Holy of Holies where God is waiting for you to listen to His still and quiet but life-changing voice?

> Those who live according to the sinful nature [flesh, outer court] have their minds [soul, Holy Place] set on what that nature [flesh] desires; but those who live in accordance with the Spirit [Most Holy Place] have their minds set on what the Spirit desires. The mind of sinful man is death, but the mind controlled by the Spirit is life and peace; the sinful mind is hostile to God. It does not submit to God's law, nor can it do so. Those controlled by the sinful nature cannot please God. (Romans 8:5–7)

God's desire is for you to have life and peace, and that you have a vibrant and growing relationship with Him. Pray that God will help you to accomplish this through His Holy Spirit. We will discuss the practical aspects of how you can become a Spiritual being over the next few chapters.

Pray This Prayer with Me:

Dear Lord, I hereby seek to renounce life within my outer court and Holy Place. I cede control of all that I am and all that I desire to You and seek to live in my Most Holy Place under the influence of Your Holy Spirit from this point on. I ask that You forgive me for thinking I could lead a meaningful life apart from You. Help me break the yoke of logical thinking when You are calling for me to trust in You for a higher order of thinking that will lead me to live an extraordinary life. In Jesus' name I pray. Amen.

1. BibleStudyTools.com, http://www.biblestudytools.com/lexicons/greek/nas/ sarkikos.html (last visited May 22, 2011).
2. Trenches New Testament Synonyms, http://studybible.info/trench/Natural (last visited May 22, 2011).
3. John 2:1–11.
4. Matthew 12:9–13.
5. Matthew 12:22, 15:31; Mark 7:31–33, 8:23, 10:51–52.
6. Matthew 8:23–27.
7. Luke 8:51–53; John 11:14–44; Luke 7:11–16.
8. Matthew 14:13–21.
9. BibleStudyTools.com, http://www.biblestudytools.com/lexicons/greek/kjv/ pneumatikos-2.html (last visited May 22, 2011).

CHAPTER 16

Taking Control of Your Temple

(Session 8b)

You are a prisoner of your appetites. Your tendencies, addictions, or interests in either the things of the world or the things of God will determine the closeness of your relationship to your heavenly Father, and ultimately your eternal destiny. As a child of God, your daily appetite should include hunger for the Word of God and a thirst for His Holy Spirit so as to constantly communicate with Him in prayer.

How Do I take Control of My Temple?

Now that you have a better understanding of the great plans God has for you as a spiritual being, as His royal priest and His temple on this earth, it is important to take control of your temple. If your nature is carnal or natural, you particularly need help in turning over your temple to the Spirit of God.

The first step in becoming a true temple of God is that you have to empty yourself of any strongholds that are currently within you, to create the conditions for the Holy Spirit to have total access. A stronghold is defined as "an area dominated or occupied by a special group or distinguished by a special quality," "a fortified place or a fortress," "a place where a particular

Strongholds dull your spiritual senses and your awareness of God

cause or belief is strongly defended or upheld," or "a place of security or survival."[1] Within your temple, a stronghold is any part of you that is dominated by something or someone other than God. It is that part of you which causes you to sin. It could be anything from a firm fixed belief about God that limits Him or restricts His role in your life—an addiction, fear, anger, unforgiveness, laziness, greed, gluttony, or pride. Essentially, it is an appetite for anything that holds you hostage or turns you into a prisoner to sin.

What exactly does God consider sin? Sinning is a willful disobedience to God, or knowing how to do good and not doing it.[2] Sin makes you a slave and leads to death. As we noted in Session 7, the law of sin and death was given to you by the school master to draw you near to God and you have been given the power to overcome it through the death and resurrection of Jesus Christ and the presence of the Holy Spirit within you. As noted by Paul: "The acts of the sinful nature are obvious: sexual immorality, impurity and debauchery; idolatry and witchcraft; hatred, discord, jealousy, fits of rage, selfish ambition, dissensions, factions and envy; drunkenness, orgies, and the like. I warn you, as I did before, that those who live like this will not inherit the kingdom of God" (Galatians 5:19–21).

Being a follower of Christ is not a license to do as you wish and to break God's law with the understanding that He will forgive you. You have been set free from the bondage of sin. "It is for freedom that Christ has set us free. Stand firm, then, and do not let yourselves be burdened again by a yoke of slavery" (Galatians 5:1).

Yes, you have been saved by grace not by your behavior. However, your salvation is to set you free from the yoke of sin so that you can have an unimpeded relationship with God.

Prisoner of Your Own Appetite?

When you keep on sinning even though Christ has set you free, you are holding yourself hostage. You are a prisoner within your own palace. Dave Wilkerson illustrates this beautifully with the summary of a book written by Thomas Costain in which he recounts the story of a king who was literally a prisoner of his own appetite.[3]

> Raynald III was a fourteenth-century duke in the country
> now known as Belgium. Grossly overweight, Raynald was

commonly called by his Latin nickname, Crassus, which translates into "fat." After a violent quarrel, Raynald's younger brother, Edward, led a successful revolt against him. Edward captured Raynald but did not kill him. Instead, he built a room around Raynald in the Nieuwkerk castle and promised him he could regain his title and property as soon as he was able to leave the room. This would not have been difficult for most people since the room had several windows and a door of near-normal size, and none was locked or barred. The problem was Raynald's size. To regain his freedom, he needed to lose weight. But Edward knew his older brother, and each day he sent a variety of delicious foods. Instead of dieting his way out of prison, Raynald grew fatter. When Duke Edward was accused of cruelty, he had a ready answer: "My brother is not a prisoner. He may leave when he so wills."

Raynald stayed in that room for ten years and wasn't released until after Edward died in battle. By then his health was so ruined he died within a year … a prisoner of his own appetite.

Are you a prisoner of your own appetite? God has paved the way for your freedom, but satan's task is to blind you and distract you from seeing the doors and windows that God has opened for you to escape. How does satan do this? By using your weaknesses and your flesh as a trap, as Raynald's brother did in sending him delicious meals he could not resist daily. You need to shed the appetite that satan is using to keep you trapped in the lifestyle that God has already freed you from. Remember to confess the truth about your salvation in Christ, and say it out loud frequently so that it resonates with you. If Jesus has set you free, you are free indeed. Do not let the devil deceive you otherwise.

"Jesus replied, 'I tell you the truth, everyone who sins is a slave to sin. Now a slave has no permanent place in the family, but a son belongs to it forever. So if the Son sets you free, you will be free indeed'" (John 8:34–36). As a child of God, you have the power to take charge of strongholds that are not of God—you cannot become the type of temple God desires until you do so. The weapon you have is the most powerful weapon and one that cannot be overcome by any stronghold: the weapon of the Holy Spirit.

"The weapons we fight with are not the weapons of the world. On the contrary, they have divine power to demolish strongholds. We demolish arguments and every pretension that sets itself up against the knowledge of God, and we take captive every thought to make it obedient to Christ" (2 Corinthians 10:4–5). Even though you are flesh and blood, you do not have to rely on physical means or on your physical or intellectual capacity to fight against strongholds that are within you or harassing you from the outside. You already have all the power you need for freedom!

Steps to Bringing Down Strongholds

Prayer is a first key ingredient to bringing down strongholds, as it will enable a connection to God the Father and make it plain to Him that you want to change. When you pray, ask God to give you the grace and the ability to resist or flee the temptation that is leading to your enslavement. This grace comes from the Holy Spirit. The most dangerous strongholds that lead to enslavement are those that become entrenched in your logical mind, which prevent you from knowing or doing God's will for your life. The mind is vulnerable, and your thought life must be guarded dearly. I strongly encourage you to personalize Paul's words in 2 Corinthians 10:4-5, related to bringing down strongholds for your situation (see prayer section at the end of the session).

Prayer is the first step to bringing down strongholds in your life

After praying, you then need to take a step in faith and take control of your temple. Whatever your trap is, be it your dangerous appetite for food, drugs, alcohol, gambling, tobacco, sex, covetousness, free spending, pornography, hoarding, need for attention, or something else, you need to work to free yourself. In your own strength it may seem and may indeed be impossible, but specifically pray that the Holy Spirit should help you. You must then get up and do your own part and avoid laziness. Seek help from Christian counselors or professionals who can help you while giving you a biblical foundation for dealing with your situation. You may also need medical attention or other specific help for your problem. Belief in God does not mean you should avoid medical help; all knowledge including medical knowledge comes from God. God is the healer and sometimes He heals miraculously but at other times He does it through the gift of knowledge that He has revealed to medical and other professionals. Choose to focus your attention on God. Read God's Word daily in the Bible and meditate on verses that empower you over sin.

Next, be careful that what you read, watch, think, and spend time on all glorify God. "Finally, brothers, whatever is true, whatever is noble, whatever is right, whatever is pure, whatever is lovely, whatever is admirable—if anything is excellent or praiseworthy—think about such things" (Philippians 4: 8).

If you spend time praying for God to help you get over a problem, and then you turn your attention to places or things that encourage the problem to persist, you are deceiving yourself and you will fall right back to where you started from. Avoid places where you will be exposed to the things that tempt you. If it is alcohol, you need to stay away from establishments that serve alcohol. If it is food, watch the type and quality of food you keep at home. If it your logical mind that is your roadblock, keep a log of the supernatural things God has done for you in the past and review it periodically to remind yourself He is not a logical God.

There is no circumstance too difficult for God. But remember that God is not a microwave oven in whom you can cook up the recipe for your healing or problem in minutes. Sometimes God heals or delivers instantly. In other situations, His healing takes time and requires your cooperation.

Often, it is in the process of a prolonged resolution to a problem that God helps you to develop the character and personality that is glorifying of Him. Do not give up simply because your situation did not change overnight; allow the Holy Spirit to work within you so that you can bear fruit. "But the fruit of the Spirit is love, joy, peace, patience, kindness, goodness, faithfulness, gentleness and self-control. Against such things there is no law. Those who belong to Christ Jesus have crucified the sinful nature with its passions and desires. Since we live by the Spirit, let us keep in step with the Spirit" (Galatians 22–25).

A fruit is a product of a plant. You can tell a plant from which a fruit came based on the type of fruit produced. When you are living as a fully spiritual temple of God, your fruit will be from a tree that can be identified clearly as the Holy Spirit. If you do not recognize any of the fruit of the Holy Spirit filled temple of God coming from you, it means you still need work and should continually pray to God to help you. Some trees take time to blossom and bear fruit, others are more bountiful sooner. While the product is the same, attention to the conditions of the soil and the nutrients added to it, the amount of water, shading or lighting provided, and protection against pests and diseases all make a huge difference in the quality and quantity of the fruit produced. This is because "strongholds" such as weeds within the soil or pests or diseases within the parent tree can prevent a bountiful crop. Similarly, the effort you put into nourishing your soil (your mind) with the right ingredients (focus on God's word, doing His will, and spending time with Him) will reduce the likelihood of strongholds and determine the quality and quantity of the fruit you produce.

Finally, you must not let the quality of the fruit you produced most recently or the duration of your failure to produce high quality fruit stop you from believing God can relieve you of the stronghold blocking your yield. For difficult strongholds, you may have to embark on a period of praying and fasting to totally focus your attention on God and be persistent like the widow.[4] In every situation, make sure you are constantly seeking God's opinion; ask Him what His will is—what are you doing here, God? With patience and time, you will be able to see what He is up to and how to overcome the stronghold.

The Grace of Christianity Is Not a License to Sin

Perhaps you are thinking, *I am a Christian, and I am baptized. I do not need to worry about all this talk of sin and strongholds since I am fully identified with Christ and all He requires of me is that I confess belief in Him. I can do as I wish as Jesus has already forgiven me all my current and future sins. It is by God's grace that I am saved and not by works. All this talk about sin and strongholds is legalism and that is what Jesus came to do away with.*

This is dangerous thinking. Yes, your salvation is purely by grace; you did nothing to earn it. However, once you become born again, your life has to reflect the values of the new family into which you have been born. If they do not, you are simply deceiving yourself about your beliefs. An apple tree cannot give birth to an orange.

Here are some clear verses from the Bible that counter this argument: "We know that we have come to know if we obey His commands. The man who says, 'I know Him,' but does not do what He commands is a liar, and the truth is not in him. But if anyone obeys His word, God's love is truly made complete in him. This is how we know we are in Him: Whoever claims to live in Him must walk as Jesus did" (1 John 2:3–6). And, "No one who lives in Him keeps on sinning. No one who continues to sin has either seen Him or known Him ... no one who is born of God will continue to sin, because God's seed remains in them; they cannot go on sinning, because they have been born of God. This is how we know who the children of God are and who the children of the devil are: Anyone who does not do what is right is not God's child, nor is anyone who does not love their brother and sister" (1 John 3: 6, 9–10, NIV 2011). Romans 6:14–17 tells us, "For sin shall not be your master, because you are not under law, but under grace. What then? Shall we sin because we are not under law but under grace? By no means!"

In the next few sessions, we will examine specific requirements on the conditions in your temple that will enable the full manifestation of the fruits of the Holy Spirit within your life: humility, obedience, faith, hope, and love.

Pray This Prayer with Me:

Dear Lord, I hereby renounce allegiance to every stronghold that is currently holding me bound and declare my total allegiance to You. I take control of every thought, word, or imagination within me and make them obedient to the Holy Spirit. I renounce sin in all its forms, and I seek to truly reflect the values of the wonderful family into which I have been adopted. Amen.

Questions to Ponder:

- At this stage in your spiritual walk, what do you think is your predominant nature—carnal, logical, or spiritual? Why do you think so?
- What type of person do you aspire to be? Why?
- Are you a prisoner of any of your appetites?
    - If so, describe one you are comfortable discussing (but during your private time make sure you consider all other entrapping appetites you may have and how they may have impacted you).
    - Do you think you can overcome this "stronghold"? If so, how?
- Is it a bad thing to rely on logic to make decisions?
    - If not, when is logic a good thing and when can logic lead you astray?
    - How can you maintain balance between using your logic and yielding to the prompting of the Holy Spirit?
- Can you recall episodes where your logic has kept you from seeing God's power at work?
    - Describe the situation.
    - What did you learn from it?

Prayer Points

- Pray that you will be transformed from a carnal or mostly logical person to a spiritual person who knows when to be logical and when to be fully yielded to the Holy Spirit and resistant to any other spirit that seeks to influence you.
- Pray the stronghold-vanquishing prayer of 2 Corinthians 10:4–5 to bring down strongholds first in your own life and then in that of a loved one who is currently bound by something keeping him or her from being a spiritual temple.

> The weapons I _____ (*insert your name*) fight with are not the weapons of the world. On the contrary, they have divine power to demolish *the* strongholds *of* _____
>
> (list the stronghold(s) and say them out loud [e.g., addiction to pornography, greed, gluttony, hoarding, pride, arrogance, poor self-esteem, jealousy, sexual immorality, tendency to brag or exaggerate, etc.]) within me (or within my friend/loved one _____) (insert name of the person if it is not you).
>
> I _____ (*insert your own name here*) demolish arguments and every pretension that sets itself up against the knowledge of God in me (or my friend/ loved one), _____ (*insert your name or your friend/loved one's name*) and I take captive every thought that I (*or my friend/loved one* _____) have to make it obedient to Christ (2 Corinthians 10:4–5; all italicized words were added by the author for instructional purposes).

196

1. http://www.merriam-webster.com/dictionary/stronghold; http://www.thefreedictionary.com/stronghold(both last visited April 9, 2011).
2. James 4:17.
3. Costain, Thomas B. *The Three Edwards,* Buccaneer Books, 1994. http://bible.org/illustration/prisoner-his-appetite. (last visited April 9, 2011).
4. Matthew 17:21 (New American Standard Bible or King James Version). For the story of the persistent widow, see Luke 18:1–5.

CHAPTER 17

The House of God is a House of Humility

(Session 9a)

Humility is the most difficult of all virtues to achieve; nothing dies harder than the desire to think well of oneself.—T. S. Elliott

What makes humility so desirable is the marvelous thing it does to us; it creates in us a capacity for the closest possible intimacy with God.—Monica Baldwin, British nun (1893-1975)

Defining Humility

Humility is defined as the quality of being modest, reverential, even politely submissive, and never being arrogant, contemptuous, rude, or self-abasing.[1] For Christians, the definition of humility is the total submission of your will to the will of God, believing that His will is better for you than your own will for yourself or the will of others for you. Humility is a difficult discipline for most people because it demands that you continuously put the needs and wants of others ahead of yours and that you quietly do things for which others seek credit. In the flesh, humility can be very draining because one of the most basic instincts of humans is the need to satisfy our own needs, desires, and egos. From a Christian perspective, humility involves faith and trust in God that when you put aside your ego, you will be rewarded by God in due time. It also involves discipline to believe this at all times, even at the risk of loss of great personal rewards in the short term.

Why should you be humble? After all, humility is at great odds with the attributes most valued in today's society where public figures and the celebrities who are viewed as our role models regularly boast and brag about themselves and their accomplishments. The explosion of reality TV shows that have mass appeal today and which base themselves on building up the importance of individuality and self-justification while demeaning others also bear witness to this fact. Humility is now seen as a major sign of weakness in our culture and is looked down upon. Imagine a candidate running for president of the United States who says in response to a question from a reporter or member of the public, "I do not have the answer. I need to pray about it, seek God's counsel, and get back to you shortly." The person would be ridiculed as indecisive, weak, and lacking self-confidence for seeking God's advice and would unlikely be elected. How does this match up to what the Bible has to say about humility?

God ultimately rewards you when you humble yourself

God Esteems the Humble

As a believer in Jesus Christ, without learning to control your ego, it is impossible for you to realize the full benefits of a relationship with the Holy Spirit because your ego will always block His ability to communicate with you and to direct you. God demands humility in order for His Spirit to be given full reign to be able to work within you and make you more like Christ. You were created to serve God, and to do so you have to be totally yielded to Him. Humility causes you to be elevated spiritually to the presence of God and allows you to have greater insight into His heart and mind so that you can accomplish more for His kingdom. "For this is what the high and exalted One says—He who lives forever, whose name is holy: 'I live in a high and holy place, but also with the one who is contrite and lowly in spirit, to revive the spirit of the lowly and to revive the heart of the contrite'" (Isaiah 57:15, NIV 2011).

God reveals that He lives in heaven (a high and holy place), but also with those who are contrite (repentant, remorseful, penitent) and lowly in spirit (humble)—through the Holy Spirit. It is when you are repentant and humble that God is allowed to *freely and completely* dwell in each of the chambers of your temple through His Holy Spirit. In the battle between your spirit and your flesh for control of your mind, humility demotes the impact of your flesh and allows God's Spirit that is already in you to be more active.

Humility Elevates You Higher than You Can Elevate Yourself

Peter reminds us that when you humble yourself, it may appear to be a setback in the short-term, but God will be the one who will elevate you in His perfect time. "Humble yourselves, therefore, under God's mighty hand, that He may lift you up in due time" (1 Peter 5:6). "In due time" means that God will elevate the humble person not only at a time that is perfect, but will also do it in such a way that there can be no setbacks. He will be the one who will fight for you.

"For the LORD takes delight in his people; he crowns the humble with victory" (Psalm 149:4, NIV 2011). Sometimes you feel a crime so egregious and unfair has been committed against you. Perhaps you have been insulted, or unjustly removed from your position at work, or denied the promotion that you deserve, or you have been personally attacked. You must always go to God first to ask Him what to do and let Him lead you step by step. If you let Him lead you and fight on your behalf, you cannot lose. If on the other hand you choose to fight your own battles without consultation from Him, he will simply put His hands behind His back and watch you fumble your way through. If you want a relationship with God and want the Holy Spirit residing in you to be influential, you have to let go of your own worldly and fleshly desires and let the Holy Spirit rule your very being. This is the meaning of "dying to flesh." There is not enough room for your own ego and God's ego within the same temple. If you do not cooperate with Him, He will not be able to influence you, but He "envies intensely" or "jealously longs" to have a closer relationship with you. The more you submit your will to God, the more He gives you the ability through His Holy Spirit to do more for Him and the more He elevates you.

> *Your uncontrolled ego is a deterrent to drawing near to God*

Or do you think Scripture says without reason that the Spirit he caused to live in us envies intensely [jealously longs]? But He gives us more grace. That is why Scripture says: "God opposes the proud but gives grace to the humble." Submit yourselves, then to God. Resist the devil, and he will flee from you. Come near to God and He will come near to you. Wash your hands you sinners and purify your hearts, you double minded ... humble yourselves before the Lord and He will lift you up." (James 4:5–10)

Isaiah 66:1–2 further highlights the importance of humility before God: "This is what the Lord says: 'Heaven is my throne and the earth is my footstool. Where is the house you will build for me? Where will my resting place be? Has not my hand made all these things, and so they came into being?' declares the Lord. 'This is the one I esteem: he who is humble and contrite in spirit and trembles at My word.'"

God is making you aware that there is nothing you can do for Him that He has not already conceived as the Creator of the Universe. Obviously if heaven is God's throne and earth is His footstool, you cannot possibly build Him a house on your own accord. He has already built the house He wants—you—as His preferred residence. The created cannot build for the creator what the creator cannot build for Himself. Humility, then, is recognizing that there is nothing you can do that will impress God as much as letting Him be the one who takes control. God wants you to take Him so seriously that you draw near to Him, always listen to what He has to say, and you always act on His word so that His plans for your life may be fulfilled.

Moses and Daniel: Examples of Humility

There are several biblical examples of persons God deliberately chose to represent Him mainly because of their humility. Moses and Daniel are two of the best examples. Moses was one of the most important leaders and prophets in the Old Testament who was responsible for leading the children of Israel out of slavery in Egypt to the land of Canaan that God promised to give to them. God used Moses to perform some of the most incredible miracles recorded in history.[2] Yet Moses was noted to be more humble than anyone who lived on the face of the earth up till that time.

"Now Moses was a very humble man, more humble than anyone else on the face of the earth." (Numbers 12:3). God used Moses in such a great way *because* he was humble and willing to submit his own will to the will of God. He was someone who trembled at God's word: "'Do not come any closer,' God said. 'Take off your sandals, for the place where you are standing is holy ground.' Then He said, 'I am the God of your father, the God of Abraham, the God of Isaac and the God of Jacob.' At this, Moses hid his face because he was afraid to look at God" (Exodus 3:5–6).

God knew who He was dealing with when He chose Moses. He chose Him because He recognized that Moses' humility would create the conditions to make Him obedient and be utilized by God for the great things he did. In contrast, Pharaoh, the king of Egypt and the most powerful man during the time of Moses and to whom Moses was sent, refused to humble himself and release the Israelites who were slaves under him, even as God performed miracle after miracle through Moses that damaged Pharaoh's land and people. The rivers of the Nile turned to blood so the water was undrinkable; the country was invaded by frogs, gnats, and flies; there was a plague on all the livestock of the Egyptians while the Israelite livestock was spared; festering boils broke out on all the Egyptian people and animals; there was a catastrophic hailstorm that destroyed crops everywhere except where the Israelites lived in Gershon; there was an insect invasion by locusts; a three-day simultaneous total eclipse of the sun and moon led to pitch darkness—and Pharaoh *still* did not let God's people go.[3]

"So Moses and Aaron went to Pharaoh and said to him, 'This is what the LORD, the God of the Hebrews, says: "How long will you refuse to humble yourself before me? Let my people go, so that they may worship me"'" (Exodus 10:3). Pharaoh's arrogance came at great cost to his people, leading ultimately to the death of every Egyptian firstborn son, while Moses' humility enabled God to work through him to deliver His people.

Daniel was another person who rose after being captured and exiled from his home in the country of Judah as a young Jewish boy to become one of the greatest men of his time as governor and lead counsel to several kings in the foreign country of Babylon. Daniel was famous for his wisdom and his ability to interpret dreams that other wise men of his time could not; he was also a major prophet God used to predict the events of the end times of the world. Daniel maintained a close relationship with God and humbled himself before God, being found to pray at least three times each day. We are told explicitly that God esteemed Daniel because of his humility.

203

A hand touched me and set me trembling on my hands and knees. He said, "Daniel, you who are *highly esteemed*, consider carefully the words I am about to speak to you, and stand up, for I have now been sent to you." And when he said this to me, I stood up trembling. Then he continued, "Do not be afraid, Daniel. Since the first day that you set your mind to gain understanding and to *humble* yourself before your God, your words were heard, and I have come in response to them ... "Do not be afraid, you who are highly esteemed," he said. "Peace! Be strong now; be strong." Daniel 10:10–12, 19 NIV 2011, emphasis added)

As a result of his faithfulness and humility, Daniel was unencumbered by being a captured slave in a foreign country. God elevated him to a high position even in exile, just as He promised. God will do the same thing for you if you learn to trust Him and release control of your temple to Him in humility.

Jesus Christ summed up the value of humility nicely in a story told to his disciples.

When He noticed how the guests picked the places of honor at the table, He told them this parable: "When someone invites you to a wedding feast, do not take the place of honor, for a person more distinguished than you may have been invited. If so, the host who invited both of you will come and say to you, 'Give this person your seat.' Then, humiliated, you will have to take the least important place. But when you are invited, take the lowest place, so that when your host comes, he will say to you, 'Friend, move up to a better place.' Then you will be honored in the presence of all the other guests. For all those who exalt themselves will be humbled, and those who humble themselves will be exalted." (Luke 14:7–11[4] NIV 2011)

In the same way, humility should be a strong desire of yours if you seek to draw closer to God. If this is not your natural disposition; pray to God that His Holy Spirit will nudge you each time you are tempted to put yourself first. Then practice obeying this nudging until such time that it becomes second nature to you. Then sit and watch if God will not reward you for your efforts with a closer relationship with Him.

In the next two chapters, we will examine the pitfall of pride—the opposite attribute of humility—and discuss Jesus Christ, the most humble man to have ever lived.

Pray This Prayer with Me:

Dear God, I acknowledge my desire to want to be in control in all areas of my life. I thank You for pointing out to me that You and I cannot both be in control of the same temple. I hereby surrender my authority to You and give You full control of this temple. Let my will yield to Your will and my desires to Your desires for my life. In Jesus' name I pray. Amen.

1. http://en.wikipedia.org/wiki/Humility.
2. Exodus 4–13.
3. Exodus 6–11.
4. See also Matthew 23:8–12.

CHAPTER 18

God Opposes the Proud

(Session 9b)

If anyone would like to achieve humility, I can, I think tell him the first step. The first step is to realize that one is proud.—C. S. Lewis

Pride Will Bring You Down

The opposite of humility is pride or arrogance. Pride is a high or inordinate opinion of one's own dignity, importance, merit, or superiority, whether as cherished in the mind or as displayed in bearing, conduct, etc.[1] Pride denies God's superiority and actually sets itself up against God. The scriptures warn us that God actively opposes the proud.

"*God opposes the proud but gives grace [shows favor] to the humble*"[2] *(James 4:6)*. You have a choice—either to be God's enemy (be opposed by Him) or to live in humility under the cover of His grace. The Holy Spirit will not impose His will upon anybody. Any inch of pride in you, your seeking to do your own thing or to go your own way means you are signaling unwillingness to be guided by the Holy Spirit, since it is impossible to submit to God's will and your own will at the same time. This is one of the reasons why Paul warned that you should not put out the Spirit's fire.[3]

Imagine a husband who no longer listens to his wife. He makes all his decisions independent of her. Even when he asks her opinion, he does not take it into consideration when he acts. After a while, she will stop giving her opinion, will she not? If you are given to bragging and boasting about how wonderful you are, and doing things your own way, then you are stealing from God's glory and acting as if He does not count. You are also setting yourself up for a big fall because God will not only leave you alone to make your own mistakes, He will also shut you out of the kingdom of heaven. "The eyes of the arrogant will be humbled and human pride brought low; the LORD alone will be exalted in that day. The LORD Almighty has a day in store for all the proud and lofty, for all that is exalted (and they will be humbled)" (Isaiah 2:11–12).

The day being described in this passage by Isaiah is the Day of Judgment, when God will judge all good and evil. This is also why Jesus revealed that only those who realize their need for Him are blessed with the kingdom of heaven: "God blesses those who realize their need for him, for the kingdom of heaven is given to them" (Matthew 5:3, NLT 1996).

While every sin committed against God is pardonable, pride is a difficult one to overcome. Pride sets us you up in equality to God, your Creator and the Creator of the universe. It is pride that causes some people to reject Jesus Christ as their hope for eternal salvation, a term Jesus referred to as having a "calloused heart": "For this people's heart has become calloused; they hardly hear with their ears, and they have closed their eyes. Otherwise they might see with their eyes, hear with their ears, understand with their hearts and turn, and I would heal them"[4] (Matthew 13:15).

Jesus' gift of salvation is for everyone, free and without condition

Jesus' gift of salvation is for everyone, free and without condition. Those who turn down the gift are in effect demonstrating pride in thinking they do not need help for their condition. Pride makes you think you do not need God because you can handle things on your own or that you are equal to God. Indeed, it was pride that caused the devil, an angel created by God who then sought equality with God, to be kicked out of heaven.[5] God will not tolerate pride from you either, no matter how talented you may be, since every talent you have is a gift from Him; even as your talents may give you a false sense of confidence and reliability on your abilities. No matter how talented you may be you cannot save yourself or deliver on the most important treasure God has promised you or those that you seek to influence—the gift of eternal salvation. Instead, your pride will lead not only to your own demise, but will also bring down several of His beloved children who will be drawn away from a close relationship with Him because of your ego. This is why God cannot tolerate pride.

The Different Faces of Pride

Pride masquerades in different fashions:

Self-Satisfaction

Pride is sometimes an excessive personal satisfaction in your own accomplishments, be they financial, work-related, or in some form of volunteerism. In this form of pride, you believe all your accomplishments are due to your own efforts. When you are successful, rather than giving God the glory and acknowledging His role in your success, you pat yourself on the shoulder and engage in self-promotion. Even as a Christian, you may consciously or unconsciously believe God cannot do what He needs to do without you. Perhaps you are a great volunteer at your church and even as you are needed and called to serve, you believe and act as if the church could not run without you. Maybe you are faithful with your tithes and offerings to the church, but you think that gives you the right to dictate to your pastor how he runs the church. You use your faithfulness in giving as a subtle form of blackmail, believing the church could not afford to do without your money or your talents. This is dangerous territory God will not tolerate because you are seeking to play the role He has reserved for Himself.

Failure to Accept Forgiveness

Ironically, for some, pride comes in the form of not accepting forgiveness from God for the sins you have committed even when God Himself has told you repeatedly that you have been forgiven. This form of pride is based on the notion that somehow you are too special, or the crime you have committed is too egregious to be forgiven. "Therefore, there is now no condemnation for those who are in Christ Jesus, because through Christ Jesus the law of the Spirit who gives life has set you free from the law of sin and death" (Romans 8:1–2, NIV 2011).

If God has said He has forgiven everyone, including those who killed His only Son, why do you think you are too important to be forgiven? There is nothing so special or hideous about the sin you have committed that God is not aware of and that He has not witnessed before. If this is you, you are denying the free gift of the grace of God and you have made your sin a god unto you. Christ's death for you has thus been rendered useless. You need to ask God to show you how you can receive forgiveness and learn to move on. Rather than wallowing in your past, read the word of God to remind you of God's promises to you as a new creation in Him.[6]

Holding on to Grudges

You may also be prideful by holding on to a grudge or not forgiving someone who has done something to you, as we discussed in chapter 9. If you are holding on to unforgiveness, you are allowing the person you are not forgiving to rent a room in your temple for free. Even if you do not see the person daily, he or she is in your mind and has control over your actions and is using up many of the valuable resources in your Holy Place. You have set the person up as a god, since he or she is replacing the rightful position God deserves in your temple. Ultimately, of course, unforgiveness is a trap that will lead you away from God's plan for your life and away from His kingdom. This is illustrated in the famous parable of the unforgiving servant Jesus told His disciples and which we discussed in chapter 9. (Matthew 18:21–35, NIV 2011)

Unforgiveness is allowing your perpetrator to rent a room for free in your temple

If Jesus was willing to forgive you of your sins and die on your behalf so you can live forever, imagine how He feels about you continuing to carry a grudge against your fellow human being. This is why unforgiveness is a major sin of pride. While forgiveness can be tough and usually takes time, especially in the case of a horrible crime, the Holy Spirit can gradually help you release the person who has wronged you. As we discussed before, forgiving him or her does not mean you condone the crime or that there will be no consequences to what he or she has done. It means you will not be consumed day and night in seeking revenge for the crime done to you, but you have released the person to God. I pray that God's Holy Spirit will enable you to release the person who is renting a free room in your Holy Place as a result of your not forgiving him or her and give you a new freedom to accomplish what God has always planned for your life.

Unwillingness to Seek Counsel

Sometimes pride takes the form of thinking you do not need help or need to seek counsel from others. If this is you, you somehow equate seeking help as being seen as a failure by others or that it would somehow make you feel vulnerable that others will notice your "weakness." Or, worst of all, you think it would destroy the carefully cultivated image you have built for yourself of what you either believe others think of you or that you think of yourself, bringing you shame. This type of pride will cause you to suffer unnecessarily and may keep others from being the blessing God has intended them to be to you.

The book of Proverbs is full of verses about the folly of not seeking advice: "The way of fools seems right to them, but the wise listen to advice," Plans fail for lack of counsel, but with many advisers they succeed," Pride goes before destruction, a haughty spirit before a fall," Listen to advice and accept discipline, and at the end you will be counted among the wise," Plans are established by seeking advice; so if you wage war, obtain guidance," As iron sharpens iron, so one person sharpens another," And so forth.[7]

This type of pride will also lead to isolation and inability to move forward with God's plan for your life. God has created humans to be of help to one another. *You cannot submit to God and yourself at the same time* If you have this type of pride, it will be very hard to ask people to pray for you or with you in agreement for the problem you have. Yet God created companionship so that you can be supported and you can be a support to others. "Two are better than one, because they have a good return for their labor: If either of them falls down, one can help the other up. But pity anyone who falls and has no one to help them up. ... Though one may be overpowered, two can defend themselves. A cord of three strands is not quickly broken" (Ecclesiastes 4:9–10, 12).

Most of the time the image people have of you is very different than what you have of yourself. Your projected image is actually much better when you humble yourself and seek counsel and help from others than if you try to hide your weaknesses. Sons and daughters are specifically advised in the book of Proverbs to get instruction from their parents,[8] and pride resulting in failure to do so will often lead to disgrace.[9]

False Sense of Superiority over Others

One other manifestation of pride is a sense of superiority over others. This could be based on your intelligence, position, skin color, country of origin, skills in a particular area, height, physical attributes, or other factors. This type of pride is closely tied to the pride described in the preceding paragraph, as it means you are likely to disregard those you deem inferior. This was the type of pride Jesus came out most strongly against when He condemned the Pharisees and Sadducees, the leading Jews of His time. Because of their position in life as priests and leaders, they looked down upon their fellow Jews and imposed unnecessary rules and restrictions upon them that made it hard for the people to follow God. Their pride made it such that protecting their high position in society was more important than seeking a true relationship to God. It was for this reason that they disregarded Jesus Christ His rightful position as their Lord and Savior, instead seeking to have Him crucified. They could not imagine tolerating someone they viewed as inferior in both upbringing and in societal standing, who was as popular and empowered by God as Jesus was. Similarly, when you view yourself as superior, you may be more interested in protecting your status than in actually receiving the very person God has sent to help you because he or she does not fit your image of how the help should come.

The story of Naaman is probably the best example of pride based on perceived superiority that almost caused someone to miss the blessing God had planned for him. Naaman was the commander of the army of the king of Aram (Syria) who was highly regarded because of his military prowess. However, he had one big problem—he also had leprosy. Upon learning from his wife's servant that there may be help from a prophet who lived in Israel, he approached the king of Aram for permission to go seek his healing there. The king granted this wish and sent Naaman with a letter to the king of Israel along with plenty of silver, gold, and clothing, asking the king of Israel to cure Naaman of leprosy. The king of Israel was offended when he received this letter, thinking the king of Aram was trying to pick a quarrel with him for asking him to do what only God could: cure a man of leprosy. However, the prophet Elisha heard of the king's anger and asked that Naaman be sent to him instead. The rest of the story is as follows:

> So Naaman went with his horses and chariots and stopped at the door of Elisha's house. Elisha sent a messenger to say to him, "Go, wash yourself seven times in the Jordan, and your flesh will be restored and you will be cleansed." But Naaman went away angry and said, "I thought that he would surely come out to me and stand and call on the name of the LORD

his God, wave his hand over the spot and cure me of my leprosy. Are not Abana and Pharpar, the rivers of Damascus, better than all the waters of Israel? Couldn't I wash in them and be cleansed?" So he turned and went off in a rage. Naaman's servants went to him and said, "My father, if the prophet had told you to do some great thing, would you not have done it? How much more, then, when he tells you, 'Wash and be cleansed'!" So he went down and dipped himself in the Jordan seven times, as the man of God had told him, and his flesh was restored and became clean like that of a young boy. (2 Kings 5: 9–14)

Naaman's pride almost cost him his healing. He first expected to be healed by royalty, and this proved futile. Secondly, he expected to be healed in a specific way personally by the prophet Elisha, but Elisha did not even show him the courtesy of a personal appearance. Finally, and perhaps the worst insult, he was asked to dip in a river that he considered inferior to the rivers in his own country! Every part of his personal pride was challenged and brought down, and yet it was only in humility that his healing came.

There is no sin you have committed that God has not witnessed before

The same is true for you. You will often have to humble yourself, allowing God to work in ways you cannot understand. He may use people that you cannot fathom, based on your current sense of yourself compared to whom God has chosen to use; and He may use methods that may shatter your perceived image of yourself. In doing this, you are acknowledging the limitation of your knowledge compared to God's and enabling God to elevate you to higher levels of blessings than you could ever otherwise conceive.

Feeling Morally Upright

For some Christians and non-Christians, pride takes the form of *looking down on others you perceive not be as morally upright as you are*. Perhaps you are a Christian who has lived your life trying your best to obey God's laws. You have not cheated anyone deliberately. You may not have stolen anything significant in your life. You do not particularly covet things belonging to others; at least you have not done so overtly externally, even though you may have privately desired things or positions belonging to others. You have not committed adultery, at least in a physical form, even though you may have fleeting attractions to members of the opposite sex. You definitely have not committed murder, even though there are times you have felt some hatred against someone for something unkind he or she has done to you. Clearly you are "better" off than the majority of people you know. So should you humble yourself? The answer is a definite yes, and the reason is simple—God is perfect, and even one sin that is committed deserves eternal condemnation.

The apostle Paul reminds us that not one human being, save Jesus, is exempt from sin: "For all have sinned and fall short of the glory of God" (Romans 3:23).

While God honors and rewards good moral behavior, your salvation is a free gift from God, not a result of your good works, so it is erroneous to think your being better than the next person in your morals or other values is what justifies you as a Christian. "For it is God who works in you to will and to act according to His good purpose" (Philippians 2:13).

Looking down on others is mocking God's creation

The apostle Paul also noted that as a Christian, you become a living sacrifice to God, which requires humility. "For by the grace given me I say to every one of you: *Do not think of yourself more highly than you ought, but rather think of yourself with sober judgment*, in accordance with the measure of faith God has given you" (Romans 12:3, emphasis added).

Why Should a "Good" Christian Be Humble?

If you fit the description of the person descried in the preceding paragraph, you need humility, because while Jesus came to fulfill the laws given by God through Moses in the form of the Ten Commandments, His ideals were actually higher and more stringent than those stipulated by the law.[10] In His famous "Sermon on the Mount" (Matthew 5), Jesus redefined the meanings of murder so that you do not have to physically carry out the act but only have to hate the person. He redefined adultery so that lustfully looking at a member of the opposite sex is the same as physically committing adultery.[11] He also redefined what constitutes lawful reasons for divorce,[12] as well as keeping your vows, retaliation, and how you should treat your enemies. In every single situation, Jesus' redefinition was much more stringent than what the Jews had understood based on the laws of Moses. Jesus' key message was to show the impossibility of keeping the law based on your own strength, and to remind all those who thought they were righteous before God that they do not quite meet the standard.

Jesus further exemplified how God derides the pride of looking down on others in His telling of the parable of the Pharisee and the tax collector:

> To some who were confident of their own righteousness and looked down on everybody else, Jesus told this parable: "Two men went up to the temple to pray, one a Pharisee and the other a tax collector. The Pharisee stood up and prayed about himself: 'God, I thank you that I am not like other men—robbers, evildoers, adulterers—or even like this tax collector. I fast twice a week and give a tenth of all I get.' But the tax collector stood at a distance. He would not even look up to heaven, but beat his breast and said, 'God, have mercy on me, a sinner.' I tell you that this man, rather than the other, went home justified before God. For everyone who exalts himself will be humbled, and he who humbles himself will be exalted." (Luke 18:9–14)

A whitewashed tomb looks beautiful on the outside, but is full of dead bones on the inside

You can only meet the standard of God through God's grace and the power of the Holy Spirit that has been deposited in you, and only when you have given Him the freedom to act by not quashing His actions.

Are You a Whitewashed Tomb or a Jar of Clay?

To keep things in perspective, a person who is prideful because he or she acts and looks good publicly but harbors sinful thoughts and behaviors in private that do not match their public image, is referred to by Jesus a "whitewashed tomb"—looking good on the outside but dead on the inside. Jesus spoke specifically against this form of pride when He accused the Pharisees of being such. "Woe to you, teachers of the law and Pharisees, you hypocrites! You are like whitewashed tombs, which look beautiful on the outside but on the inside are full of dead men's bones and everything unclean. In the same way, on the outside you appear to people as righteous but on the inside you are full of hypocrisy and wickedness" (Matthew 23:27–28).

Jesus was particularly harsh on the Pharisees because of their demanding rules for others that they themselves were not keeping and because they did not understand the concept of grace. By contrast, when you are fully submitted to God in humility and have the full power of the Holy Spirit within you, you may look fragile on the outside (humble, meek), but you are full of light and power on the inside—you are like a jar of clay full of treasure.

> For God, who said, "Let light shine out of darkness," made His light shine in our hearts to give us the light of the knowledge of the glory of God in the face of Christ. But we have this treasure in jars of clay to show that this all-surpassing power is from God and not from us. We are hard pressed on every side, but not crushed; perplexed, but not in despair; persecuted, but not abandoned; struck down, but not destroyed. (2 Corinthians 4:6–9)

Which one would you prefer, to have a "treasure in your jar of clay" or to be a "whitewashed tomb"? You already have the treasure of the Holy Spirit within your temple of clay. You now have to make sure you allow Him full authority to run your temple. May what is in you always be much more than what people can see on the outside.

Pray This Prayer with Me:

Dear Lord, I confess that I am full of pride and have not always released all the situations in my life to You. I ask forgiveness for this and pray that You will help me remember where all my strength and blessings come from. Help me to be full of the treasure of the Holy Spirit in each of my three chambers within the jar of clay that is my body—instead of being a whitewashed tomb. I relinquish all control to You today. In Jesus' name I pray. Amen.

1. http://dictionary.reference.com/browse/pride (last visited April 9, 2011).
2. See also 1 Peter 5:5; Proverbs 3:34.
3. 1 Thessalonians 5:19.
4. Also quoted by the Prophet Isaiah in Isaiah 6:10.
5. Isaiah 14:12–15; Ezekiel 28:11–18.
6. Acts 10:43; Ephesians 1:7; Colossians 1:13–14; 1 John 2:12; Matthew 26:28; Hebrews 8:12; 1 John 1:9.
7. Proverbs 12:15, 15:22, 16:18, 19:20, 20:18, 27:17.
8. Proverbs 4.
9. Proverbs 11:2.
10. Matthew 5.
11. Matthew 5:27.
12. Matthew 5:32–33.

CHAPTER 19

Jesus Christ, the Greatest and Humblest Man to Ever Live

(Session 10a)

Jesus of Nazareth, without money and arms, conquered more millions than Alexander the Great, Caesar, Mohammed, and Napoleon; without science and learning, He shed more light on things human and divine than all philosophers and scholars combined; without the eloquence of school, He spoke such words of life as were never spoken before or since, and produced effects which lie beyond the reach of orator or poet; without writing a single line, He set more pens in motion, and furnished themes for more sermons, orations, discussions, learned volumes, works of art, and songs of praise than the whole army of great men of ancient and modern times.—Philip Schaff,
Protestant theologian and Church historian (1819-1893)

The Incarnate Definition of Humility

The best example of humility is found in our Lord Jesus Christ. His arrival as the Messiah was the most eagerly and widely anticipated and predicted event in the history of the Jews and of humanity.[1] In fact, His birth was so frightening to the jealous King Herod, who was the king of Judea at the time Jesus was born, that Herod tried to kill Him at birth.[2] Most successful people are known for being especially talented in one or maybe two specific areas, such as sports, painting, sculpting, acting, banking, law, teaching, building, preaching, medicine, cooking, computer sciences, etc.

However, the same people are often limited or average in other areas. It is rare to find a human being who is famous for being an outstanding lawyer and doctor at the same time or for simultaneously being a great painter and chef. Jesus was different in that he had no limitation in any talent area. The lofty expectations on His life were more than surpassed by the extraordinary accomplishments of His short life—a greatness that would have given him the right to be a very proud man.

The Greatest Man by Any Measure

Jesus is the greatest man ever to have lived by any measure possible because His greatness encompassed all the professions of His day. He is the greatest physician ever to have lived, possessing expertise in every medical specialty and healing *every* kind of disease brought before him with 100 percent success rate.[3] Today, there are specialists that deal with individual areas of medicine. Yet Jesus cured skin diseases, healed blood disorders, cured blind eyes and deaf ears, healed neurological, orthopedic conditions and psychiatric conditions, exorcised demons, instantly performed plastic surgery without instruments, and even raised dead people back to life without the benefit of CPR.[4]

At the same time, Jesus was a master chef who needed only a few ingredients to feed and satisfy crowds of thousands.[5] He was the greatest fisherman of all time, being able locate and catch large schools of fish without the benefit of special modern sonar equipment.[6] He was the greatest legal mind of His times, able to argue with the leading experts of the law and win every case brought before Him.[7] He was the greatest chemist to ever live, converting water to the finest tasting wine without the use of any grapes or chemical reagents and without needing to age the wine ahead of time.[8] He also restored vision to the blind using only mud and saliva as the ingredients for His "eye drops."[9]

He was the greatest physicist to ever live, with the ability to calm raging storms with simple commands, and the ability to not only walk on water but to stop others from sinking when they attempted walking on the same body of water.[10] He was the greatest prophet to ever live, speaking the words of God the Father with absolute authority and predicting his own death and resurrection with perfect accuracy.[11] He was adored and a hugely popular man, with large crowds following his every move[12] and was the greatest teacher to ever live.[13] No man in any profession could stand up and be compared to this man whose only formal education was as an apprentice in carpentry. Because of these remarkable accomplishments, no one could have questioned it if Jesus had shown great pride in Himself.

And Yet, the Humblest Man Ever

So, without question, Jesus was the greatest man to ever live. Somehow, this great man also was the most humble man to ever live! He had the opportunity to be whatever He wanted to be in society and to obtain the highest positions. Some of his followers even wanted to make Him their king by force.[14] Others became so jealous of His abilities that they plotted to kill Him because his huge popularity threatened their own positions in society.[15] In spite of all this clear evidence of His extraordinary power and status, we are told that Jesus was very humble and He is the one we are to emulate.

Jesus Christ is both the greatest and most humble man to ever live

> In your relationships with one another, have the same mindset as Christ Jesus: Who, being in very nature God, did not consider equality with God something to be used to His own advantage; rather, He made himself nothing by taking the very nature of a servant, being made in human likeness. And being found in appearance as a man, He humbled himself by becoming obedient to death—even death on a cross! Therefore God exalted Him to the highest place and gave Him the name that is above every name, that at the name of Jesus every knee should bow, in heaven and on earth and under the earth, and every tongue acknowledge that Jesus Christ is Lord, to the glory of God the Father. (Philippians 2:5–11, NIV 2011)

Jesus Christ came to earth as a man who knew He was in very nature God and yet did not use His position to His own advantage. His sole purpose in life was to glorify God the Father. Even when confronted with having to die on a cross for a crime He did not commit, He chose to do it out of obedience and subservience because it was what God the Father wanted Him to do. As a result of His humility, God rewarded Him with the highest possible position of honor in heaven as the supreme ruler of the universe. When a man as great as Jesus when He walked the earth was as humble as described, what gives you or me the right to not humble ourselves? In the same way Jesus was rewarded for His humility, you can be sure God, who did not spare Jesus for your sake, will also reward you when you humble yourself.

A Man like Any Other?

Some people argue that Jesus was great because He was God and did not require humility to die to His flesh since He was not a normal man and was not subjected to the same desires and feelings as other men. In this line of argument, Jesus would not have needed help from anyone including the Holy Spirit since He was God. The evidence shows that exactly the opposite is true. Even though Jesus is God, He came to earth as a man and went through all the emotions and susceptibilities of a man. He wept,[16] was hungry,[17] thirsty,[18] sorrowful,[19] and got upset[20] just like any other man. We are also told that He was tempted in every possible way that we are but did not yield to sin.

"For we do not have a high priest who is unable to empathize with our weaknesses, but we have one who has been tempted in every way, just as we are—yet he did not sin" (Hebrews 4:15, NIV 2011).

Powered by the Holy Spirit

If Jesus was just a person like you and me, how was He able to accomplish such greatness with so much humility? We are explicitly told that Jesus was "full of the Holy Spirit" (Luke 4:1) when his ministry began, strongly hinting that the Holy Spirit had a major role in His ministry. In relation to being "full," it should be noted that Jesus is the first person in the Bible to be referred to in this way. The reference to fullness connotes the fact that the Holy Spirit was not limited to the Most Holy Place in Jesus but was present in all compartments of His temple including His outer court, Holy Place and Most Holy Place due to Jesus' total yielding.

The first reference to Jesus being full of the Holy Spirit or even having any relationship to the Holy Spirit was after He had publicly humbled Himself in full obedience to God's will through the process of water baptism. John the Baptist was a prophet who had been sent to prepare the way for Jesus Christ.[21] He was responsible for baptizing large numbers of the Jews into repentance, including the leading Jews of the day (Pharisees and Sadducees), in preparation for the coming of the Messiah. Baptism is a symbolic public declaration of death to one's old life of sin and rebirth as a new creature in God. It was a form of humble identification, initially to God only (John's baptism), and then to the trinity of God the Father, God the Son, and God the Holy Spirit (subsequent baptisms). John was highly respected by the Jews as a prophet, but he knew his role was to prepare the way and be subservient to Jesus, the long-awaited Messiah. Yet when the time came, Jesus the Messiah came to John, His messenger, to be baptized. John publicly tried to dissuade Jesus from this illogical act of the lesser person baptizing the greater one, arguing that he should be the one baptized by Jesus and not the other way around.[22] The obvious question is: Why did Jesus, if He was not a man, need to be baptized? Jesus responded to John by saying, "Let it be so now; it is proper for us to do this to fulfill all righteousness" (Matthew 3:15). In effect, Jesus was saying, "It is part of my Father's plan for my life, so I submit to it." Jesus did what He was expected to do as a man in order to fulfill God's righteousness, even though it meant humbling Himself. It was at this precise moment of total humility and submission to God's will in baptism by John that the perfect conditions were set up that enabled the Holy Spirit to come and rest on Jesus.

"As soon as Jesus was baptized, He went up out of the water. At that moment heaven was opened, and He saw the Spirit of God descending like a dove and alighting on Him.[17] And a voice from heaven said, 'This is my Son, whom I love; with Him I am well pleased'" (Matthew 3:16–17).

Power comes from the Holy Spirit through humility

This was the turning point in Jesus' life from being a mere man to a man empowered by God. From this point of the Holy Spirit resting on Jesus, several of His divine actions are described in relation to the influence of the Holy Spirit. Immediately following the impartation of the Holy Spirit upon Him, He received power which enabled Him to be able to fast for forty days and nights in the wilderness and to resist the devil's attempts to try and get Him to disobey God on three separate occasions (Matthew 4:1–11).

This same Holy Spirit that was deposited in Him enabled Jesus to subsequently become the greatest man who ever lived. Throughout His life, Jesus' continued demonstration of humility enabled the full influence of the Holy Spirit to be functional in Him. He did not seize the reign of power on earth as He had been expected to do by His followers, even though He had the ability and the following to do so because He recognized God the Father's dominion. He did not "lord over" others and demand people come to Him in order to be healed as He could have as the healer, but often went into others' homes to effect healing.[23] Indeed, it would have made more sense if Jesus hung around and sought favor from the elite of His society so He could attain status and "enjoy" the benefits that come with this. Instead, He was mostly found among the downcast in society—the "tax collectors and sinners,"[24] a scenario that was unimaginable and annoying to the religious leaders of His time. This showed the extraordinary sense of purpose Jesus had in fulfilling His Father's mission, a purpose that could only be fulfilled by His unrelenting yielding of His outer court (flesh) and Holy Place (soul) to the Holy Spirit. This model of total yielding to the Holy Spirit in humility is the model for you and me as Christians who should be seeking greatness where it truly counts, in the kingdom of God.

Jesus' Active Demonstration of Humility

One of His most famous moments of humility was when Jesus washed His disciples' feet. Foot washing was an ancient act of kindness usually performed by servants toward their masters' guests and is described as an act of humility and kindness in several parts of the Bible.[25] Abraham, a man honored repeatedly by God and called "a friend of God," offered to wash the feet of three men who had, unbeknownst to him, been sent by God.[26] Lot, Abraham's nephew, also offered to wash the feet of the two visitors who turned out to be angels who had been sent to destroy the towns of Sodom and Gomorrah for their pervasive and extreme evil behaviors.[27] Abigail, the wise wife of King David who referred to herself as King David's servant prior to becoming his wife, was credited with humility and kindness for making herself available to wash the feet of King David and his servants.[28]

So the significance of Jesus' condescension to wash His disciples' feet was an extraordinary example of servitude that was not lost on His disciples, and they tried avidly to dissuade Him from doing so, since He was clearly their Master.[29] Jesus, however, used this opportunity to teach His disciples about humility toward one another. "'Do you understand what I have done for you?' he asked them. 'You call me "Teacher" and "Lord" and rightly so, for that is what I am. Now that I, your Lord and Teacher, have washed your feet, you also should wash one another's feet. I have set you an example that you should do as I have done for you'" (John 13:12–15).

In setting the example of humility, Jesus showed and warned us that serving others in love and humility to God is the key to greatness in the kingdom of God. In this very personal demonstration, Jesus was teaching His disciples and all His subsequent followers to remember to put others ahead of themselves. "The greatest among you will be your servant. For those who exalt themselves will be humbled, and those who humble themselves will be exalted" (Matthew 23:11–12, NIV 2011). The way you serve others shows that you have put down your ego and put others needs ahead of your own.

The ultimate humility demonstrated by Jesus was of course His willingness to subject Himself to the brutal punishment He received for a crime He did not commit, and to undergo a trial by people who did not have the authority to put Him on trial, when He could have destroyed all his persecutors with a single command to heaven.[30] Instead, He endured a horrible death because He wanted to spare you and me from the eternal torment of hell. His humility to be obedient to His Father even unto death was empowered by His faith and trust in God His Father.

Jesus' humility was rewarded "in due time" by His resurrection and ascension into glory in heaven. Your humility will be equally rewarded if you allow God to take full control of your life. This is the example we are all to emulate if we want to be fully actualized as the house of God.

Pray This Prayer with Me:

Dear God, my heavenly Father, I am in total awe of the humility demonstrated by Your Son and my Savior Jesus Christ, who swallowed His entire ego and chose to endure torture and death so I could live. Thank You very much, Lord Jesus, for Your example. Give me the ability to always remember You when my ego starts to threaten to take over my temple, and to always remember that everything I have accomplished or could ever accomplish is not because of me but because of You and Your Holy Spirit resident within me. Amen.

1. Luke 3:15; Isaiah 53.
2. Matthew 2:1–18.
3. Luke 5:15; Acts 5:16; Matthew 4:24; Mark 1:34, 3:10; Luke 6:18.
4. Matthew 4:24, 11:5, 9:20–22, 9:23–25, 14:34–36, 15:21–28; Luke 22:49–51, 6:18, 7:22; Mark 5:15–16, 5:21–43, 1:34, 8:22–25; John 5:1–8.
5. Matthew 14:13–21, 15: 29–38; Mark 8:1–9.
6. Luke 5:1–11.
7. Mark 5:29–32, 5:33–39; John 8:2–11; Matthew 22:15–46.
8. John 2:1–11.
9. John 9:5–6.
10. Matthew 8:23–27, 14:22–33.
11. John 6:14, 2:19–22, 11:1–44; Luke 16:17; Matthew 17:9.
12. Matthew 4:25, 13:2, 19:2; Mark 10:1; Luke 5:15, 8:42, 11:29, 14:25.
13. Matthew 13; Mark 1:21–22.
14. John 6:15.
15. John 11:45–51.
16. John 11:35.
17. Matthew 21:18.
18. John 19:28.
19. Matthew 26:37–38.
20. Matthew 21:12–13.
21. Luke 3:1–15.
22. Matthew 3:13–15; Luke 3:21.
23. Luke 7:1–10; Mark1:29–31.
24. Luke 5:27–31.
25. Genesis 18:4, 19:2, 24:32, 43:24; 1 Samuel 25:41.
26. Genesis 18:4.
27. Genesis 19:2.
28. 1 Samuel 25:41.
29. John 13:6–9.
30. John 19:1–3, 16–30.

CHAPTER 20

The House of God Is a House of Obedience

(Session 10b)

Resolution one: I will live for God. Resolution two: if no one else does, I still will.—Jonathan Edwards, American Christian preacher and theologian (1703-1758)

As obedient children, do not conform to the evil desires you had when you lived in ignorance. But just as He who called you is holy, so be holy in all you do; for it is written: "Be holy, because I am holy."—1 Peter 1:14–16 (NIV 2011)

Obedience Is a Prerequisite for Manifestation of the Holy Spirit

We have established in earlier chapters that in order to fulfill God's perfect will for your life, you need to receive the Lord Jesus Christ as your personal savior, and yield your Most Holy Place to the Holy Spirit of God. We have also established that humility is a prerequisite for "dying to your flesh" and enabling God's Spirit to work through all the parts of your being. In this chapter, we will discuss another key ingredient that you need in order to become a complete House of God—*obedience*. On the night before He was crucified, Jesus promised to send the great gift of "the counselor," the Holy Spirit, the third person of the triune nature of God to all those who "love Him *and obey* what He commands." "If you love me, *you will obey* what I command. And I will ask the Father, and He will give you another Counselor to be with you forever—the Spirit of truth. The world cannot accept Him, because it neither sees Him nor knows Him. But you know Him, *for He lives with you and will be in you*" (John 14:15–17, emphasis added). Notice that Jesus promised that the counselor would live with and inside those *who love and obey Him.*

This concept of obedience as a prerequisite for the Holy Spirit is further reinforced in the book of Acts: "We are witnesses of these things, and so is the Holy Spirit, whom God has given to those who *obey* Him" (Acts 5:32, emphasis added). God's promise that you will be His house, His church, His temple, or the abode of His Holy Spirit is conditional upon your acceptance and love of Jesus *and* your obedience to Him. God not only desires your eternal salvation (accomplished through faith in and acceptance of Jesus Christ), which is a free gift from Him. He also wants a close relationship with you so as to be able to use you for expanding His kingdom while you are on Earth. To accomplish this demands obedience on your part.

Slave to Sin or Slave to God?

There are two levels of obedience if you want to fully walk with Christ as a spiritual being. The first is obedience to receive the free and unconditional gift of God in accepting Jesus Christ as your savior. There is nothing you can do to earn this gift; no amount of good works will earn you your eternal salvation. "For the wages of sin is death, but the gift of God is eternal life in Christ Jesus our Lord" (Romans 6:23); "For it is by grace you have been saved, through faith—and this not from yourselves—it is the gift of God—not by works, so that no one can boast" (Ephesians 2:8–9).

Love of God is a springboard of obedience to Him

However, once you do give your life to Christ, in order to achieve the highest level of relationship with Him and to fulfill the perfect purpose for which you were created, you must show the nature of the new person you have become by obeying His commands. You can then claim the dominion God has always intended for your life. Prior to giving your life to Jesus Christ, you were a slave to sin, which leads to eternal death, but when you gave your life to Jesus Christ, you became a slave to righteousness, which leads to eternal life.

Don't you know that when you offer yourselves to someone as obedient slaves, you are slaves of the one you obey—whether you are slaves to sin, which leads to death, or to obedience, which leads to righteousness? But thanks be to God that, though you used to be slaves to sin, you have come to obey from your heart the pattern of teaching that has now claimed your allegiance. You have been set free from sin and have become slaves to righteousness. ... When you were slaves to sin, you were free from the control of righteousness. ... But now that you have been set free from sin and have become slaves of God, the benefit you reap leads to holiness, and the result is eternal life. For the wages of sin is death, but the gift of God is eternal life in Christ Jesus our Lord. (Romans 6:16–18, 22–23, NIV 2011)

In other words, your actions reflect who you obey. Before Christ, you had no option but to sin, since you were a slave to sin and free from the influence of righteousness (that which comes from the Holy Spirit). When you received Christ and the Holy Spirit came into you, God's laws became written upon your heart and became a part of you; as a result you are now free from the influence of sin. "I will give you a new heart and put a new spirit in you; I will remove from you your heart of stone and give you a heart of flesh. And I will put my Spirit in you and move you to follow my decrees and be careful to keep my laws" (Ezekiel 36:26–27).

The Kingdom of Sin and the Kingdom of God

Obedience to sin is your natural and expected state when you are not yet born again. As an analogy, think about the difference in rules and laws when you are under the authority of different nations. In some Middle Eastern countries, for example, it is the law that women must show modesty by covering their head in public with a traditional item of clothing known as *hijab*. The women living in these nations are therefore under obligation of this law and must wear the hijab.

For many women, after having to wear the hijab all their lives, it becomes an integral part of their identity. Not only is it the law that they wear it, they become so used to wearing it that they feel exposed when they remove it. On the other hand, other women long to be able to be able to remove the hijab and walk around without it on, but they are under obligation to continue to wear it as long as they reside in their native country. If one of these women was able to pay the price of changing countries and she moves and becomes a legal citizen of another nation that does not demand the hijab, she is now freed from the obligation of the hijab. She can move around in her new nation without fear of breaking the law. She is the same person, but she is under a new authority and no longer subjected to the laws of her old kingdom.

Similarly, when you are under the authority of the kingdom of sin, you have to be obedient to your sinful ways. When you give your life to Jesus Christ who paid the ultimate price to liberate you from the kingdom of sin into the kingdom of God, He endows you with the Holy Spirit who ensures that you are no longer under obligation to obey the laws of sin or to be under fear of condemnation.

> Therefore, there is now no condemnation for those who are in Christ Jesus, because through Christ Jesus the law of the Spirit who gives life has set you free from the law of sin and death. For what the law was powerless to do because it was weakened by the flesh, God did by sending his own Son in the likeness of sinful flesh to be a sin offering. And so he condemned sin in the flesh, in order that the righteous requirement of the law might be fully met in us, who do not live according to the flesh but according to the Spirit. (Romans 8:1–4)

The law of lift is needed to overcome the law of gravity

These verses refer to two laws based on two different kingdoms: the law of life in the Spirit, which gives new life to those who are in the kingdom of Christ Jesus, and the law of sin and death, which leads to the death of those who remain under the influence of the kingdom of sin. When you choose God's kingdom, you come under the law of life in the Spirit and are freed from the obligation of the law of sin and death! "For He has rescued us from the dominion of darkness and brought us into the kingdom of the Son He loves" (Colossians 1:13).

234

The Law of Life in the Spirit Frees from the Obligation of the Law of Sin and Death

Imagine that you choose to live on the thirtieth floor of a magnificent high-rise building. As a result of your choice, you gain some clear benefits, including a beautiful panoramic view of your city and the prestige of having a higher floor address. However, there are some drawbacks as well. One main drawback is that you cannot simply choose to walk outside your building without falling quickly and uncontrollably due to the force of gravity. Similarly, you cannot just step inside your building and directly enter your apartment. You first have to either do some work climbing stairs or take an elevator that takes you to your floor.

Given this scenario, imagine that you decide suddenly that it is ridiculous for you to have to go down to the main floor prior to walking out of your building or for you to go up before entering your suite while those living on the first floor can simply walk in or out of theirs. Of course you realize this has to do with the law of gravity, but you conclude that this law is unfair and discriminatory. You could decide to lobby your local or state government to pass a new law decreeing that the law of gravity is discriminatory and declaring it to be abolished. As it turns out, it does not matter how much you dislike this law, or what your legislators have to say about it. If you choose to disregard it and walk out of your thirtieth floor, you are going to plunge rather quickly! Even if you are eloquent and charismatic enough to persuade the legislators that the law is unfair, and they pass a law stating that the law of gravity is unfair, you are still going down if you choose to step out of your building from your floor. You cannot, on your own accord or talents, choose to overcome the law of gravity. The law is a natural law that is fixed and unchangeable.

The law of life in the Spirit overcomes the law of sin and death

The law of gravity is similar to the law of sin and death. Your dislike of God's law that states that any of your sins will lead to eternal death is not going to change the consequence of the law. You may be upset that this is a harsh law or that it is unfair because on balance your sins do not seem that bad to you compared to the sins of others. You are still going to pay the full price if you have a single sin. However, going back to the law of gravity, there is a way to overcome gravity, just as there is a way to overcome the law of sin and death. This is through another natural law called the law of lift, which is rooted in two different natural laws discovered centuries ago by two brilliant scientists, Sir Isaac Newton (Newton's third law) and Daniel Bernoulli (the Bernoulli equation). The law of lift allows you to overcome the law of gravity. The law of lift is employed to varying degrees in designing aircraft, elevators, escalators, hydraulic forks, etc. When the law of lift is in play, the effects of the law of gravity can be superseded. In other words, when you step inside an elevator, you get to go up instead of down, or you get to go down in a controlled fashion with gravity rather than tumbling down. You can also go thousands of miles up in the air in the confines of an airplane or helicopter without tumbling down. Here is the catch. You can only overcome the effects of the law of gravity if you are within a container (elevator, airplane, etc.) that buoys you from the effects of gravity through the law of lift. You cannot do it in your own flesh or simply by expressing your disdain for the law.

Similar to the law of lift, there is another of God's laws known as the law of life in the Spirit.[1] When you are operating under the law of life in the Spirit, the law of sin and death is overcome. The Holy Spirit, who is the third person of the triune God and resident in you, enables you to escape from the clutches of the law of sin and death. However, just as with the law of lift, there is a catch. You cannot overcome the consequences or the power of sin on your own, but only with the Holy Spirit resident within you.

When you have the Holy Spirit within you, you become hidden in Him and are enabled to prevail over any sinful circumstance in your life, conditional on your obedience to His rules and promptings. When you are in an elevator or an airplane, you have to obey the rules put in place that enable the law of lift to continue to operate. You cannot choose, for example, to disregard the rule of keeping the cabin doors closed within the airplane you are in while you are flying at thirty thousand feet above sea level simply because it is inconvenient for you and you want fresh air. You will go down! The same is true for the law of life in the Spirit. It will save your life, but you must be obedient to the rules of God.

The Ten Promises of God

The Ten Commandments (Exodus 20) given by God through Moses can then be viewed in two very radically different ways depending on which kingdom you belong to and which laws you are operating under. If you belong to the kingdom of sin, it is impossible to obey or overcome the Ten Commandments because you are under obligation to the sinful or satanic influences in your outer court. The Ten Commandments are a major burden to you because you are being asked to disobey the rules of the kingdom to which you belong.

In contrast, when you become a follower of Christ, the Holy Spirit whom God has given to live within your Most Holy Place is there to remind you that you are no longer under any obligation to sin. In the kingdom of God to which you belong, you have been given the desire and the power to obey the Ten Commandments through the Holy Spirit that resides in you and you can now view the laws as guaranteed promises for your new kingdom.

> A thief broke into a church to help himself to the church's coffers. Upon preparing to carry away his loot, he felt a prompting and stopped in front of a large display of the Ten Commandments in the church's sanctuary. As he read through these commandments, he felt the strong presence of the Holy Spirit and had a profound encounter with Jesus Christ. Having met with His savior and receiving a deposit of the Holy Spirit, he became convicted the commandments were not a set of difficult rules put in place for him to follow but were a set of promises from God that he would be able to resist all future temptation. Thus, "thou shalt not covet" was not a burdensome commandment but a promise from God that he would not need to covet. This revelation revolutionized his life, and he became a changed man that night with no further urges to steal. (HDD, modified from anonymous)

The same is true for you. Because of the Holy Spirit, who is now in you, the Ten Commandments have now become for you the ten promises of God. You do not need to worship any other gods or idols anymore. You do not have to curse using God's name anymore. You do not have to hold hateful or murderous thoughts about your enemies anymore. You do not have to commit adultery anymore. You do not have to steal anymore. You do not have to give false testimony or lie anymore. You do not have to covet your neighbor's belongings anymore. You are no longer under obligation to gamble, engage in prostitution, give your body over to drugs or alcohol or denigrate yourself! You can now look at each of God's commandments and not be intimidated by them, recognizing that they are not only for your benefit but are promises to you of what the Holy Spirit will do for you when you are confronted with the temptation.

Obedience Is a Choice

Of course, because you are no longer under obligation to do something does not mean you cannot and will not do it, and you may choose to continue to obey the rules and laws of your former kingdom. In the analogy of the women who live in the nation where the hijab is demanded, when one emigrates to another nation where such a rule does not exist, she may still *feel* a strong obligation and choose to continue to wear the hijab. Similarly, as a Christian, you are no longer under obligation to sin, but you may choose to obey sin because you feel you need to because you enjoy it, get some rewards from it, or it may have become such an integral part of you that even when you have been given the freedom not to do so, you are not quite able to do so without help.

You have all the power you need to be obedient to God's law through the Holy Spirit as a Christian, but doing so still remains your choice. It is a matter of what your focus is on—pleasing God by focusing on your Most Holy Place or pleasing yourself or the world in your outer court. "Those who live according to the flesh have their minds set on what the flesh desires; but those who live in accordance with the Spirit have their minds set on what the Spirit desires. The mind governed by the flesh is death, but the mind governed by the Spirit is life and peace" Romans 8:5–6, NIV 2011).

Victory over bad habits is immediate for some, but gradual for others with the Spirit's help

This is why some believers in Jesus Christ fail to overcome burdens or generational curses in their lives even after receiving Jesus. You have been given the freedom and power to overcome these burdens by relying on Jesus Christ and the Holy Spirit, but you have not chosen to exercise your newly found freedom and power. This involves obedience in reading God's word, remembering who you are in Christ and not accepting that the things that held you hostage prior to Christ can still hold you hostage when you are in Christ. Just because several generations of your family were alcoholics or failed to have stable marriages or died young does not have to mean the same will happen to you when you receive Jesus. You are a new creature, under new rules and regulations. However, if your goal is to continue to willfully live according to your sinful nature by doing things your old ways after you have been set free by Christ, you are denying the authority of the kingdom to which you now belong and will be denied the blessings God promises for your life. "[Jesus] replied, 'Blessed rather are those who hear the word of God *and* obey it'" (Luke 11:28, emphasis added).

Obedience to the will of God does not mean you become perfect the moment you give your life to Jesus Christ. All Christians are on a lifelong journey to perfection that only gets realized fully upon going home to heaven. For some people giving up obedience to old habits, generational curses, and behaviors or powerful addictions from their previous kingdom is instantaneous once they receive Christ and receive the presence of the Holy Spirit.

Tony[2] was at his wits' end and ready to take his own life. He hated himself, having lost everything important in life including his marriage and his children because of his addiction to drugs and alcohol. Indeed, he felt as if he was a "dead man walking." He was living a life totally separated from the knowledge of God. He's not sure why, but he was drawn to the First Assembly of God of Greater Lansing in East Lansing, Michigan. That day, the pastor of the church, Curt Dalaba, welcomed him and spent time with him, letting him know about the redeeming grace of Jesus Christ and how Christ's love frees men from all sorts of bondage. According to Tony, "My life began on that day." In obedience, he gave his life over to Jesus Christ and now has God's Spirit living in Him, as He became a member of God's kingdom. He has not felt any desire to use drugs since that day and soon became an active member of the church, with a strong sense of God's calling on His life.

For others, giving up current obedience to bad habits proves much more difficult to do. No human being is perfect, but God has commanded you to aim for perfection—which means following the example of the life Jesus led.[3] However, He does not expect perfection overnight, but expects you to be making the utmost daily effort possible to change. This can only be accomplished by total yielding yourself to the Holy Spirit. God can see deep inside your heart. He knows when you are making a strong effort to be obedient and to change your ways, even if you fall down sometimes. Remember who you are in Christ! You have the power now to overcome and you should confess this new truth daily with your mouth if you must to enable you to shed the vestiges of your previous kingdom.

There is however, great danger in claiming to have Jesus Christ living within you and not giving room to the Holy Spirit to remake you into the model citizen of the kingdom to which you now belong. If you are a Christian who is deliberately disobeying God's word and continuing to do your own thing and living to please yourself as if you were still in the kingdom of sin, you are mocking God, and God will not be mocked. "Do not be deceived: God cannot be mocked. A man reaps what he sows. Whoever sows to please their flesh, from the flesh will reap destruction; whoever sows to please the Spirit, from the Spirit will reap eternal life. Let us not become weary in doing good, for at the proper time we will reap a harvest if we do not give up" (Galatians 6:7–9, NIV 2011).

Obedience leads God to bless you here on earth and guarantees your position in heaven

In order to be obedient to God, you need to know what God's word says. This means you need to regularly "eat" God's word by reading your Bible daily. You also need to spend time listening to God during your regular prayer time so you can recognize His voice when the Spirit nudges you to move. The Holy Spirit will only confirm principles within God's Word in the Bible and will *never* contradict it. If you say you are being obedient to God by following instructions that contradict His word, you are under deception.

Finally, obedience takes practice. If you constantly practice doing what God tells you to do even in the little things, you are much more likely to be obedient in the big things.[4] The greatest part of obedience is that God will never leave you stranded when you are following His instructions. Whatever God's call to you may be: obedience to preach the gospel to your neighbors, to be more loving, to stop lying, stealing, swearing, to be more generous or to be faithful in your tithing, to let go or to hold on to your current circumstance, God will enable you to fulfill it and will never let you falter. He will always back you up and strengthen you to do what He has called you to do and provide all you need to see it through to completion. If this is your desire, I pray that God grants you the hunger, desire and passion to start the process of living a life that is in full obedience to Jesus Christ beginning from today. You will then experience the full blessings of being in Christ.

Jesus, the Most Obedient Man Who Ever Lived

While you were transferred from God's kingdom to the kingdom of sin through the disobedience of Adam, you were redeemed back to the kingdom of God through the obedience and sacrifice of Jesus Christ. Jesus, the only true Son of God (the rest of us were adopted), was the perfect example of obedience to God. "For just as through the disobedience of the one man the many were made sinners, so also through the obedience of the one man the many will be made righteous" (Romans 5:19).

Jesus was sent to earth to accomplish the most difficult task ever given. His job was to give up His supreme and elevated position as the prince of the kingdom of God, come to earth as a mere man, and suffer cruel pain, torture, and then death in order to regain God's kingdom for humanity. Yet as we noted in the previous chapter, Jesus was completely humble, obedient, and totally submitted to God, choosing to die on the cross for you and me because that is what God the Father wanted Him to do. "And being found in appearance as a man, he humbled himself by becoming obedient to death—even death on a cross!" (Philippians 2:8)

This same Jesus whose obedience and love paid the price that bought you out of the kingdom of sin into the kingdom of God now clearly demands that you follow His footsteps out of love and appreciation for Him in what He did for you. "Jesus replied, "Anyone who loves Me will obey my teaching. My Father will love them, and We will come to them and make our home with them. Anyone who does not love Me will not obey my teaching. These words you hear are not my own; they belong to the Father who sent Me" (John 14:23–24, NIV 2011).

It does not matter if you are the most loyal attendee of your church on Sundays and have heard hundreds of sermons or that you are excellent at praising and worshipping God. While you are called to do all these things as a Christian, if you are not following God's commands He does not see you as righteous. "For it is not those who hear the law who are righteous in God's sight, but it is those who obey the law who will be declared righteous" (Romans 2:13).

Benefits of Obedience

Obedience to Jesus has two main benefits:

Guarantee of Blessings on Earth and Eternity in Heaven:
The first benefit of obedience is that it sets you apart in holiness as a child of God and will guarantee your eternal position in heaven, while also leading to blessings for you while on earth. "But now that you have been set free from sin and have become slaves of God, the benefit you reap leads to holiness, and the result is eternal life" (Romans 6:22).

There are more than 250 verses in the Bible dealing with obedience. Indeed, all of God's promises to you are conditional upon your obedience. This includes His promise of salvation which is conditional upon your accepting and believing in Jesus Christ as your savior. "For God so loved the world that he gave his one and only Son, that *whoever believes in him* shall not perish but have eternal life" (John 3:16, emphasis added). Abraham's obedience to God when called to sacrifice his covenant son, Isaac, led to provision of a life full of blessings.

> The angel of the LORD called to Abraham from heaven a second time and said, "I swear by myself, declares the LORD, that because you have done this and have not withheld your son, your only son, I will surely bless you and make your descendants as numerous as the stars in the sky and as the sand on the seashore. Your descendants will take possession of the cities of their enemies, and through your offspring all nations on earth will be blessed, because you have obeyed me." (Genesis 22:15–18)

In contrast, Lot's wife became a pillar of salt as a result of disobedience when angels were sent by God to destroy Sodom and Gomorrah for their pervasive wickedness and sinfulness. "When he hesitated, the men grasped his hand and the hands of his wife and of his two daughters and led them safely out of the city, for the LORD was merciful to them. As soon as they had brought them out, one of them said, 'Flee for your lives! Don't look back, and don't stop anywhere in the plain! Flee to the mountains or you will be swept away!' But Lot's wife looked back, and she became a pillar of salt" (Genesis 19:16–17, 26).

King David was famous for his obedience to God, always seeking His face before making any decisions. As a result, God blessed David with material wealth, lifelong victory over his enemies and a lineage that included the Messiah. King Saul who preceded David failed to obey God and was specifically told that he lost his throne as a result of his disobedience.[5] All the verses and the consequences noted of men and women throughout the Bible who either obeyed or disobeyed God lead to one inexorable conclusion: obedience to God is associated with blessings and disobedience to Him with curses.

The Law of Obedience and Blessings

This first law of obedience simply states that obedience to God guarantees you blessings from Him! In the first fourteen verses of Chapter 28 in the book of Deuteronomy,[6] God clearly lays out blessing after blessing that He will provide to those who obey Him. These blessings include causing you to stand out among your peers; a fertile womb and blessings for your children; extraordinary productivity in your workplace; extraordinary provisions to meet all your needs; prosperity, and freedom from debt; victory against those who oppose you and possession of the land on which you live; and a Spirit of excellence and leadership.

While these blessings in Deuteronomy Chapter 28 are part of the Old Testament law, the underlying principle of "God blesses obedience to Him" is still valid today. This is evident in Romans 8:4, which says "the righteous requirement of the law might be fully met in us, who do not live according to the flesh but according to the Spirit." When we follow (obey) the Holy Spirit in our daily lives, God considers us to have fully met the requirement of the law, thus allowing His blessings to be released. This idea is reinforced in Galatians, where the spiritual underpinnings of the natural law of sowing and reaping are explained. "Do not be deceived: God cannot be mocked. A man reaps what he sows.[8] Whoever sows to please their flesh, from the flesh will reap destruction; whoever sows to please the Spirit, from the Spirit will reap eternal life.[9] Let us not become weary in doing good, for at the proper time we will reap a harvest if we do not give up" (Galatians 6:7–9, NIV 2011).

We do not complain when we plant a corn seed and a corn plant sprouts up—it is what we expected. We would be genuinely mystified, however, if we planted a corn seed and a pumpkin plant grew instead! We have an innate sense of how sowing and reaping are related in the natural world. This can help us understand, then, how the same principle applies in the spiritual world. Sowing to please the Holy Spirit (obedience to Him) brings rewards, the greatest being eternal life, but also the rewards enjoyed on this earth as the fruit of our joyful obedience to our loving God.

The Law of Disobedience and Curses

The second law of obedience simply states that disobedience to God guarantees curses from Him! In fifty-three verses within Deuteronomy Chapter 28, beginning in verse 15,[7] God highlights numerous curses that will come to you as a result of disobedience to Him. These include failure to be productive at work in spite of your best efforts; failure of the land in which you work to yield its goods for you; failure for you to bear children, or if you do, bearing children that are a burden and a curse to you rather than a blessing; ongoing diseases and famine; constant fear of your enemies and guaranteed defeat by them; inability to succeed in anything you do; overt poverty and a form of slavery that includes burgeoning debts and a life without joy or hope; and a life subjected to tragedy after tragedy and ultimate failure to fulfill the purpose for which you were created.

The striking thing about both laws is that God has not only set them in motion as natural laws, He has warned you in advance about the consequences. He has given you a choice to proactively make between the consequences of the two laws—a choice between life and death. "This day I call the heavens and the earth as witnesses against you that I have set before you life and death, blessings and curses. Now choose life, so that you and your children may live and that you may love the LORD your God, listen to his voice, and hold fast to him. For the LORD is your life, and he will give you many years in the land he swore to give to your fathers, Abraham, Isaac, and Jacob" (Deuteronomy 30:19–20, NIV 2011).

Sowing to the Holy Spirit reaps great benefits

You may frown as a believer on the notion that these blessings and curses could possibly apply to you since you have received Jesus and are under a new covenant. Belief in Jesus Christ freely guarantees salvation that is independent and irrespective of your past sins. However, it is clear that Jesus did not come to do away with the laws of God but to fulfill them. As we noted in the previous session, Jesus' interpretation of the laws of God were more stringent than what the people had believed up till His time on Earth. "But," you may say, "Galatians 3:13 says Christ redeemed me from the curse of the law, so I don't have to worry about negative consequences such as those in Deuteronomy 28 happening to me, even if I disobey God. I am under grace." You would be absolutely right that you are under grace. But as we saw earlier, grace is not God promising to close His eyes to our willful disobedience. If I willfully disobey, God is neither obligated to bless me nor is He obligated to shield me from the natural consequences that my actions of sowing "bad" seeds will set in motion. Thus, the redemption from the "curse" in Galatians is not in conflict with the consequences of disobedience that serve as warnings in Deuteronomy 28.

On the contrary, the love poured on us by God has the effect of causing our hearts to long to make Him smile. When we sense His love for us, it creates in us a desire to obey—out of our love for Him. If you are a parent, you can understand how this works. Given the choice, you would much rather have your children do what you say simply because they love you, than for them to grudgingly obey you just because they don't want to get in trouble. Motivation for obedience is one difference between Old Testament obedience to the law and New Testament obedience to grace. Ephesians 5:1 describes it this way: "Therefore be imitators of God [copy Him and follow His example], as well-beloved children [imitate their father]" (Ephesians 5:1, Amplified). What motivates you more to obey God today: just because you love Him and want to make Him smile, or because you don't want something bad to happen? Which would you prefer to be your own children's motivation to obey you?

Getting to that lifestyle of obeying God simply because we love Him and do not want to hurt Him in any way may take time; changes to our character can be painfully slow. Many times we obey as an act of faith, because it is the right thing to do, whether we feel like doing it or not. God will bless our obedience done in faith, even when we do not feel the rush of emotion. He understands that sometimes that is all we can do. But He also does not lower the bar, because He knows that we will eventually grow up to a more love-motivated obedience. He knows that often it is the continued practice of obedience that molds our character so that we can truly appreciate the feelings of love for God that will follow. This may be one reason that Jesus made it clear in several passages of the Bible that He also expects obedience from all who proclaim belief in His name. "[Jesus] replied, 'Blessed rather are those who hear the word of God and obey it'" (Luke 11:28).

"Jesus replied, 'Anyone who loves me will *obey* my teaching. My Father will love them, and we will come to them and make our home with them.

Anyone who does not love me will not *obey* my teaching. These words you hear are not my own; they belong to the Father who sent me'" (John 14:23–24, NIV 2011, emphasis added).

"And this is love: that we walk in *obedience* to His commands. As you have heard from the beginning, His command is that you walk in love" (2 John 1:6, emphasis added). In fact, Jesus' last words to His disciples prior to being taken to heaven was for them to teach the world obedience to Him. "All authority in heaven and on earth has been given to me. Therefore go and make disciples of all nations, baptizing them in the name of the Father and of the Son and of the Holy Spirit, *and teaching them to obey everything I have commanded you*. And surely I am with you always, to the very end of the age" (Matthew 28:18–20, emphasis added). By giving you the Holy Spirit, He has made it much easier to be obedient, but you first have to yield to Him.

Get Ye out of Crisis Mode

There are people in life, even believers, who always seem to be in crisis mode. Everything seems to be difficult for them. They struggle through their lives and constantly have instability in their jobs, marriages, and in their daily routines. They have built their temples' foundation on the sand of disobedience and as a result fail to reap the benefit of God's blessings.

It is never too late to follow God

Is this you? *If so, it is never too late to rebuild your temple with the rock of Jesus as your foundation.* Obedience to Him is the key to building the strongest possible foundation for your life. When the storms of life come along, you will be well anchored to endure them. There is no crisis you can encounter in life that you will not be able to endure when your mind is set on following Jesus. On the other hand, claiming to be a follower of Christ but not doing what He says will set you up for a fall when even minor problems occur.

> Why do you call Me, "Lord, Lord," and do not do what I say? I will show you what he is like who comes to Me and hears my words and puts them into practice. He is like a man building a house, who dug down deep and laid the foundation on rock. When a flood came, the torrent struck that house but

could not shake it, because it was well built. But the one who hears My words and does not put them into practice is like a man who built a house on the ground without a foundation. The moment the torrent struck that house, it collapsed and its destruction was complete. (Luke 6:46–49)

Millions of people, including professing Christians, have turned their backs on obeying Jesus and have snuffed out His Holy Spirit, even those who are loyal church attendees. As a result, they are struggling in a world full of pain, difficulties, hatred, bitterness, and unanswered prayers. They are looking for more miracles in spite of all the wonderful miracles going on around them, which their hardened hearts will not allow them to see or participate in. Are you one of them? Is the Holy Spirit able to manifest in you still or is His power put out by your ongoing mastery of your own life, and failure to utilize the power you have in your new kingdom under Jesus? Are you trying to be the master of your own destiny, or have you relinquished control to Jesus? Remember, you cannot have two people giving different directions for the destination of an automobile. One has to give in to the other, or chaos ensues. When you resist God's commands you are wrestling with the king for control of your life, and He will ultimately yield control to you. However, in this scenario, you are determining your own destiny—which is suffering here on earth and eternal separation from God. "Blessed are they who do His commandments, that they may have right to the Tree of Life, and may enter in through the gates into the city (Revelation 22:14, KJV).

May God grant you the grace to enable total obedience of your outer court and Holy Place to the firm, loving, totally secure, and rock-solid foundation of Jesus Christ.

Ability to Be Used by God

The second benefit of obedience is the ability to be used by God. When you obey God you are doing what you were programmed to do, and accomplishing His greatest purpose for your life—to draw others to Him. "Because of the service by which you have proved yourselves, others will praise God for the obedience that accompanies your confession of the gospel of Christ, and for your generosity in sharing with them and with everyone else" (2 Corinthians 9:13, NIV 2011).

When you do this, you are helping fulfill the Great Commission, a principle we will explore further in future sessions.

Pray This Prayer with Me:

Dear God, Please help me become a house of obedience. Give me the courage to believe and trust You so I can always do what You have asked me to do, as written in Your Holy Book, the Bible, and revealed to me through Your Holy Spirit. Help me understand that I am a new creature in a new kingdom and have new laws that free me from the clutches of the laws of my old kingdom. Help me also to grasp the implications of my disobedience to You to my destiny. I am so grateful to You for the role model I have in Jesus for perfect submission to Your will. Amen.

Questions to Ponder:

- What, if any, is the connection between humility and obedience?
- If the Holy Spirit is already deposited as a free gift in all Christians, why then do you need to be obedient to God?
- Is there a "hijab" in your life that you are holding on to from your old life, even after you have been set free from the burden of "wearing" it? Discuss what this is and why you have trouble letting it go.
- Does it make sense to you to view the Ten Commandments as the ten promises of God?
- What are the implications of viewing the Ten Commandments this way?
- Have you experienced any of the blessings associated with obedience? If so, which blessings?
- Have you experienced any of the problems associated with disobedience? If so, which ones?

Prayer Points

- Pray that God will help you be fully obedient to *all* His laws so you can attain all the blessings that come with it.
- Pray that God will help you to overcome any spirit of disobedience in your life and to enable you to trust Him when your tendency is to disobey.
- Pray that God will use obedience within you as a light to draw others into His kingdom.

1. Romans 8:1–4.
2. A true account; however, his real name has been changed to protect his identity.
3. Matthew 5:48.
4. Luke 16:10.
5. 1 Samuel 13:13–14.
6. See also Leviticus 26:1–13.
7. See also Leviticus 26:14–46.

CHAPTER 21

The House of God Is a House of Faith, Part 1

(Session 11a)

If the devil has got your faith, then he has got everything.
—Curt Dalaba, Pastor, Assemblies of God, Michgan.

Now faith is being sure of what we hope for *and certain of what we do not see.*—Hebrews 11:1 (emphasis added)

Faith Is Belief and Complete Trust in God

Faith is the next key attribute to becoming a spiritual house of God. Having faith is a natural progression from humility and it is also closely tied with obedience.

Faith is *complete trust and belief in God.* Being a desirable house of God involves learning to listen to, believe in, and act on promptings from the Spirit of God, who is living within your Most Holy Place, instead of the multitude of voices in your outer court. Your mind is your most valuable asset; you must learn to guard it jealously. The person or thing you listen to the most is the one most likely to influence you and motivate you to act. Failure to have God's voice as the predominant voice you listen to all the time and failure to actually believe in God's words when you do hear them are two of the biggest deterrents to building your temple on the foundation of Jesus Christ. It does not matter how genuine or eloquent you are, if you are trying to counsel someone for his or her own good but he or she does not listen to what you are saying or believe a word of it, you are wasting your time with the person. The person is unlikely to comply with your instructions or persuasions. The same is true of God and the Holy Spirit as they relate to you.

Demonstration of Christian faith is likely the single most important attribute other than Christian love that sets you apart as a spiritual being. It shows that you have fully turned from the visible distractions of your outer court and are firmly focused on the one enthroned on the mercy seat in your Most Holy Place. In your outer court, you are bombarded with the ways and thoughts of those around you: persons in your family, place of work, and those whom you let in via radio, television, Internet, etc. In your Holy Place, you have to rely on your logic, which tries to interpret everything you encounter only in a way that makes sense to you based on your experiences. In your Most Holy Place, however, there exists the supernatural God who does things in miraculous ways that do not conform to your logic or the persuasive voices coming in from your outer court. Faith demands a close and intimate relationship with God such that you trust Him and His methods even though they defy your logic.

Faith is borne of the understanding that God is God, the one who created the universe and all that is in it. There is no challenge you can face that God cannot help you overcome. There is nothing you can conceive of that He cannot do better for you. That is why without faith it is *impossible* to please Him. "And without faith it is impossible to please God, because anyone who comes to Him must believe that He exists and that He rewards those who earnestly seek Him" (Hebrews 11:6).

In other words, if you do not trust God and believe His promises to you are true and specifically for you, you are denying His integrity and His honesty; as a result you are insulting Him. The same way a parent expects their child to believe them when they make a promise, God expects the same from you. As we noted in the previous session, if you are in Christ, you are a new creature. You are no longer under the clutches of the rules of your old kingdom, but you have to let go of the habits of your old kingdom and embrace the rules and benefits of the new one. You have to believe that the rules of your old kingdom no longer apply to you, and that you are entitled to all the benefits of your new one, the kingdom of God. If you do not, you will struggle through every trial in life because you will never be able to see beyond your previous understanding of your situation and will miss out on the extraordinary methods God has put in place to help you. Both belief and disbelief reveal a lot about you.

Underpinning belief is the recognition that God is infinitely smarter than you and that the way He does things are radically different from yours. "'For my thoughts are not your thoughts, neither are your ways my ways,' declares the LORD. 'As the heavens are higher than the earth, so are my ways higher than your ways and my thoughts than your thoughts'" (Isaiah 55:8–9).

If you truly understand that God's ways are very different from yours and that He is not logical and cannot be put "into a box," you will soon learn to completely trust Him and allow for situations in your life to unfold as He intends them, even when you do not know exactly how He will handle them. When you are confronted by the thrashing storms of life, you will learn how to approach them with confidence that the God of grace will take care of you and you will come out stronger on the other end.

Without faith it is impossible to please God

Disbelief, on the other hand, means you have trapped God within the limited box of your intelligence and cannot fathom that He is able to act outside of your understanding.

Faith Is a Gift of the Holy Spirit

Faith does not come naturally to everyone and can be downright scary for some because it involves transferring control from your outer court, where you can see everything and from your Holy Place, where everything makes sense to you, to your Most Holy Place, where you have to totally rely on God. It is especially hard for people whose primary personality is logical to believe what they cannot see or what they do not understand. However, faith is something that builds on itself, and once God shows Himself true in one situation, it is easier to trust Him in other circumstances. If you never practice using it, your faith will never grow.

God has actually made a way for you to increase your faith—by offering it to you as one of several gifts through His Holy Spirit. The Holy Spirit gives different gifts as He determines you to need them including wisdom, knowledge, faith, healing, miraculous powers, prophecy, distinguishing between spirits, ability to speak in different tongues, and interpretation of tongues.[1] As with all talents and gifts from God, not everyone is given the same amount because God needs people with different talents in order to have a complete and fully functional kingdom.[2] However, once you learn to walk closely with God, He will often release each of these gifts to you as needed for a specific situation.

Eagerly Desire Faith

You can "eagerly desire"[3] a specific gift of the Spirit, especially one that you are not particularly strong in at the present time for use in serving God. Eagerly desiring a gift means you earnestly seek God's help in building up this gift in your life.[4] If it is more faith that you lack and desire, then you should pray constantly for God to increase your gift of faith. You should also "hunger" for faith and go after it with determination. Hang around men and women who have faith. Read and meditate about men and women of God who were noted for their faith and model your behavior after them. A great place to start is by reading Hebrews 11, the chapter of the Bible known as the "faith hall of fame," where ordinary men and women like you are commended for their extraordinary faith.

You can read in more depth about each of the people mentioned in this chapter of Hebrews in the specific part of the Bible where their lives and exploits are described. Practice working your faith by learning to trust God, starting with little things so that you can be confident that you will have faith when you need it for your big trials. Even if it may seem that you have failed initially, you must continue to desire and work on this aspect of the Spirit until it comes to you in full measure. Do not be discouraged because you prayed for more faith and the next day you still have trouble believing God fully. Most people who seem to have full measures of a gift of the Spirit did not receive the gift overnight. They have practiced and developed the gift over and over again until it became their natural character.

For some people, a specific spiritual gift seems to come naturally because this is a primary (major) gift God has given them. Just as an athlete seeking to become excellent in any sport has to work hard to improve his or her skills, it also takes hunger and perseverance to build up the spiritual gifts, even if it is one that comes naturally to you. Be like a little child when it comes to faith. Little children are amazing for their belief in acting on what they are told. Here is a story of one such boy as recounted by a missionary who ran a camp the boy attended:

Jeremy[5] had terrible vision caused by a degenerative eye disease, which he was born with and for which he needed special prescription glasses. He was invited to a Christian camp, where he heard the gospel message around a campfire during the first night for the first time in his nine years, and he gave his life to Christ. The message that night included the promise that Jesus is able to heal all of Jeremy's sins and diseases. That same night, Jeremy's glasses fell off and were accidentally trampled on by an unknowing camper. Unfortunately, Jeremy could not see a thing without his glasses, and there was no chance he would be able to get a new pair prior to camp being over. As a result, he needed to be led all around the camp by one of the counselors.

This camp counselor felt very bad for him and offered to pray for God to give him a new pair of glasses. To the counselor's amazement, Jeremy told him it was not necessary because Jesus was going to heal his eyes. The counselor was apprehensive and concerned about the boy getting disappointed and losing trust in God if his eyes were not healed, especially as a new believer. Nonetheless, he prayed with Jeremy that God would heal his eyes.

By the next day, the most amazing miracle of God occurred. This boy who could barely make out distinct images all his life and had needed to be led around camp the night before had suddenly become the talk of the camp. When he woke, he could see perfectly without his glasses. When asked what happened to him, Jeremy said simply, in a matter-of-fact manner, that Jesus had healed him! This boy demonstrated the power of simple faith. He was told that Jesus had forgiven him of all his sins and was able to heal his diseases. He believed what he was told. The Holy Spirit within him nudged him to pray to receive his healing and he did. As a result a miracle occurred.

Jesus calls you to have the faith of a little child

That is why Jesus asked all believers to be like little children when it comes to our faith. "And [Jesus] said, Truly I say to you, unless you repent (change, turn about) and become like little children [trusting, lowly, loving, forgiving], you can never enter the kingdom of heaven [at all]. Whoever will humble himself therefore and become like this little child [trusting, lowly, loving, forgiving] is greatest in the kingdom of heaven" (Matthew 18:3–4, Amplified). You too can see God do great things in your life, but you need to have the faith of a child.

Faith Involves Certainty that God Will Act
but Uncertainty in How He Will Act

When Moses led an exodus of more than two million Israelites out of slavery in Egypt, they camped by the Red Sea as they were rapidly pursued by *all* the army of King Pharaoh, including all the horses, chariots, horsemen, and troops of Egypt. Very quickly, the army caught up with the utterly terrified Israelites, who saw no hint of an escape route for themselves. They were trapped by Pharaoh's army behind them and the Red Sea in front of them and they very quickly believed they were all going to perish. There were no ships to climb onto and sail away from this mighty army. Even if there had been ships, they would hardly have saved more than a mere fraction of the hordes of Israelites.

God always finishes what He begins

There was absolutely no way out, which magnified the panic and drove the Israelites to utter fury toward Moses for putting them in this predicament. The people of Israel, in facing their outer courts, could only see the magnitude of the challenge that confronted them. Moses' eyes, on the other hand, were firmly focused on His Most Holy Place where he resolutely believed God would move in a very different and miraculous way to save His people. Moses did not know exactly what God was going to do, but his existing relationship with God led him to believe and have complete trust that God would come through for him as He had done several times in the past. As a result, Moses was able to step up to a challenge that overwhelmed his peers and take control of the situation. "Moses answered the people, 'Do not be afraid. Stand firm and you will see the deliverance the LORD will bring you today. The Egyptians you see today you will never see again. The LORD will fight for you; you need only to be still'" (Exodus 14:13–14).

It is obvious from these comments, "The Lord will fight for you; you only need to be still," that Moses did not know exactly *how* God was going to deliver the Israelites. If he had known, he would have been more specific about the delivery method. He just knew from his relationship with God that God always comes through and that He finishes what He begins. He had not led the people of Israel to the Red Sea after performing so many miracles in Egypt only to have them humiliated and taken back or slaughtered by the Egyptian army.

Similarly, the more situations in your own life that you can release to God and allow Him to act on your behalf, the more you are likely to build up your faith and trust God to act on your behalf during all the challenging situations and times you face.

Faith Involves Obedience

In the middle of panic and consternation by the Israelites trapped behind the Red Sea, Moses cried out to God. God then gave Moses specific instructions to follow in order to activate a method of deliverance that was previously inconceivable to any human mind. *God will do the same for you when you trust Him.*

> Then the LORD said to Moses, "Why are you crying out to me? Tell the Israelites to move on. Raise your staff and stretch out your hand over the sea to divide the water so that the Israelites can go through the sea on dry ground." ... Then Moses stretched out his hand over the sea, and all that night the LORD drove the sea back with a strong east wind and turned it into dry land. The waters were divided, and the Israelites went through the sea on dry ground, with a wall of water on their right and on their left. (Exodus 14:15–16, 21–22)

This passage illustrates three very important attributes of faith.

Faith usually demands action on God's Word. You must not only believe God but must *act* on His Word. In retrospect, we all know the end of Moses' exodus story, and it now seems natural that Moses raised up his staff and stretched out his hand in obedience as commanded by God in order to part the sea. However, to the Israelites, this must have been a strange and ridiculous response to the situation they were being confronted with. Here they were, tired, hungry, and terrified while being pursued by a very powerful enemy they knew well. This enemy had kept them in slavery for four hundred years and had exerted his powers at will over them during this period, and they were well aware of the consequences awaiting them once they were captured and taken back as slaves.

To magnify matters, they were standing face to face with a formidable natural enemy in front of them in the form of the Red Sea. They surely knew that the waters of the Red Sea were too deep to wade through, with an average depth of 1,608 feet and up to 7254 feet in some parts. Faced with these hopeless choices, all the angry eyes were firmly fixed on Moses.

The people must have been dumbfounded to watch and see that the only thing the man who had put them in this predicament could do was to lift up a staff and stretch out his hands toward the imposing sea. While God gave Moses these "crazy" instructions, the Israelites were not privy to any of them. Even though they were not educated in any of the laws of physics, what Moses was doing simply could not have made any sense to them. Yet Moses did not question God's judgment and ask the logical "are you serious?" question in response to God's command. Instead, he immediately acted on God's command, raising his staff and stretching out his hand just as he had been commanded. Even as he was doing this, it is likely Moses was expecting angels to descend from heaven and surround the pursuing army, or that fire would come down and devour them. Instead, God moved mysteriously as only He can.

Believe God? Then do what He says!

A whistling sound of a gentle eastern breeze soon built into a powerful, howling storm. The storm methodically formed waves that did not come down to the shore as might have been expected to pound the mesmerized Israelites. Instead the waves began to separate the sea into two vertical columns, inch by inch, crafting and sculpting the most famous avenue of passage from slavery into freedom ever recorded. Before their unbelieving eyes, the Israelites watched in awe as one of the most amazing miracles in recorded history was performed. The sea that had been a barrier to their freedom was now a dry and safe corridor that led them away from their unrelenting enemy.

In the same manner as Moses, only your complete trust and obedience can be used by God to perform miracles in your life during every trial you go through. *Belief and trust are only useful to you if they compel you to act.* If you say you have belief and complete trust in God, and you do not do what He is asking you because it does not make sense, is against your own idea as to what should happen, or it may make you seem foolish to others, then you are deceiving yourself and you will never accomplish anything for Him. He in turn will never seem to be coming through for you. You will struggle and the trials of life will soon overwhelm and exhaust you.

This is why James, a leader of the early church in Israel and the brother of Jesus said, "For as the body without the spirit is dead, so faith without works is dead also" (James 2:26, KJV).

If Moses had simply told the Israelites that he believed God *would* save them, but he did not follow through on the command given by God, the Israelites would have perished, even though that was not God's intent for their lives. Similarly, many people who say that God no longer performs miracles or does anything special in their lives are people who claim to have faith but are not tapping in and listening to what God is asking them to do. Sometimes, God puts the answer to your situation right in front of you, and asks you to do something simple to actualize it, but the simplicity or the lack of logic in what is demanded stops many people from getting their solution. Others are too busy trying to do things in their own way to follow God's commands to follow. Others yet say they have faith, but they refuse to do anything because they expect God to spoon feed them. God can put the food in front of you, but *you* have to eat it. *Which category do you fall in?* Faith should be a strong motivator in your life that leads you to action (or works) in a way that does not always make sense in earthly terms because the action is in response to God (1 Thessalonians 1:3).

Faith in action sometimes means keeping still. Faith in action does not mean you must always be *physically* doing something. Sometimes the action demanded by God may be to do something physically unique and possibly against the grain when all others around you are doing nothing (e.g., Noah building an ark when there was not a single sign of rain). At other times faith calls for you not to be doing anything in the flesh, but to be active in praying, listening and waiting on God while others are busy actively doing something that God has not called you to do (e.g., panicking in the middle of a storm or fleeing in a certain direction). Praying for discernment between the two is very important.

While Jesus was often doing things in obedience to God, His faith in His heavenly Father often led Him to do nothing when everyone around Him was urging Him to act. This includes one such occasion toward the end of His earthly ministry when soldiers came with the Jewish high priests to arrest Jesus in the garden of Gethsemane. One of His disciples, Peter, felt a need to do something to protect Jesus, using his sword to cut off the ear of the servant of the high priest who was with the soldiers. Jesus could have called down angels from heaven to destroy his captors. However, He did not take any action, even as He was continuously struck, spat on, and slapped[6] because His eyes were firmly fixed on His Most Holy Place where

God the Father had instructed Him to endure all this without acting—so that you and I could live forever. "'Put your sword back in its place,' Jesus said to him, 'for all who draw the sword will die by the sword. Do you think I cannot call on my Father, and He will at once put at My disposal more than twelve legions of angels? But how then would the Scriptures be fulfilled that say it must happen in this way?'" (Matthew 26:52–54).

Jesus endured humiliation and even death because His eyes did not deviate from God.[7] He saw through the glaze of pain with the eyes of faith, the joy that His Father was setting before Him.[8] That empowered Him to endure. Faith demands complete belief such that when God either asks you to do something or to be doing nothing; your only response will be to obey fully. Sometimes the instruction God gives is for you to "Be still and know that I am God."[9] At other times, it is to "raise your staff and stretch out your hand over the sea." The key principle is obedience to what God has called you to do. Acting when God has told you to rest is as much folly as resting when He has given clear instructions to act. Whether you are resting or acting, you must always be praying and listening to what God is telling you to do.

Faith is being certain of what you cannot see

Faith is clear spiritual vision. When you learn to develop your faith, you will have a clear spiritual vision about God's ability, even when there is no physical clarity about what He will do. Sometimes, God will take you on a journey that could be very unsettling, even if you have learned to trust Him and believe that He will take care of you. This journey would be outright terrifying if you have no true or child like belief in Jesus. This journey could be through physical illness, persecution, the sudden loss of your job, loss of a loved one, or some other trial. Your true level of faith will determine how you respond. While it is normal to have some trepidation about how God will work, there should never be any reason for panic for those who know and trust Him. God knows what you hope for and will give you a certainty about your future that you would not otherwise have, as noted by the author of the book of Hebrews.

"Now faith is being sure of what we hope for and *certain of what we do not see*" (Hebrews 11:1, emphasis added).

The certainty is belief that God will come through. The certainty of faith is both a gift and a fruit,[10] both coming from the Holy Spirit, and which is reinforced by keeping a close relationship with Him in prayer, regular fasting, and reading His word. It is accomplished by keeping your eyes firmly on your Most Holy Place where the Holy Spirit resides.

All great men and women of faith learn to believe and trust God and accomplish extraordinary things because their "spiritual vision" supersedes their physical vision.

Elisha was one of the most powerful and spiritually connected prophets in Israel during the times of the Old Testament. He was so connected with God and what God was doing that he often knew what was going to happen before it did. He was thus a messenger that God used to alert the king of Israel about the plans of the enemies of Israel before they could be executed against Israel. In one such occasion, Ben-Hadad, the king of Aram, was at war with Israel (2 Kings 6:8–18). As the king made plans to attack Israel, Elisha knew all that was going on and was able to send the information about his plans to the king of Israel. In fact, it was almost as if he was in the room with the king of Aram when the plans were being made. This infuriated the king of Aram, who believed there was a spy amongst his officers. However, the officers pointed out to the king that it was Elisha giving away all the secrets without being told a word about them.

Elisha had clear spiritual vision. As a result of Elisha's clear spiritual vision, the king of Aram decided to capture him to stop his perceived treachery. During the night, with a strong army of his men on horses and chariots, the king surrounded the city of Dothan, where Elisha was located. Elisha's servant woke up in the morning, and all he could see was a huge army surrounding the city, and he was terrified. However, Elisha, with his clear spiritual vision could see more than the physical realm, and as a result was able to reassure his servant as noted in the following passage: "'Don't be afraid,' the prophet answered. 'Those who are with us are more than those who are with them.' And Elisha prayed, 'Open his eyes, LORD, so that he may see.' Then the LORD opened the servant's eyes, and he looked and saw the hills full of horses and chariots of fire all around Elisha. As the enemy came down toward him, Elisha prayed to the LORD, 'Strike this army with blindness.' So he struck them with blindness, as Elisha had asked" (2 Kings 6:16–18, NIV 2011).

So while his servant only saw the enemy in the physical realm, Elisha saw what God was doing to counter this in the spiritual realm. God is able to do the same for you and for me, but we need to have a close relationship with him borne out of obedience and regular communication.

Moses had clear spiritual vision. Similarly, it was Moses' spiritual vision that caused him to persevere in delivering the children of Israel from bondage. "By faith [Moses] left Egypt, not fearing the king's anger; he persevered because he *saw* Him who is invisible" (Hebrews 11:27, emphasis added). No one would argue that it is impossible to see something that is invisible. It is very clear that the "sight" being referred to here is a spiritual one. Similarly, as a believer, you must learn to fix your eyes on Jesus and see Him for who He is. He is bigger than any problem you may be facing; surrender your situation to Him and then watch Him move on your behalf.

"Let us fix our eyes on Jesus, the author and perfecter of our faith" (Hebrews 12:2). Your spiritual eyes are what you should fix on Jesus, the perfect role model for faith. They will help you to endure while God is carrying you through your journey. Spiritual eyes are sharpened by trusting God even for the little things in your life. Learn to pray to God to help you in the small and the big trials you are going through. Regularly record the things He has done for you, so they can serve as a reminder of His abilities when the big trials come. You will then be able to resist the temptation to believe the other voices that are likely to come to you from your outer court into your mind during the storms of your life, telling you God cannot help you. God will surely deliver you from every storm that comes your way through your ongoing faith in Him.

Pray This Prayer with Me:

Dear God, I pray that You give me a clear spiritual vision so I can see all of Your plans for me and that my faith will be strengthened both during quiet and buoyant periods of my life, and also during turbulent periods when I am going through trials and challenges. Make every challenge I face in my life an opportunity for my faith in You to increase. Help me to always know when to be still and when You are calling me to action, and to be found obedient in both situations. In Jesus' most precious name I pray, amen.

1. 1 Corinthians 12:7–11.
2. 1 Corinthians 12:12–20.
3. 1 Corinthians 12:31.
4. Luke 11:13.
5. The name has been changed.
6. Matthew 26:67–68.
7. Matthew 26:47–54.
8. Hebrews 12:2.
9. Psalm 46:10.
10. Galatians 5:22.

CHAPTER 22

The House of God Is a House of Faith, Part 2

(Session 11b)

Man: "Seeing is believing." God: "Believing is seeing, amen."

Faith Goes against the Grain

Another principle of faith to be learned from the miracle of the parting of the Red Sea is that faith usually goes against the grain. When you are following through on your faith in God, it is possible you will be the only person who believes in what God has told you or asked you to do. None of the children of Israel believed Moses could save them against the vast and advancing army of the Egyptians. Here's what they had to say to Moses: "Was it because there were no graves in Egypt that you brought us to the desert to die? What have you done to us by bringing us out of Egypt? Didn't we say to you in Egypt, 'Leave us alone; let us serve the Egyptians'? It would have been better for us to serve the Egyptians than to die in the desert!" (Exodus 14:11–12)

Moses could easily have said, "My goodness, everybody believes we are doomed. I must be nuts to think otherwise. Why am I going ahead with this plan when millions of others think it is a crazy plan?" When you are acting on faith in God, you will often be going against the crowds and conventional wisdom. If you allow popular opinion or conventional wisdom to dictate your obedience to God, your faith will be rendered useless. Moses went against the grain because the relationship he had with God was more powerful and more important to him than his popularity and his standing with his people. His eyes were firmly fixed on his Most Holy Place. Similarly, you must hold on to your relationship with God above any other relationship you have in order for God's miracles to be accomplished in your life.

In the Gospels, there is a story of a woman who had been having problems with bleeding for twelve years who heard that Jesus was in town. She had already spent years seeking all the help she could get and had spent most of her earnings on doctors, to no avail. She joined the large crowds of people who were trying to tap into Jesus' obvious powers for healing and other problems they had. However, while others were simply in awe of Jesus, waiting for Jesus to do something, this woman was motivated to take action by her fixed, firm belief that touching Jesus would heal her.

> A large crowd followed and pressed around Him. And a woman was there who had been subject to bleeding for twelve years. She had suffered a great deal under the care of many doctors and had spent all she had, yet instead of getting better she grew worse. When she heard about Jesus, she came up behind Him in the crowd and touched His cloak, because she thought, "If I just touch His clothes, I will be healed." Immediately her bleeding stopped and she felt in her body that she was freed from her suffering. (Mark 5:24–29)

In the same way, God will heal you when you believe in Him and then take action based on your belief.

Belief in God plus Action Equals Miracles

This woman had a lot of reason to have lost all hope. She could have been facing her outer court where all she would have seen was the impossibility of her situation, the reminder that she had already tried everything humanly possible and was actually getting worse. She could have had the fear of disappointment and ridicule by others if the illogicality of her faith in Jesus had been flawed. Instead, she turned and faced her Most Holy Place where all she saw was Jesus. She went against the grain. In her indomitable spirit, she was firm in her belief that she would be healed, but it was her action that led to her relief. In a beautiful illustration of faith in action, belief ("If I just touch His clothes, I will be healed") married action (she made her way through the crowds and touched Him) and a miracle was born. There were others in the crowd who were also pressing, but they were waiting for Jesus to do something to receive their own healing. This woman believed and acted and ended up being singled out by Jesus for her faith.

"[Jesus] said to her, 'Daughter, your faith has healed you. Go in peace and be freed from your suffering'" (Mark 5:34). The severity and duration of her problem was not a deterrent to her, and neither was it to God. All God saw was the total faith coupled with action in this woman. Similarly, your faith must always spur you to obedience as the evidence of your complete trust in God, no matter how big your problem is and you must be prepared to go against the grain if the situation demands it. A word of caution: what you believe God has asked you to do must never conflict with the Word of God as written in the Bible. If you believe God is asking you to do something that is directly contradictory to His word, you are very mistaken.

Faith Comes from Hearing

We are told that the woman with the bleeding problem received her healing by touching Jesus. However, she came to Jesus "when she heard about Jesus."[1] Hearing about Jesus and what He has done for other people is a very important aspect of building your faith. "Consequently, faith comes from hearing the message, and the message is heard through the word about Christ" (Romans 10:17, NIV 2011).

This is one of the many reasons it is important to read your Bible regularly. There are numerous examples in it of God moving in the lives of those who trust in Him.[2] It is also why Christians should record and share their testimony of what God is doing in your lives, so as to encourage someone else who may be going through the same thing. Record what God has done in your life and share it with others. You never know how your word of encouragement will be used by God to increase the faith of someone who is struggling with their faith at that very moment.

Faith Is Your Spiritual Console

As a further illustration of faith, I want to introduce to you the concept of faith as your "spiritual console." Consider all the powerful computers sold by sweet-talking salesmen and saleswomen in retail stores and through glitzy advertisements on the Internet, on TV, or in print around the world every day. The ability of the salesperson to sell you a computer depends on the persuasive power of his or her words in convincing you that the computer in question has the ability to make a difference to your life. This person's job is to make you understand the special capacity of each computer in meeting your perceived expectations, or at least to validate your good judgment of the one you are interested in prior to separating you from your money before you leave for home with your new gadget.

This new computer is then proudly brought home with great expectation and hope of its power to improve your life and great intentions to be used for different purposes. These may be perhaps to play games, possibly for work, and often for other purposes such as communicating and networking with your friends or reading the latest news. Within the heart of your new computer is something called the central processing unit, or CPU. This is the part of the computer that carries out all the instructions for the programs installed on the computer. The CPU is the "software execution" arm of the computer, the part that gets things done. When you turn on your computer, the CPU is standing ready to process any commands you give to it to activate the game, drawing, or other special programs on your computer. The CPU is thus a very important part of your computer.

However, there is another key component of your computer known as the console. The console is the part of your computer that allows you to "talk" and "listen" to your CPU. The console contains the input device used to manually operate, and to give and receive instructions to your CPU. Common examples of consoles are the keyboard on your laptop or desktop computer, or the remote controller used to play popular video games such as the Nintendo Wii games.

You need to do something with the console in order to execute the programs on your computer. It does not matter how much you trust all the information you got from your sales agent about your computer's abilities; how powerful and fast you believe the CPU is, or how wonderful all the latest games on the computer are. If you do not utilize the console the computer's CPU will be useless to you. You must use the console to ensure that your CPU does what it is programmed to do. When my children are playing their Nintendo Wii games, they use the console to tell the video game they are playing what to do. This is actualized by holding the remote wireless controller in one hand and waving it around or turning it purposefully to send instructions to the CPU of their Wii. They are rewarded by seeing characters on their video screen jump over mountains and rivers, or tennis balls fly over nets or racing cars speed across tracks at supernormal speeds. If they were not interacting through their remotes and getting results that reinforce their actions positively, not only would their behavior seem very odd indeed, they would also soon quit playing the game and condemn the game box as useless because they would not get any results. Furthermore, if they do not have or they were to lose their console, they could not play any of their games.

This is the essence of faith. Faith is your "spiritual console." You may say you trust God and believe He is able to do everything you desire of Him. However, until you actually tap into your spiritual console, which is your faith, you are deceiving yourself and depriving yourself of the power of God in your life. The wireless remote is not responsible for the wonderful games that can be played on the Wii. Those games are there ready to be tapped, but without the console, the games are useless.

Faith enables you to interact with the "fully loaded" God in you

Many people never tap into their spiritual console in order to execute the power God has released into their lives and then complain that God does not do anything. God's power is there whether you do anything or not. It is only when you tap into it that something happens for you. Moses by raising his staff and waving his hands over the Red Sea was utilizing his spiritual console. Jesus by waving His hand and saying, "Quiet, be still" to rough sea waters was also tapping into His spiritual console. If you are wondering why there is no display or any evidence of power in your life, it could simply be because you are stuck with reading about how powerful your God is, but you have never yet bothered to activate your spiritual console to access His power. The woman with the longstanding bleeding problem tapped into her spiritual console by reaching out and touching Jesus and she received her healing. Can you imagine abandoning your fully loaded new computer because when you turn it on, the programs do not run by themselves?

Similarly, a "fully loaded" God is useless to you without you activating your spiritual console known as faith. Belief is a necessary but insufficient component of faith. Faith goes beyond belief in the power of God and extends into demonstration of trust in action. Even the demons believe that Jesus Christ is the Son of God and they fear and tremble when they are in His presence.[3]

Steps toward Activating Your Faith

1. Get Plugged In

In activating your spiritual console of faith, first you have to get plugged in. If your computer is not plugged into an electrical outlet, it will not work. Similarly, if you are not plugged into your source of power, Jesus Christ, you will not experience any miracles in your life. You get plugged in by reading God's Word, praying, and communicating with Him every day.

2. Get Turned On

Even if your computer is plugged in, if it is not turned on, it will not work for you. Similarly, since you are the temple of the Living God and His Spirit is within you, you have to learn to "turn on" the Holy Spirit living within you. You have to learn to suppress all the external influences that are drowning out your ability to hear the voice of the Holy Spirit within you so that He is fully released to be active and to guide you. You do this by learning to meditate quietly and listen to the small still voice within you every day, and obey what He is telling you (*consistent with the Word of God!*). Getting turned on is predicated on obedience as we discussed in the previous session. If you are not following the rules for booting your computer, it will not come on no matter how eager you are to play all the games or use all the programs on it, or even how good you are in doing so. Similarly, obedience to God's laws is a key ingredient to activating faith. If you are not following His rules, the influence of the Holy Spirit in you will be snuffed out and you will not experience any miracles in your life.

Practice activating your spiritual console

3. Get Tapping!

Once you have your computer plugged in and turned on, the next step is to get tapping and give instructions to your CPU either through your keyboard or through your touch screen or a remote wireless controller, to activate whichever program you want to use on it. Similarly, with God, you have to activate your spiritual console by doing what God has asked you to do, either from your prayer time, reading the Word, or listening to the Holy Spirit. Many people give up on God because they believe in Him but do not understand why He does nothing in their lives. God will do nothing in your life if you do not cooperate with Him and do your part, even if you are plugged in and turned on. Even the free gift of salvation requires that you do your part and accept Jesus Christ as your savior. If you have complete trust in God, you should be constantly seeking His opinion in prayer and reading His Word and then doing what He tells you to do, even if it seems silly or stupid to others. Your faith should always stir you to action—or "active inaction," one way or another, based on instructions you receive from God. "Active inaction" is when you are very active in praying and listening to instructions from God while waiting on Him.

In these situations, it appears to the outside world that you are doing nothing, but you are actively waiting on the Lord. The more you practice using the console on your computer, the better you get at using it to get the most out of the games and other programs on your computer. Similarly, the more you move beyond the belief part of faith and practice obeying God's commands, the more you will see God move in your life.

Activating My "Spiritual Console"

On several occasions, I have had to activate my own spiritual console. One such occasion occurred on September 13, 2008. I sat in the passenger seat, preparing to return home with my friend Doug Carr after attending a Christian men's retreat at Camp Michawana in Michigan with a group of other believers. We had enjoyed a wonderful weekend of prayer, praise, and teaching by Tom Herman, an ex-cop turned evangelist and author. Our stay had been "blessed" by torrential showers of rain that confined us indoors, ensuring that we were able to share quality time of indoor games and personal stories but which had also caused several large branches to fall off trees and land on the roads and create cloudy mists that substantially reduced driving visibility.

As we were about to leave the camp, I felt a strong nudging from the Holy Spirit to pray and dedicate our one-hour journey back home to the Lord. I obeyed and said out loud a brief but specific prayer, thanking God in advance for a safe trip home, and declaring that there would be no accidents, no delays, and no vehicular breakdowns on the way home, to which Doug said a big amen. As we drove from the camp into the dark and misty evening about thirty-five or forty miles per hour, we commiserated on a wide-ranging variety of topics. After traveling for just about one mile, we made our way around a blind curve when suddenly around the curve we were confronted by a very large tree lying horizontally across the road. Based on our speed and distance from the tree, it was clear that we were on a direct and inevitable collision path with the trunk. On the side of the road we were on was a ditch with barely enough car room between it and the tree trunk, and there was no room to pass on the other side. Just as it seemed there was no escape, Doug somehow managed to make a quick swerving motion that was just wide enough to maneuver the vehicle around the tree and narrowly prevent us from falling into the ditch. However, as the car avoided both the tree and the ditch, there was a grinding sound following which the car went a short distance and then came to screeching halt.

Meanwhile, in a van right behind us were some other friends, Nicholas Olomu, Javon Jones, and John Schafer. They were clearly oblivious to the tree in their path and were coming full tilt toward it. As I saw the beam of their front lights flash behind us, I instinctively jumped out of our car and started to run toward them, waving and praying avidly for the same hand that delivered our car from disaster to deliver theirs as well. Miraculously, without seeing me, Nick made the same swerving motion at the last moment around the log and away from the ditch and came to a halt behind Doug's car. After praising God for the averted tragedies, and shifting the log as much as we could off the road, we all approached Doug's car, in which he was fully engaged in a futile attempt to restart the engine. The car was completely stalled and Doug was trying to call General Motors' "OnStar" customer communication service to access the car's built-in computer system to diagnose the cause of his stalled vehicle and to receive help to get it going again. He repeatedly made the call, but there was no response.

Reactivating My Spiritual Console

Having already had one part of our pre-travel prayers answered (*there will be no accidents*), I decided to continue to utilize my spiritual console so that the rest of the prayers would be fully addressed (*there will be no breakdowns and there will be no delays*). I called all the other men around the car and asked that we all lay hands on the car, and we all activated our faith in praying together in agreement that the car would restart. To the rest of the "normal" world, this would be a silly and foolish act, laying hands on an inanimate object to restore "life" to it. However, as we finished praying, I asked Doug to restart the car, fully expecting God to answer our prayer.

God did answer immediately, but not in the way we had expected. The car did not start, but instantaneously after our prayer, the OnStar agent who had been unreachable earlier suddenly called back. She immediately took remote control of the car's computers and was immediately able to diagnose that the problem with the car was a problem with the emission valve. Based on this comment, Doug, an amateur expert on cars realized the catalytic converter may have become unplugged from underneath the car during the harsh motion involved in getting around the log. He handed a flashlight to Javon, who looked underneath and confirmed the diagnosis with a clearly visible plug lying on the ground. Lying on a blanket on the ground under the car, he connected the plug back to the converter, after which we were all thrilled to hear the beautiful sound of the engine revving again. The rest of our prayers now completely answered with no breakdowns and no substantive delay, we gave glory to God for the warning of the Holy Spirit prior to our departure and for His answering our prayers so specifically when we activated our spiritual console. We were able to make it back home in just over the hour it would have taken without this incident.

Just as God responded to our faith on this and other occasions, you can be certain that He will also respond to yours as you practice tapping into your spiritual console. The more you take a step of faith, the more you will be rewarded by God and be able to unleash all the great opportunities and powerful things He has planned for your life. You need to practice this regularly so you can learn to trust God in the little and the "silly" things so you can gain courage during the major storms of your life. May your spiritual vision be so clear that your focus is always on the powerful and trustworthy God in your Most Holy Place instead of the magnitude of the problems in front of you.

Jesus Christ, the Master of Demonstrating His Faith

The master of demonstrating faith in God and utilizing His spiritual console to the fullest was of course our Lord Jesus Christ. As a result of His close relationship with God the Father, Jesus constantly showed His faith by doing things in unconventional ways. His faith in God led Him to challenge all the logical assumptions of His time. When it was time to pay the temple taxes, Jesus "saw" money in a fish's mouth with His spiritual eyes. His belief and complete trust that God had shown Him this image of the fish, then led Him to ask Peter to go fishing at the lake and to open the mouth of the first fish he caught. Peter's faith in Jesus led him to activate his own spiritual console and obey, even though Peter would surely have wondered about the conventionality of looking for money in a fish. As a result of his faith, and in spite of the "stupidity" of it, when he did catch the first fish, and the fish's mouth was opened, there was enough money in it to pay the taxes for both Peter and for Jesus.[4]

It was also activation of His spiritual console that enabled Jesus to walk on water; to feed five thousand men, women, and children with two loaves of bread and five fish; to turn water into wine; to heal the blind, the deaf, and the lame; to raise people from the dead; and to cast out demons. As noted before, the ultimate demonstration of faith in God was the complete trust Jesus had in God when He allowed Himself to be crucified on the cross even though He did not want to die. While love kept Jesus *on* the cross, it was faith that led Him *to* the cross. It was faith that God knew what He was doing and that the long-term rewards of the journey He was on were greater than the monumental inconvenience of the suffering He endured. Jesus, who is the perfect role model, was called the pioneer and perfecter of faith exactly for this reason.

"And let us run with perseverance the race marked out for us, fixing our eyes on Jesus, the pioneer and perfecter of faith. For the joy set before Him He endured the cross, scorning its shame, and sat down at the right hand of the throne of God. Consider Him who endured such opposition from sinners, so that you will not grow weary and lose heart" (Hebrews 12:1b–3).

Notice that for all the glory of the miracles Jesus performed, His most remarkable act of faith was enduring the scorn of men and the cross. He trusted God even to the point of His death because He took an eternal view and believed that God's plan was the best for Him. This is what you are also called to do, trust your heavenly Father whose love for you has no parallel on earth, and always take an eternal view, remembering that you are only a temporary resident in this world. Fix your eyes on the most precious price in store for you, a crown of glory that will be presented to you when you begin your eternal life in the presence of the Creator of the universe in heaven. You will be in a place where there will be no more storms to contend with, no more tears to shed and no more diseases to battle with.[5] Instead, you will be in a place more beautiful than your mind could ever conceive. May the God of heaven give you a clear spiritual vision to have your eyes fixed on heaven in the same way our Lord Jesus did!

The Calmness of Faith

When you are fully exercising your faith, others may confuse it as a sign that you do not care, or more likely that you do not fully understand the gravity of the situation that confronts you. Once when Jesus was with His disciples on a boat, He was comfortably asleep in the stern while a furious storm with large waves slammed the boat and nearly swamped it. The terrified disciples woke Jesus up and asked Him, "Teacher, don't you care if we drown?" (Mark 4:38b). The disciples focused on their outer court and became intimidated by the power of the danger that confronted them. Jesus woke up and calmly rebuked the wind and the waves with three words—"Quiet! Be still!"—and the wind died down completely (Mark 4:39–41).

Why did Jesus not panic? Because His eyes were firmly on His Most Holy Place where He had complete belief and trust in God the Father. He was confident of safety based on the time He had spent praying and talking to God and the fact that He had experienced the power of God previously. He knew that He had command over all the elements through the power of the Holy Spirit resident in Him. Most importantly, He knew God's plan for His life was not for Him to drown while on a boat. He had this confidence based on His close personal relationship with God and a full understanding of God's intent for His life.

Similarly, as I have developed a regular habit of praying and fasting and committing every situation I am confronted with to God, I have found amazing calmness in tough situations where people around me have panicked, even when I am the one in the center of the storm. It does not mean I do not have momentary periods of fear. It just means I can overcome the fears through remembering God's promises and what He has done for me in previous situations. When you have a regular habit of praying before you do anything including going on any journey, whether short or long, you have the full confidence that God will watch over you, no matter what the circumstances may be. While others may panic when there is severe turbulence on your plane ride, you can have full assurance that God will keep you safe. If you have committed your work situation to God and you know that you are in His will where you are, you have nothing to fear, even when your enemies threaten you and your faith is being challenged.

Breast Cancer Healed through Faith

When one of our family friends, a physician with strong Christian faith was diagnosed with breast cancer, she simply turned into her Most Holy Place, going into her prayer closet and committing days and weeks to praying and to trusting in God. The type of cancer she had was considered the most aggressive form and there was evidence it had spread beyond the local lymph nodes, suggesting a poor prognosis. She was strongly encouraged by her colleagues to leave town and seek out the best possible cancer doctors and clinics to receive her treatment. Her colleagues were bewildered when she did not seem concerned about the pathology reports and they were the ones who were "bothered" enough to call around to confer with colleagues elsewhere about how to proceed. They thought she was being cavalier about her diagnosis and did not understand the gravity of her prognosis.

She, on the other hand, fully understood but chose to stand on her faith in God. She simply took the route of "active inaction," receiving instructions from God in prayer that it was okay to receive her care locally and found peace in her faith and astounded everyone by the way she "sailed" through the treatment. Had she received word from God to go elsewhere to receive her treatment, she would have gone, but these were not her instructions. As a result, her recovery time was miraculously short and she was back at work at almost record time. Everyone marveled at her calmness and other women with similar diagnoses have subsequently sought her out to get encouragement and gain strength for their own journey.

She is now several years out from her diagnosis and cancer free. While she seemed calm and unconcerned about the gravity of her situation to everyone, our friend drew her strength from her relationship with Jesus Christ and her focus was always on her Most Holy Place. Recently, a physician colleague who had observed how this woman handled her trial and saw the light of Jesus continuously flowing through her as she continued on her journey of faith was so moved by her living testimony that they established a foundation in her honor to help children with cancer! I pray that you will also find calmness and hear the voice of God to similarly guide you through the storms of your life in turning toward your Most Holy Place, so that you reach God's goals for you and can also be an inspiration to others.

Does Faith Mean God Will Always Do What You Want?

Having faith does not always mean God will do what you want Him to do. However, it does mean He will always do what is best for you, whether you know it at the time or not. Faith should lead you to trust and follow God whether He does what you want or not. Jesus did not "want" to die but died out of love for you so that you could live and out of total conviction that He would be resurrected, conquer death forever, and receive an eternal reward as king of the universe. This was also the attitude of three Jewish boys, Shadrach, Meshach, and Abednego, who refused to bow down and worship the image of the king of Persia, even when they were threatened with being thrown into a fiery furnace. They had total confidence that God would rescue them. However, their eternally minded attitude was that even if God did not rescue them, they would not bow down because they did not want to destroy their long-term relationship with Him. They recognized that if God did not come to save them, He must have a bigger plan for them. Furthermore, they realized that life would not be worth living if they destroyed the most important relationship in their lives, their relationship with God. Thus, they were not afraid of King Nebuchadnezzar's threats.

"Shadrach, Meshach and Abednego replied to him, 'King Nebuchadnezzar, we do not need to defend ourselves before you in this matter. If we are thrown into the blazing furnace, the God we serve is able to deliver us from it, and He will deliver us from Your Majesty's hand. But even if He does not, we want you to know, Your Majesty, that we will not serve your gods or worship the image of gold you have set up'" (Daniel 3:16–18, NIV 2011).

Faith in God means you will never be afraid of any human being or any situation. Yes, you will have momentary fears, but the fears will not linger when you recognize that the one who is in you is greater than anyone who is in the world.[6] This can only happen if you consider your relationship to God as being more important than any other relationships you have. If you are married, your spouse should be your primary human partner, but it is your primary relationship with God that will sustain your marriage.

God came through for Shadrach, Meshach, and Abednego, and not a hair on their heads was harmed when they were thrown into the fiery furnace, even though the soldiers who threw them in there were instantly killed. Protection came for these boys because they valued their relationship with God more than life itself. I pray that you will learn to value your relationship with God more than your life itself, as this is what will sustain your life.

Building Up Your Faith

In order to build your faith, the first step is to hunger to draw near to God so you can fully appreciate who He is and what He is capable of doing (Hebrews 10:22). It is impossible to have complete trust in someone you do not know and who you do not have a relationship with. When you draw near to God through prayer, fasting, reading His word, and praising Him, God draws near to you in return.[7] The conditions are then created that allows His Holy Spirit to move from your Most Holy Place and spread to your remaining chambers—your Holy Place and your outer court. When your outer court gets influenced by the Holy Spirit, you will automatically be able to influence the world around you instead of being influenced and will draw others to God. You will receive divine vision directly from God who will guide you with specific instructions that you cannot possibly conceive on your own, and enable you to accomplish extraordinary things for His kingdom.

"Call to me and I will answer you and tell you great and unsearchable things you do not know" (Jeremiah 33:3). God is ready to do marvelous things in your life as you build up your faith in Him!

Pray This Prayer with Me:

Dear Father, I thank You so much for giving me faith as my spiritual console. Teach me how to always use this faith as a console to access Your full power so that Your plans for me will be activated. Help me to always keep my eyes on You so that my faith will not be snatched away. Help me have a calmness that is beyond human understanding in every situation I am in, no matter what others around me may think or how they may be reacting so that Your mighty name can be glorified in my life. In Jesus' mighty name I pray. Amen.

Questions to Ponder:

- Why should God be concerned if you do not believe His promises and act on them?
- Is it easy for you to believe God can overcome problems that seem impossible to you?
  - If the answer is no, how can you overcome this?
- Have you ever eagerly desired one of the spiritual gifts?
  - If so, which one, and how did you pursue getting this gift?
  - How had God rewarded you so far?
- Do you believe God is able to do miracles through you today just as He did through Moses and Jesus in biblical times?
- Has God ever done a miracle through your activating your spiritual console of faith?
  - If so, describe one such occasion.
- How can you keep your faith in God when everyone around you is panicking or moving in a certain direction?
- Have you ever utilized "active inaction" in your faith work?
  - If yes, describe how it felt to those around you.

Prayer Points

- Pray that God will enable you to completely trust and believe in Him and to obey Him when He calls you to act either through His word or through His Spirit nudging you in a manner consistent with His word.
- Pray that you will develop a close relationship with Jesus Christ that will enable you to emulate the type of faith He had when He walked the earth.
- Pray that God will increase your faith and enable it to grow like a mustard tree from a mustard seed.
- Pray that God will make it clear to you the occasions on which He wants you to act and those occasions on which He wants you to "be still and know *He* is God."
- Pray for clear spiritual vision to see what God is trying to do even when it is not obvious to you or others in the physical world.
- Pray that your church, workplace, neighborhoods, and nation will be filled with children of God who have an exuberant spirit of Jesus-like faith that will be transformative to them and to those around them.

1. Mark 5:27.
2. Hebrews 11.
3. James 2:19.
4. Matthew 17:24–27.
5. 2 Corinthians 4:17–18.
6. 1 John4:4.
7. James 4:8.

CHAPTER 23

The House of God Is a House of Hope, Part 1

(Session 12a)

When you say a situation or a person is hopeless, you are slamming the door in the face of God.—Charles L. Allen, American Methodist minister (1913-2005)

We have this hope as an anchor for the soul, firm and secure. It enters the inner sanctuary behind the curtain.—Hebrews 6:19

Defining Hope

Hope is defined as the feeling that you can have what you want or that future events will turn out for the best. It also sometimes describes a person or thing in which you center your expectations.[1]

Naomi was a woman who lost all hope in her life. She had left Bethlehem in Judah with her husband, Elimelek, and two sons, Mahlon and Kilion, to live temporarily in the foreign country of Moab because of a major famine that hit Bethlehem during her times.

Her hope for her future was anchored in her family taking care of her in her old age. Without social security or other source of income, most women in those days relied on relatives to look after them in their old age. Unfortunately for Naomi, her husband died early during her arrival in Moab, leaving her as a widow to care for her sons Mahlon and Kilion. Her hopes were rejuvenated when both Mahlon and Kilion got married to two wonderful Moabite women, Orpah and Ruth. However, ten years later Mahlon and Kilion also died, and along with them died any hope Naomi had for a bright future since neither her nor her daughters had any source of income.

Later on, Naomi heard that the conditions in Bethlehem had improved significantly, such that she decided to return home. Her daughters-in-law Orpah and Ruth prepared to go with her, but in her state of hopelessness, Naomi discouraged them from coming with her. She did not see a future for the foreign women without their Jewish husbands in Judah, because as foreign women, especially from a nation (Moab) that was viewed over generations as an enemy to Israel, they were unlikely to be accepted and would likely have been rejected and "condemned" to live as widows for the rest of their lives.

If Naomi had any other sons, things might have been different. In those days, if a man died and had an unmarried brother, the next unmarried brother was eligible to marry the widowed wife of the brother.[2] If there was no brother, the nearest closest male relative (known as a "guardian or kinsman redeemer") was eligible to marry the woman. Naomi did not even have this hope since she had no other children and she was too old to get married again. These were her words: "Return home, my daughters; I am too old to have another husband. Even if I thought there was still hope for me—even if I had a husband tonight and then gave birth to sons—would you wait until they grew up? Would you remain unmarried for them? No, my daughters. It is more bitter for me than for you, because the LORD's hand has turned against me!" (Ruth 1:12–13, NIV 2011).

Naomi had left Judah with a husband and two sons and great hope for her future but returned home to Judah almost "empty." While Orpah returned to her people, Ruth refused to go back and committed her life to being with Naomi. While Naomi had become a bitter woman because she had lost all hope for her future, Ruth's love in staying with her rekindled some of the hope Naomi had lost.

The Christians' Blessed Hope

Similarly, before giving your life to Christ, the storms of life can drain all hope from your life. You are also on a trajectory where there is no certainty of an eternity spent in the presence of God. When you give your life to Christ you receive the grace of a free and unwarranted gift, the gift of eternal life. You also receive the gift of a close friend (the Holy Spirit) who promises to love you and never leave you no matter what your circumstance in life may be. You do not earn or deserve this gift and friendship, but they are yours by virtue of the work Jesus did on the cross.

"But when the kindness and love of God our Savior appeared, He saved us, not because of righteous things we had done but because of His mercy. He saved us through the washing of rebirth and renewal by the Holy Spirit, whom He poured out on us generously through Jesus Christ our Savior, so that, having been justified by His grace, we might become heirs having the hope of eternal life" (Titus 3:4–7).

Jesus Christ is your "guardian redeemer"

As a result of God's gracious gift of Jesus, as a Christian you now have what is known as the "blessed hope." This is hope that is grounded in certainty that the same Christ that died and was resurrected for your sake will return at a future date. As a result you and all who believe in Him will be taken up with Him to spend eternity in a beautiful place called heaven.

"For the grace of God has appeared that offers salvation to all people ... while we wait for the blessed hope—the glorious appearing of our great God and Savior, Jesus Christ" (Titus 2:11, 13, NIV 2011). Jesus Christ is your guardian redeemer, the one who gives hope to anyone who believes in Him for a secure future both here on earth and eternally in heaven.

The Blessed Hope Is a Sure Thing

The blessed hope is not like the hope that is used in common language today, which always has a degree of uncertainty about it. Every human being hopes for something or some situation that is better or perceived to be more desirable than their current situation. Coaches often have their players visualize what winning would look like so that they can have something to look forward to. Every parent has high hopes for their children accomplishing great things in their lives. In neither of these scenarios nor any other type of hope based on humans is there a certainty that the hope will be fulfilled. Nonetheless, if you do not have hope for anything in life, then you have lost all reason for being alive. There is a grave emptiness associated with losing all hope; a void which only God can fill and which only He does in miraculous ways for those who trust in Him.

There is recognition that all human hope apart from the blessed hope is without certainty and may or may not be realized. Naomi's hope in life was somewhat rekindled by her friendship with Ruth and Ruth's selfless love for her. However, once they were both back in Judah, the stark reality of life had to be dealt with and they needed a source of food. As a result, Ruth volunteered to go and pick the leftover crops from a nearby field. As it turned out, the field belonged to a man named Boaz, who was a relative of Naomi's. Ruth started picking leftover crops from the field after the men working for Boaz had harvested their crops. She had no idea the field belonged to Boaz, nor did Boaz have any idea who Ruth was. When Boaz discovered Ruth on his field and inquired about her, he found out not only that she was a foreigner but that she had shown such great love and kindness to Naomi. Surprisingly, Boaz did not shun Ruth as would have been expected by cultural norms of the day but more than returned the same kindness to Ruth that she had shown Naomi. Boaz not only allowed Ruth to continue to pick crops, he ordered his men to leave extra crops for her.

Naomi's hope for the future was brightened significantly when Ruth returned home with more grain than she could have expected. Naomi discovered that the man who showed this kindness to Ruth was an unmarried close relative of hers who could be a guardian redeemer for the family and rescue both Ruth and Naomi from a life of poverty and the shame of not having offspring. "Her mother-in-law asked her, 'Where did you glean today? Where did you work? Blessed be the man who took notice of you!' Then Ruth told her mother-in-law about the one at whose place she had been working. 'The name of the man I worked with today is Boaz,' she said. 'The LORD bless him!' Naomi said to her daughter-in-law. 'He has not stopped showing his kindness to the living and the dead.' She added, 'That man is our close relative; he is one of our guardian-redeemers'" (Ruth 2:19–20, NIV 2011).

The word for *guardian-redeemer* in Hebrew is a legal term for someone who has the obligation to redeem a relative in serious difficulty. From a situation of a future filled with total destitution, Naomi was now in a situation where there was someone who could possibly be a provider for her and especially for her daughter-in-law. Naomi then hatched a plan consistent with the customs of the day where Ruth made it clear she would be willing to get married to Boaz if he would claim her as a guardian-redeemer, to enable their hope for a secure future to be realized.

In the most unlikely of circumstances, a destitute foreign Moabite woman ended up marrying a wealthy Jewish man much older than her. Even as the scenario was unfolding, there was no guarantee that Naomi's hope would be realized through her plan. Indeed, as it turns out, there was another man who was a closer relative and had "rights of first refusal" to marry Ruth, but he quickly backed out once the situation became clear to him and it was noted that Ruth a Moabite woman was part of the package he had to rescue. Boaz on the other hand, responded to Ruth's kindness and Naomi's ingenuity and ultimately the most amazing story unfolded of a Jewish man marrying outside the culture and taking a Moabite woman (Ruth 3–4). Ruth subsequently gave birth to Obed, the father of Jesse and the grandfather of King David. Ultimately, of course, Ruth was a direct ancestor of our Lord, Jesus Christ.

Just as Boaz was the guardian redeemer for Naomi and Ruth, Jesus Christ is the guardian-redeemer for all humanity. Each of us is in serious "legal" difficulty with our sins having separated us from any hope of a future in heaven, but Christ's blood purchased our future for us.

The Christian blessed hope is built firmly on the foundation of Jesus Christ who, through *His* death and resurrection, paved the way for *your* victory over death and eternal condemnation. Because Jesus' life, death, and resurrection were so compelling in revealing who He is, and because He continues to change lives today just as He did in times past and has shown Himself to be always true, you should have every confidence that He will return as promised and that your eternal salvation is guaranteed. Furthermore, as a Christian, you have been gifted with the Holy Spirit of God who was responsible for Christ's resurrection and who now resides in your Most Holy Place.

"And if the Spirit of Him who raised Jesus from the dead is living in you, He who raised Christ from the dead will also give life to your mortal bodies through His Spirit, who lives in you" (Romans 8:11).

Jesus has given you a deposit on this blessed hope of eternal life—the deposit of the Holy Spirit, which is all you need to enable you to live a life of certainty while you are on earth. "[Now] we have this [hope] as a sure and steadfast anchor of the soul [it cannot slip and it cannot break down under whoever steps out upon it—a hope] that reaches farther and enters into [the very certainty of the presence] within the veil" (Hebrews 6:19, Amplified).

An anchor is a device used to connect a vessel such as a boat to the bed of a body of water to prevent the vessel from drifting due to wind or current[3]. What the boat is anchored to will determine the degree of protection that will be afforded during storms. In this passage, we are told that your hope in Christ (the blessed hope) is a sure and steadfast anchor of your soul which will never break or fail. In other words, this particular hope is guaranteed to deliver on the promise of future salvation. In the next phrase, it is clear why this anchor is secure – because it is not an anchor that just holds on to the surface of the bed of the body of water which can be easily disentangled.

This particular anchor reaches farther and goes much deeper, entering into the very certainty of the presence within the veil. Behind the veil of course is the Most Holy Place in which resides the mercy seat and the presence of God's Spirit within your temple. In heaven's Tabernacle, Jesus Christ and God the Father are the presence behind the veil. Nothing is going to separate your soul from God because God is the bed on which the anchor to which your soul is hooked lies.

While you live, your hope in life—the hope that anchors your mind or your Holy Place with secure confidence—is based on the presence of the Holy Spirit in the hidden place behind the veil within your Most Holy Place. Your ability to interact fully and yield to the Holy Spirit within your temple will enable you to have full confidence not only of the future salvation of your soul for eternity but also assurance of hope in the fulfillment of God's plans for your life while you are on earth. "And hope does not put us to shame, because God's love has been poured out into our hearts through the Holy Spirit, who has been given to us" (Romans 5:5, 2011).

You can count on this: your hope in Jesus Christ will *never* put you to shame.

Hope Helps You Overcome

As a believer, the presence of the Holy Spirit within your temple should give you confidence that you will overcome even extreme conditions in your life. The love of God that is also characteristic of His Spirit enables you to persevere, to tolerate extraordinary circumstances and to triumph over impossible situations in your life. You can have the assurance that when you have asked God about His plans for your life and your life revolves around a vision or plan that has been validated by God through prayer and His word, then He will give you the strength and courage toward the realization of this vision.

Faith is complete trust and belief in God. It is what motivates you to step out and do what God has asked you to do, even when you cannot visualize what God is doing. However, hope is the assurance from God who does not tell lies that there is something better planned for you at the end of your faith journey; so that you can have the assurance that your faith journey will not be a useless and meaningless journey.

This sentiment was expressed by Paul in his letter to Titus: "Paul, a servant of God and an apostle of Jesus Christ to further the faith of God's elect and their knowledge of the truth that leads to godliness—in the hope of eternal life, which God, who does not lie, promised before the beginning of time" (Titus 1:1–2).

If there is no hope of eternal life, your having and manifesting faith that leads to godliness during life on earth would be a futile exercise. While going on your journey of faith, you will face discouragement, fear and doubts about what you are doing. Hope is what enables you to keep moving forward when these negative elements creep in. Hope is the flame of light that flashes each time you are about to give up when your battery meter is reading empty as you navigate the dark and perilous tunnels of life. It is the image that God sends to you of the fertile oasis of lush greenery that awaits you as you thirstily wade through the dry and sparse deserts of your life.

Just when your faith is beginning to wither, hope is what gives you endurance and keeps you on the journey as noted by Paul in his letter to the Thessalonians: "We continually remember before our God and Father your work produced by faith, your labor prompted by love, and your endurance inspired by hope in our Lord Jesus Christ" (1 Thessalonians 1:3).

Hope then, is when God gives you a glimpse of what that end result of your faith walk will look like. In the journey of life, the blessed hope of eternity in the presence of God in heaven should motivate you to continue to do good works and to trust God even when the day to day doubts and challenges of life creep into your Holy Place. In your own flesh, you do not possess this ability to have the hope to endure all situations. However, when you cooperate with the power of the Holy Spirit, you can "overflow" with hope in all situations.

"May the God of hope fill you with all joy and peace as you trust in Him, so that you may overflow with hope by the power of the Holy Spirit" (Romans 15:13).

Jacob, an Example of Hope Inspired by Love

Hope that is inspired by the love of God and specific obedience to Him is infallible. One of the most famous examples in the Bible of hope guided by love and instruction from God is the story of Jacob. Jacob had just received a blessing from his father, Isaac, who then gave him this command:

Hope is a glimpse of the end result of your faith walk with God

Do not marry a Canaanite woman. Go at once to Paddan Aram, to the house of your mother's father Bethuel. Take a wife for yourself there, from among the daughters of Laban, your mother's brother. May God Almighty bless you and make you fruitful and increase your numbers until you become a community of peoples. May He give you and your descendants the blessing given to Abraham, so that you may take possession of the land where you now reside as a foreigner, the land God gave to Abraham." Then Isaac sent Jacob on his way, and he went to Paddan Aram, to Laban son of Bethuel the Aramean, the brother of Rebekah, who was the mother of Jacob and Esau. (Genesis 28:1b–5, NIV 2011)

Jacob honored his father and did as he was told and set out to find a wife at the place his father had instructed him. While his father had blessed him and sent him on this journey, Jacob had no clue as to what he would actually encounter on the other end. In the middle of his journey of obedience, Jacob became tired and needed rest and some hope of a successful outcome for his journey and indeed for his future. As he lay down to rest, he had an incredible encounter with God that gave him all the confidence and hope he needed.

When he reached a certain place, he stopped for the night because the sun had set. Taking one of the stones there, he put it under his head and lay down to sleep. He had a dream in which he saw a stairway resting on the earth, with its top reaching to heaven, and the angels of God were ascending and descending on it. There above it stood the LORD, and he said: "I am the LORD, the God of your father, Abraham, and the God of Isaac. I will give you and your descendants the land on which you are lying. Your descendants will be like the dust of the earth, and you will spread out to the west and to the east, to the north and to the south. All peoples on earth will be blessed through you and your offspring. I am with you and will watch over you wherever you go, and I will bring you back to this land. I will not leave you until I have done what I have promised you." (Genesis 28:11–15)

In the midst of Jacob's fatigue, and very likely when he was having some degree of uncertainty about how his journey would turn out, God gave him hope through a picture of the gate of heaven with angels (*representing protection*) ascending and descending a ladder to earth. God also confirmed that his father, Isaac's, request to God that God should bless Jacob and make him fruitful had been heard.

Then Jacob made a vow, saying, "If God will be with me and will watch over me on this journey I am taking and will give me food to eat and clothes to wear so that I return safely to my father's household, then the LORD will be my God and this stone that I have set up as a pillar will be God's house, and of all that you give me I will give you a tenth." (Genesis 28:20–22, NIV 2011)

Jacob's experience so far also highlights the principle of obedience to God's commands—in this case, honoring your parents as an important precondition to receiving God's blessings. In this example, Jacob had not received anything yet, but God's Words of hope gave him a glimpse of his abundant future and assurance of protection.

Today, you have the full benefit and constant blessing of the Holy Spirit of God living within you and able to give you hope for all situations in your life, conditional on your obedience to God. When you seek His counsel through prayer, reading of His Word in the Bible, and are obedient to His instructions, then you too will receive all the hope you need for the faith journey of your life.

Hope Motivated by God's Love Never Leads to Shame

"Hope deferred makes the heart sick, but a longing fulfilled is a tree of life" (Proverbs 13:12). The love of God that has been poured into your heart through the Holy Spirit gives you the type of confident hope that does not lead to shame[4]. Overflowing with this type of hope may lead the world to misunderstand you and think you are a foolish optimist, and indeed may lead others to ridicule you or seek to take advantage of you. However, hope that is guided by the love of the Holy Spirit, involving situations that you have sought guidance from God will never lead to your shame. The hope that God had given Jacob about his future was put to test when he reached Paddan Aram, the place where he had been instructed to go find his future wife, Rachel. When Jacob saw Rachel, he was totally taken and smitten and immediately found himself in love with her (Genesis 28:18). In a story of extraordinary endurance, Jacob then worked for his uncle Laban for seven years in order to have the right to marry Rachel.

"So Jacob served seven years to get Rachel, but they seemed like only a few days to him because of his love for her" (Genesis 29:20). As a result of Jacob's obvious dedication and endurance guided by the hope he had of marrying his beloved Rachel, Jacob persevered. However, this same hope caused his uncle Laban to seek to take advantage of Jacob.

"Hope deferred makes the heart sick, but a longing fulfilled is a tree of life"

Then Jacob said to Laban, "Give me my wife. My time is completed, and I want to make love to her." So Laban brought together all the people of the place and gave a feast. But when evening came, he took his daughter Leah and brought her to Jacob, and Jacob made love to her. And Laban gave his servant Zilpah to his daughter as her attendant. When morning came, there was Leah! So Jacob said to Laban, "What is this you have done to me? I served you for Rachel, didn't I? Why have you deceived me?" Laban replied, "It is not our custom here to give the younger daughter in marriage before the older one. Finish this daughter's bridal week; then we will give you the younger one also, in return for another seven years of work." And Jacob did so. He finished the week with Leah, and then Laban gave him his daughter Rachel to be his wife. (Genesis 29:21–28)

The hope that came as a result of Jacob's love for Rachel led to him serving fourteen years for the reward of marriage to her. He endured the deception and delayed gratification of being with the woman he so desperately wanted because of the love and confidence he had that Rachel was worth the wait. Today, you have the gift of the blessed hope of spending eternity with someone who loves you more than anyone in your life has ever loved you and who will provide much more joy and happiness than anything you could ever imagine in your mortal flesh. This blessed hope, motivated by the love of God for you is what should drive most of your life as a Christian, to endure and remain calm and steady during the storms of life, understanding that God will surely come through for you in righteousness. "For through the Spirit we eagerly await by faith the righteousness for which we hope" (Galatians 5:5, NIV 2011).

Jesus Christ is the basis of your hope, for He willingly died and rose again to defeat satan and death forever and to make certain the victory that you are now guaranteed when you go under the cover of His wings. Jesus is thus called "our hope" and "the hope of glory" (1 Timothy 1:1; Colossians 1:27) in the Bible. Christ's resurrection makes Him the "first fruit" of those who have fallen asleep and the guarantee of the same resurrection to all who believe in Him (1 Corinthians 15:20). Nothing can separate you from God's love and ultimate destiny for you, which is manifested by Jesus Christ, your hope. "For I am persuaded beyond doubt (am sure) that neither death nor life, nor angels nor principalities, nor things impending and threatening nor things to come, nor powers, nor height nor depth, nor anything else in all creation will be able to separate us from the love of God which is in Christ Jesus our Lord" (Romans 8:38–39, Amplified).

This means that because Jesus Christ is the basis of your hope, the anchor of your soul, there is no power in this world or the spiritual world that can derail your destiny, even though there may seem to be temporary periods in your life when your hope is deferred. May your hope in Christ Jesus grow continuously throughout your life!

Pray This Prayer with Me:

Dear God, I thank You that because of the blessed hope, I can face tomorrow with certainty. Help me to always understand the certainty of the hope I have in my Lord, Jesus Christ, a hope that never fails. Thank You for increasing to full measure the presence of the Holy Spirit to inspire me with hope through every trial here on earth. I pray this prayer in the name of my Lord, Jesus Christ, amen.

1. http://dictionary.reference.com/browse/hope (last visited April 10, 2011).
2. Deuteronomy 25:5; Genesis 38:8; Ruth 3, 4.
3. http://en.wikipedia.org/wiki/Anchor. (Accessed Nov 20, 2011.
4. Romans 5:5.

CHAPTER 24

The House of God Is a House of Hope, Part 2

(Session 12b)

Some day you will read in the papers that D. L. Moody, of East
Northfield, is dead. Don't you believe a word of it. At that moment
I shall be more alive than I am now. I shall have gone up higher, that
is all; out of this old clay tenement into a house that is immortal, a
body that death cannot touch.—Dwight L. Moody

Keeping a Heavenly Focus

In order to fully appreciate the blessed hope, you need first to pray that
God gives you a strong vision or revelation of a picture of the heaven in
which you have hope, and then constantly keep this vision in your mind at
all times. "Where there is no vision, the people perish: but he that keepeth
the law, happy is he" (Proverbs 29:18, KJV).

You need to be convinced that heaven is real and appreciate the
incredible beauty that awaits you when you get there. Jacob endured seven
years of toiling because he had the vision of marriage to Rachel constantly
on his mind which gave him the hope he needed. Similarly Naomi's hope
meter was greatly enhanced by a vision of the possibility of Ruth being
rescued by Boaz. It is only with a clear vision of the reality of heaven that
you can strive for all things godly and endure all the storms of life while
you are on Earth. This vision will enable you to hold on lightly to all your
earthly treasures and possessions while recognizing that this world and
all its prizes, imperfections, and struggles is a temporary home and when

you depart, you will take nothing with you. The focus of your heart will be on what you treasure the most. If all your perceptions of what life is about are tied up onto your treasures on Earth, you cannot have a heavenly perspective.

"Do not store up for yourselves treasures on Earth, where moth and rust destroy, and where thieves break in and steal. But store up for yourselves treasures in heaven, where moth and rust do not destroy, and where thieves do not break in and steal. For where your treasure is, there your heart will be also" (Matthew 6:19–21). Your ultimate destiny is to serve and expand God's kingdom here on earth while waiting for the blessed hope. This is why it is very important to fully understand that you yourself as the temple or tabernacle of God here on earth are a replica of the real tabernacle of God in heaven. God's designs of you and of the Jewish Tabernacle are based on the design of the Tabernacle in heaven in which Jesus is the high priest.[1] With this realization, you should strive to know what the real Tabernacle in heaven is like so that it can motivate your own tabernacle here on earth.

The Majestic Beauty of Heaven

So what is so special about this heaven in which Jesus serves as the high priest? While the full picture will be revealed to us only when we die, we do already know that it is a place of indescribable beauty and tranquility. It is a place where we will always be in the presence of the most High God, Jehovah whose appearance will constantly lift up our spirits. It is an appearance that is of such glorious beauty that it can only be described in terms of precious stones such as jasper and ruby.[2] It is a place where God Himself will be the direct source of a beautiful and consistent light that shines day and night, a light that is brighter than the sun,[3] yet there is no scorching from its heat.[4]

It is a place of such brilliance that the walls have the appearance of jasper, the streets and structures are made of crystal clear gold, and the foundations are decorated with all types of the most precious stones—jasper, sapphire, agate, emerald, onyx, ruby, chrysolite, beryl, topaz, turquoise, jacinth, and amethyst.

It is a place where there are no thieves or corruption, no shame or deceit, no tears or mourning, no hunger or thirst or pain and where everyone is sheltered in an indescribably beautiful mansion prepared by our Lord Jesus.[5] It is a place where the symbolism of the acacia wood used in the Jewish temple is fully realized as people—representing individual temples from every nation, tribe, people, and language—are united in the constant worship of the God who created us and the universe.[6] And the most amazing part of all this is that it is a forever place. There will be no dips or valleys in the joy that we will experience there, no days that are worse than others. Every day will be special unto itself and we will live the life God intended for all His creation forever.

Stephen, the first Christian to be martyred in the Bible had such a strong vision of heaven given to him by the Holy Spirit that it inspired him to boldly share the gospel, even at the point of his death.[7] Similarly, you must always seek to keep your focus on this beautiful place of your eternal destiny to motivate your life today. The alternative to heaven is a place reserved for those who have no hope because they have failed to acknowledge Jesus Christ in this world. "He said to me: 'It is done. I am the Alpha and the Omega, the Beginning and the End. To the thirsty I will give water without cost from the spring of the water of life. Those who are victorious will inherit all this, and I will be their God and they will be my children. But the cowardly, the unbelieving, the vile, the murderers, the sexually immoral, those who practice magic arts, the idolaters and all liars—they will be consigned to the fiery lake of burning sulfur. This is the second death'" (Revelation 21:6–8, NIV 2011).

Heaven is a place of indescribable beauty and majesty

Consequences of the Blessed Hope

There are certain consequences of being a house built on the blessed hope. The first is that you should strive to be joyful in everything that you do and in every situation of your life because your eternal future is secure.[8] This is why you are told to "rejoice in the Lord always" by the apostle Paul.[9] This means that no matter what trial or situation you may be going through in life, your attitude should be one of joy. You have this joy based on confidence of hope in your future that transcends any experience you may have on Earth. This is very different from what the world expects of you. Your joy should be borne of the fact that you know that your God, who has already gone through the trouble of sacrificing His only Son so you can live forever in heaven, will not allow you to now go through a trial for which there is no purpose.

"And we know that in all things God works for the good of those who love him, who have been called according to his purpose" (Romans 8:28). If your focus is on the mercy seat within your Most Holy Place where your hope of glory resides, you will come through every situation in your life better, stronger and more glorious because all the work for your victory has already been done by Jesus Christ on the cross at Calvary. This is why Christians are "more than conquerors" (Romans 8:37). We gain our victory in the work done by someone else—our Lord Jesus Christ, who is faithful to oversee all of us who are the temples in which He resides. We then get all the spoils of the victory of Jesus.

"But Christ is faithful as the Son over God's house. And we are His house, if indeed we hold firmly to our confidence and the hope in which we glory" (Hebrews 3:6, NIV 2011).

Next, the blessed hope is an anchor that should keep you from wavering in your faith. "Let us hold unswervingly to the hope we profess, for He who promised is faithful" (Hebrews 10:23).

This calls for continuous reading, meditating on, and memorizing of the Word of God to remind you of God's faithfulness and promises, and for keeping a journal of when God comes through for you so that it can strengthen you and remind you of what He has done when your faith is again challenged. This is how you gain courage and strength to overcome all situations in your life, no matter how daunting they may appear.

The Grace of Salvation Is Not a License to Sin

Your blessed hope should also be your strongest motivation for personal purity and holiness. Since you have been given a free gift and assurance of salvation and you have the witness of the Holy Spirit living within your Most Holy Place, your ongoing *deliberate* sinning is viewed worse by God than those who have never experienced the gift and truth of salvation. God is primarily a God of love, but if He has done everything to rescue you from the pit of hell, and has freely given you His Holy Spirit to be with you always and to guide you through life, you are showing incredible contempt for Him when you continue in deliberate sin.

> If we deliberately keep on sinning after we have received the knowledge of the truth, no sacrifice for sins is left, but only a fearful expectation of judgment and of raging fire that will consume the enemies of God. Anyone who rejected the

law of Moses died without mercy on the testimony of two or three witnesses. How much more severely do you think someone deserves to be punished who has trampled the Son of God underfoot, who has treated as an unholy thing the blood of the covenant that sanctified them, and who has insulted the Spirit of grace? For we know Him who said, "It is mine to avenge; I will repay," and again, "The Lord will judge His people." It is a dreadful thing to fall into the hands of the living God. (Hebrews 10:26–31, NIV 2011. See also I Thessalonians 4:3–8)

Notice the emphasis on the word "deliberate" sin in the verses above. While your goal as a Christian is to achieve purity, God knows that achieving such purity is a lifelong process for all believers. God is a God of love and forgiveness and He has forgiven all your sins both current and future ones for which you are repentant. However, as a Holy God, He will not overlook the ongoing pursuit of deliberate sin. Because of the gift of the blessed hope, you need to persevere in righteousness so that your confidence in God can be rewarded in due course.[10]

Hold on Lightly to Earth and Firmly to Heaven

Next, the blessed hope should encourage you to hold on very lightly to your temporary earthly possessions and be very generous to God's kingdom while you are here on earth. Jesus Christ noted that while your salvation is a free gift from God, your treasures in heaven are tied to how well you treat and care for the poor, being motivated out of the love of God while you are here on earth.[11]

Finally, the blessed hope should keep you from excessive grief when a loved one in Christ goes to be with the Lord. "Brothers and sisters, we do not want you to be uninformed about those who sleep in death, so that you do not grieve like the rest of mankind, who have no hope. For we believe Jesus died and rose again, and so we believe God will bring with Jesus those who have fallen asleep in him … therefore encourage one another with these words" (I Thessalonians 4:13–14, 18).

Losing a loved one is never an easy process to deal with, even if he or she lived a long life. Losing a loved one who does not know the Lord is especially painful and should cause grief to all believers. However, having a loved one die unto the Lord is not a permanent loss, which should be the biggest source of comfort to all believers, with security in the knowledge that they are eternally in the presence of the living God, and in the country in which they are true citizens.

"But our citizenship is in heaven. And we eagerly await a Savior from there, the Lord Jesus Christ, who, by the power that enables him to bring everything under his control, will transform our lowly bodies so that they will be like his glorious body" (Philippians 3:20–21). I pray God will give you a full and clear vision of heaven, the place of your true citizenship, to motivate you to persevere in hope for every situation in your life.

Pray This Prayer with Me:

Dear Father, I thank You so much for the blessed hope of eternal life in my Lord and Savior Jesus Christ. I recognize that this hope is not futile or uncertain as is the hope held separate from knowledge of You. Thank You for instilling in me the grace to persevere in the blessed hope. Give me a strong vision of heaven all the days of my life so I may share in the rewards You have promised to those who believe and trust in You till the end. Amen.

Several other key biblical verses dealing with the issue of our blessed hope in the Lord Jesus Christ are noted in the references listed at the end of this sentence and are worthy of meditating upon.[12]

Questions to Ponder:

- Read Hebrews 6:19.
  - What is meant by the Christian blessed hope being an anchor for your soul?
  - Why is the hope described here said to be firm and secure?
  - What is the implication of this hope being an anchor that reaches into the inner sanctuary?
- Naomi's hopes for her future were anchored on human beings.
  - Have you had your hopes in the future dashed by relying on anyone?
  - Describe one such episode and what you learned from it.
- Both Naomi and Jacob relied on love to give them hope.
  - What is the connection between love and hope?
  - Why is love important in giving hope to someone who has lost it?
- Do you think of heaven much?
  - How can a clear picture of heaven help give you hope?
  - How can you keep this image of heaven with you at all times?

Prayer Points

- Pray that God will give you a strong conviction of the certainty of the Christian blessed hope.
- Pray that your hope for your future will be anchored not merely on your retirement earnings, or your stock portfolio, but on the certainty of Jesus Christ.
- Pray that God's love will shine through you to bring hope to others and through others to bring hope to you at all times.
- Pray that God will give you a clear and powerful vision of heaven that will motivate your perseverance in every situation you face in your life.

1. Hebrews 8:1–6.
2. Revelation 4:3.
3. Acts 26:13.
4. Revelation 7:16.
5. Revelation 21:4, 27; 7:9–17; Matthew 6:19–21; John 14:2.
6. Revelation 7:9.
7. Acts 7:54–60.
8. Romans 12:12.
9. Philippians 4:4.
10. Hebrews 10:36–39.
11. Matthew 19:16–26.
12. Romans 5:2b; Hebrews 3:6; 2 Thessalonians 2:16; Hebrews 10:22–23; Ephesians 2:10; Galatians 5:5; Colossians 1:5; Romans 8:25, 12:12; 1 Peter 1:7; 1 Thessalonians 1:3; 1 Corinthians 13.

CHAPTER 25

The House of God is a House of Love, Not Fear

(Session 13a)

I stand in awe of a God whose overwhelming love for me, a sinner deserving death, leads Him to sacrifice His most precious possession— His only natural son Jesus Christ to die so that I would not have to die. Confronted by this humbling reality, my least means of showing my gratitude is by loving Him back and by loving other sinners just as He loves me.

These things I command you, that you love one another.—John 15:17 (NKJV)

The Greatest Show of Obedience Is by Loving God

In previous sessions, we established that Jesus Christ, the greatest and most humble man to ever live, empowered by the Holy Spirit resident within His temple *chose* to be fully obedient to God and to die on the cross for your and my sins. As a result of this magnificent free and unwarranted act of love, your destiny and mine were forever changed because there is now no condemnation for anyone who accepts and believes in Jesus Christ as their savior. "For God so loved the world that He gave His one and only Son, that whoever believes in Him shall not perish but have eternal life" (John 3:16).

Our natural response to such a wonderful free gift from God should be such love and gratitude as to want to serve Him and obey Him for the rest

309

of our lives. Jesus himself repeatedly noted that if you claim to be grateful for what He has done for you, you will love him and show your gratitude by obeying Him, and this in turn would enable Him to come and take full residence in you.

"If you love Me, keep My commandments. ... He who has My commandments and keeps them, it is he who loves Me. ... Jesus answered and said to him, 'If anyone loves Me, he will keep My word; and My Father will love him, and we will come to him and make our home with him. He who does not love Me does not keep My words; and the word which you hear is not Mine but the Father's who sent Me'" (John 14:15, 21a, 23–24, NKJV).

While there is a deposit of the Holy Spirit in all Christians when you give your life to Jesus Christ, total obedience to Him is important in enabling each of the three chambers of your temple to be totally influenced by God's Spirit. Your obedience demonstrates your love and enables you to become an extension of God Himself. "And so we know and rely on the love God has for us. *God is love.* Whoever lives in love lives in God, and God in Him" (1 John 4:16, emphasis added).

In obedience, He not only resides in you, but you also get to reside in Him! God is faithful and He keeps His covenant of love to a thousand generations of those who love Him and keep His commandments.[1] This means that in your obedience, there is nothing that can separate you or your children or children's children from the love of God.[2] As an extension of Him, you are God's ambassador and God expects you to demonstrate this same love He has for you toward others. When Jesus was asked by one of the Jewish leaders of His time which one of the commandments is the greatest one, His reply was unambiguously about our need to love God and our neighbor: "'Teacher, which is the greatest commandment in the Law?' Jesus replied 'Love the Lord your God with all your heart and with all your soul and with all your mind. This is the first and greatest commandment. And the second is like it: Love your neighbor as yourself. All the Law and the Prophets hang on these two commandments'" (Matthew 22:36–40).

Love Is the Key "Sparkplug" of Your Temple

The act of loving God and others is the sparkplug that fires up the Holy Spirit dwelling within your Most Holy Place. It will spread into the other chambers of your temple in such an explosive way that the light hidden within you escapes and radiates brightly to the world around you. Your love of others is the key act of obedience that opens the floodgates of heaven and enables God the Father to be fully manifested here on Earth. It is the most special ingredient in the believer's life that transforms you from an ordinary person to an extraordinary one that is able to expand the kingdom of God. Through love, God used one man to change the course of history and save billions of people from the guilt of eternal condemnation. Similarly through your own obedience in loving others, God will use you in transforming the lives of others and enable you to accomplish more than you could ever plan or hope for through any act based on your own mortal efforts. If you love Him, God will reward you abundantly and bless you as you become one of His key ambassadors.[3] "No eye has seen, no ear has heard, and no mind has imagined what God has prepared for those who love Him" (1 Corinthians 2:9, NLT).

Faith, hope, and love are all very important and intertwined attributes of being a spiritual Christian that are not intended to and cannot exist separately from each other. However, while each is essential, the one that truly sets you apart in the kingdom of God is love. "And now these three remain: faith, hope and love. But the greatest of these is love" (I Corinthians 13:13).

Indeed, the Bible teaches (1 John 4:8) that if you do not love others, you cannot know God!

How Do You Love God?

One obvious question is what is love and how do you show your love for God? The love being referred to here is not the type of love used in our common language that is closely tied to experiences or emotions (*phileo*, or brotherly love). Phileo love is an important type of love that God has put in your heart to enable you to have affection for and enjoy your family members, close friends, favorite objects, pets, etc. It should not surprise anyone that you love your spouse or your child or sibling. This is phileo love, a characteristic that every human being is innately born with.

However, phileo love is not a love that motivates you to act in a universal manner toward everyone. Instead, the love being referred to by Jesus is Christian love known as *agape*. Agape love is love that motivates you to seek the best for others, irrespective of how you feel toward them.

Demonstrating agape love is a fundamental tenet of the Christian faith. We are called to hate sinful behavior in all its form, but to love the sinner no matter what they have done, just as God detests all sin, but loves all of humanity irrespective of their sinfulness. This is a tough behavior at best for most believers to model because we often forget to draw the line between the sin and the sinner, or we act in such a manner that others perceive we are condemning the sinner with the sin even when our intent may not be so.

As always, the role model for us in demonstrating agape love should be Jesus Christ who clearly came out strongly against sin, but loved God and all humanity including you and me so much that He gave up His life for us. He did this even for those who hated him and those who still continue to hate him because He wants to give everyone a chance at redemption and an eternity spent in heaven. You and I are called to have the same self-sacrificing *love* as a reflection of our appreciation of Jesus' love for us. Agape love then, is based not on how you feel, but love that motivates acting in spite of how you feel because of what God has commanded you to do. This is how you show agape love toward God:

You love God when you seek to know Him thoroughly and to do His will diligently, without concern for your reputation or what others may think of you.[4]

You love Him when you desire to spend quality time daily reading and memorizing His words and meditating on His promises for your life.

You love Him when you worship and praise Him, and when you pray and fast regularly so that "His kingdom" may come in your life and the lives of those around you.[5]

You love Him when you are willing to put aside your own selfish ambition in the firm belief and complete trust that His ambition for you is better than any plans you may have hatched for yourself.[6]

You love Him when you are willing to put aside your own ego and put other people's needs ahead of your own.[7]

You love Him when the only thing you like to boast about is God and His goodness to you and others.

You love Him when you forgive and pray for others who have hurt you, remembering that He forgave you for doing worse to Him.[8]

You love Him when you refuse to keep a record of those who have wronged you, because you understand that when you say you love God but you hate a brother or sister who has hurt you, you are a liar.[9]

You love Him when you remember the poor and the hungry and the destitute while you are balancing your checkbook each month and you do not send away those who genuinely need your help when you have the ability to help them.

You love Him when you not only say that you believe in Jesus, but your actions back up your words in faithfully doing what He has commanded.[10]

You love Him when you are willing to obey *all* His commands and not just those that seem palatable to you at the time you are faced with the choice to do so.[11]

You love Him when you always trust Him enough to persevere on the journey He has called you to take in life, even when the circumstances seem dire to you.

You love Him when you always have hope that He will do what He has promised, no matter how the circumstance you are facing looks to you at the time.

You love Him when you do not discuss others behind their back in a way that denigrates them.

Agape love does not depend on how you feel about someone

You love Him when you are so excited about your relationship with Him and what He has done for you that you are always palpably excited to share the good news with others.[12]

You love Him when you love the poor as much as the rich and you do not show favoritism to those who seem able to reward you for your efforts ahead of those who do not.[13]

You love Him when you become a channel that spreads His love to those around you through your giving, sharing, and caring.

I encourage you to meditate on the "love chapter" (1 Corinthians 13), which includes the apostle Paul's description of the attributes of agape love.

The Holy Spirit of Love

While it may at first seem impossible to love God and your neighbor in the manner prescribed above, it becomes easier when you recognize that God has given you all you need in His Holy Spirit, who has been deposited in you so that you can accomplish this goal. The secret to agape love is in learning to stay close to the Holy Spirit, so that you can unleash His full power into all three parts of your temple to act in a loving manner at all times. The Holy Spirit is constantly longing to break out of your Most Holy Place to be your lamppost. The reality of humanity is that you naturally turn your attention to and focus on what you love the most.

There is a saying that goes, "Show me where a man spends his money, and I will show you what he loves." When you love God, your time and money will reflect this love, just as God's actions throughout time have reflected His love for you and me. This is why God spends so much of His time chasing after His children and continues to pursue us in spite of our imperfections—because He deeply loves us unconditionally and desires a close relationship with us.

Get this firmly into your mind:

The Creator and king of the whole universe and the embodiment of love is very much in love with you. Once you catch the full significance of this statement, you should have no option but to want to turn your focus from your outer court to your Most Holy Place where the Holy Spirit— your greatest lover and best friend resides at all times. When you do this, it is akin to your watering and fertilizing the powerful seed planted in the fertile ground of your heart. The Holy Spirit will then be freed to spread His roots throughout all the chambers of your temple, sprout, germinate, and burst out of you. And when The Holy Spirit is fully blossomed within you and consumes you, you will take on His glow and possess all His qualities. Under these conditions, you will ultimately bear sweet and productive fruit that will make it obvious from which tree you came, the fruit of the tree of the Holy Spirit.[14] Among these fruit, there are nine characteristics, the first one of which is love. "But the fruit of the Spirit is love, joy, peace, patience, kindness, goodness, faithfulness, gentleness, and self-control. Against such things there is no law" (Galatians 5:22–23).

Each fruit has an aroma. Love is the primary aroma by which you will be recognized by those around you as being from the tree of the family of Jehovah, the only living God.[15]

Love Is the Dominant Fragrance of the Holy Spirit

Love then is the leading and dominant fragrance of the Holy Spirit. It is a sweet aroma that leads people to recognize the presence of God in you. You will be easily recognizable as a follower of Christ because of your love. As your focus turns to the Holy Spirit, you become in sync with Him and you will receive the desire and the power to reflect His characteristic of agape love (2 Timothy 1:7). Interesting enough, as you show agape love to others, God then enables you to develop phileo love toward them as well. Your love of others will no longer be a legalistic or ritualistic action but will be motivated differently. It is no different than when you first fall in love with another person. You are motivated to do things for them, not because you feel obligated to, but because you want to. You are anxious to tell your friends about this person, and even if you do not, they can tell by the look on your face that you are in love. King David, a great lover of God, said of God: "Because your love is better than life, my lips will glorify you" (Psalm 63:3). Love of God, rather than obedience born out of obligation, is the key to living the life God has called you to live.

"This is how we know that we love the children of God: by loving God and carrying out His commands. This is love for God: to obey His commands. And His commands are not burdensome, for everyone born of God overcomes the world. This is the victory that has overcome the world, even our faith" (1 John 5:2–4).

"Everyone born of God" means everyone who has been "born of the Spirit of God."[16] It was not the nails that kept Christ on the cross but love for you and me—infused in Him by the Spirit of God. He stayed there in loving obedience to His Father when His whole flesh, Spirit, and Soul were being tormented and begging for release. Just as the Holy Spirit enabled Jesus' love and obedience to glorify God the Father, this same Spirit instilled in you will enable you to glorify Jesus Christ, His Son.[17] He will make obedience to loving others a strong desire of yours and you will experience a new and overwhelming hunger to pursue God in your life and to tell others about Him.

The Creator and king of the whole universe is very much in love with you!

May God grant you the grace to express the full extent of His love throughout your life.

Fear Is a Spirit Unleashed by Satan to Oppose Love

One of the biggest hurdles most believers face when it comes to loving God or others is fear. *Fear is a spirit that opposes love, and it is not from God but comes from the enemy.* "For God has not given us a *spirit* of fear but of power and of love and of a sound mind" (2 Timothy 1:7, emphasis added). While the Spirit of God gives you the desire and power to love and obey Him, to love yourself and others, and to be of a sound mind, the spirit of fear does the exact opposite.

Fear takes away all your desire and power and makes you of unsound mind.

Fear paralyzes you from wanting to take any step of faith and obedience to God because it shows you how narrow the plank you are about to step on is and how far you will fall if you miss your step.

Fear plays in advance for you all the people who will ridicule you and marvel at your folly, when you take a position that is not conventional to the wisdom of the day.

Fear plays back all the failures of your past and asks you why you think you can now succeed.

Fear shows you how big and powerful the enemies you are about to take on are, how much more resources they have at their disposal, and how they can seemingly determine the course of your future, and then dares you to take them on or to challenge them.

Fear reminds you how stupid you will look to everyone around you when you are building a boat in your backyard that God has asked you to build, because there is not a whiff of water around to float it on or any obvious known mechanism by which the boat can even be moved from your yard toward the sea.

Fear shuts you up when you are witness to something awfully wrong that is being perpetrated right in front of you by reminding you that you are just one person and you cannot possibly change the situation.

Indeed, fear reminds you that if you do intervene, it will come at great personal cost and loss, your life will be put under an intense and unwanted microscope and you will be ridiculed and ostracized.

Fear will remind you of that one time when you trusted God for something important and tell you that He did not deliver it the way you expected Him to, when you expected Him to, or never at all.

Fear ridicules your basic notion of faith in God and makes sure you see how big and overwhelming the mountain in front of you is, exposing every treacherous cliff, valley, and peak on it and daring you to believe you can overcome it.

Fear tells you that you will become somewhat of a pariah, or worse still that you will come under sustained attack that you cannot overcome by putting your trust in the Living God.

Fear Aims to Shift Your Focus from God

The goal of the spirit of fear is to ensure that you do not believe any of the promises God has deposited in you through His Word and His Spirit.

In essence, fear is a very powerful and controlling spirit and the weapon satan has fully mastered to unleash at will, in order to paralyze most Christians and people, stopping them from accomplishing the full purpose for which God created them. Fear is a spirit of intimidation whose main goal is to remove your focus from your Most Holy Place where your solutions are, and fix it instead on your outer court where there is no possible hope. The ultimate goal of fear is to derail the destiny God has planned for you!

Love Overcomes Fear

The secret of overcoming the spirit of fear is a four letter word spelled L-O-V-E, as in *agape love*. Imagine a scenario where your daughter (or son or close relative, such as niece of nephew if you have no children) has requested a special gift for her birthday. On the happy day, she rips open the present and finds you have acceded to her request and purchased exactly what she wanted. She is beaming from ear to ear and her joy reinforces your own sense of good judgment in giving her this gift. For the next ten days, she holds on to this gift everywhere she goes, showing it to her friends, passersby, and to anyone who cares to make eye contact with her. "Mommy (or Daddy) gave this to me for my birthday," she proudly declares. One day as you are taking a walk with your precious princess along a trail, you pass by a railroad track just a few yards away that runs parallel to your walking path. Your little girl is joyously tossing up and catching her new toy in the air as she walks along. Like a mother bear guarding her cub, you instinctively position yourself between her and the railroad track, fearing the danger of her drifting too close to the track.

However, in one carefree moment of launching her toy up, your girl overshoots her ability to retrieve it on its downward journey and it rolls directly onto the path of the railroad track just as a train is fast approaching. Instinctively, she starts to go after her toy, totally oblivious to the clear and present danger of the train treacherously whistling along on its journey toward her.

You are instantaneously confronted with two distinct choices, with absolutely no doubt as to which one you are about to make. The first choice is to go after your daughter's toy. After all, you have witnessed the joy that has come these past few days as a result of this gift. However, this choice has only a modicum of appeal. Your potential reward of delight for your child in retrieving the toy is superseded by your fear and respect of the damage that could be caused by the onslaught of the fast-approaching engine and the danger to your daughter. The other and much more appealing choice you have is to go after the girl and protect her from the looming and imminent danger. For this choice, there is a greater element at work, your overwhelming need to protect your beloved one, which is borne out of the strong parental love you have for her.

The same fear and respect of the fast-approaching train is at work in both of the choices you have to make. In the first scenario, fear is a sensible motivator that precludes you from putting yourself in harm's way over an object, no matter how precious it may be to you or your daughter. You do not love the object enough to overcome the fear of the potential serious injury from the train. In the second scenario, love becomes your motivator as you run after your daughter, knowing you would overcome your fear and jump in front of that train if you needed to if that is what it would take to pull her out of harm's way. Your intense love for your child helps you to overcome any fear you may have in the face of clear and present danger. True love always conquers fear when your love and relationship with the person involved is stronger than the perceived danger associated with the circumstance. After the December 14, 2012 Sandy Hook elementary school killings, many stories emerged of courageous teachers, and other workers whose love for the kids placed under their watch motivated them to overcome their own worst fears and insert themselves in harm's way to protect their children. These acts of profound bravery and love saved the lives of several children while costing some of these heroic adults their own lives.

In your relationship with God, your love for Him and faith and confidence in Him must be stronger than your concern about your relationship with others or concerns about material loss or loss of status. In other words, your love for God needs to be so much more than ordinary, such that you are willing to suffer loss for Him. To reach this, you first need to believe God's words that He loves you and will always watch over you. "There is no fear in love. But perfect love drives out fear, because fear has to do with punishment. The one who fears is not made perfect in love" (1 John 4:18, NIV 2011).

In the same way, the perfect love Jesus had for you and for God the Father is what kept Him on the cross, not the nails that were used to pierce his hands and feet. Love is thus the key ingredient to overcoming fear. Even though it is natural to be afraid at times, the Spirit of love enables you to move forward in spite of your fear.

The Paralyzing Power of Fear Can Ruin Your Destiny

One of the best illustrations of the disabling and paralyzing power of fear contrasting with love and confidence in God is found in the book of Numbers.[18] In this story, God sends twelve leaders, one from each of the tribes of Israel to go spy and scout out the land of Canaan He had promised to give to them as an inheritance. When they returned from the land, all the men agreed that the land was indeed beautiful and fertile just as God had promised them, and they even brought back some of its delicious fruit for everyone to see. However, there was more in the land than the scouts had bargained for.

The land was also full of "giant men" who were much bigger and taller than they had ever seen. For ten of the scouts, their focus came off God and the land He had promised them and instead fell on the size of the men who were living in Canaan at the time. This focus of the men soon filtered through from their outer courts into their minds where the images of the men they saw soon became so exaggerated that they became paralyzed with fear. The fear from these ten men spread like yeast to all the chambers of their temple. This fear, having escaped their temples, was then spread to the remaining Israelites whom they were able to convince that the benefits of the land God had promised them were not enough to overcome the clear and present danger of the perceived giants who lived in the land.

In contrast, two of the men, Joshua and Caleb, never stopped believing and loving God and their focus remained on Him. They did not focus on the giants but on the God who is much bigger. As a result of their fear, none of the Israelites of that generation except for Joshua and Caleb entered the Promised Land. In the same way, fear will keep you from fulfilling God's promises to you and His destiny for your life, while the love of God will enable you to become who He called you to be.

Turning Off the "Faucet of Fear"

If the Spirit God has given you is one of power and love and of a sound mind, why do you often feel the opposite—afraid and timid? Why do you often feel fearful, powerless, and loveless and perhaps even question the soundness of your own mind? It is probable you have welcomed the spirit of fear into your temple with open arms and given it a special room in your Most Holy Place, which you should have reserved only for God's Spirit of love. You may have continuously fed and nourished the spirit of fear to the point where it is not anxious to go anywhere else. Why should it? You have opened a direct access from your outer court to your Holy Place and into your Most Holy Place where fear is welcomed to operate at liberty. Since you have given such free reign to so powerful an enemy, it will take a more powerful force to displace him. The only force more powerful than the spirit of fear is the Spirit of love. To take back control of your temple, you have to turn it over to the Spirit of love, which is the Holy Spirit, who is fully empowered to cast out your spirit of fear.[19]

How do you do this? Think of your temple as it is currently, dominated by the spirit that often causes you to fear. You are like a house in which a faucet has been turned on, and the water from the faucet has not only filled the bathtub, it has now spilled onto the bathroom floor and is overflowing into your bedroom and the living room. Indeed, you have a serious flood problem going on in your home.

The first step in the control of any flood is to turn off the faucet from which the water is pouring out. This means you have to turn off anything that feeds fear into your temple. It could be that it is time to stop watching those news channels that remind you of the doom and gloom that is awaiting you as you step out into the world. Stop listening to those radio stations where the hosts are shouting at one another and telling you about the evils about to befall you. Stop reading those horror books that pour fear into your mind. Stop watching those horror movies that deposit fear into your temple. Stop spending time with people who work hard to instill fear into you or who have fully welcomed the spirit of fear into their temple and are constantly expressing it to you. *You must turn off the faucet!*

Mopping Up the "Flood of Fear"

Turning off the faucet will cut off all the new supply of fear into your temple. Unfortunately, there is still plenty of fear already deposited into your temple's tub and into all your rooms such that even after the faucet is turned off, your temple will remain moist and moldy and you may not perceive any difference in yourself. How do you dry up this remaining amount of fear? You need to mop it up and then blow away the remnants. You can only mop away the flooded rooms by using the words and promises of God in the Bible. Spend time reading God's word and reminding yourself that God is bigger than any mountain of fear you may be facing. Do not just read the Bible, but meditate on key verses that have meaning to you and memorize them, especially the promises made by God related to fear until they become part of you. Reinforce the mopping by repeating the key verses several times each day and practice standing on His word. Whenever the spirit of fear tries to pop back up, you can knock it down with the appropriate promise from the word of God just as Jesus did with God's Word when He was tempted by satan in the wilderness.[20]

For example, when fear starts to creep in, say out loud God's promises, such as the following verses (emphasis added):

"God has not given *me* a spirit of fear but a Spirit of power and of love and of a sound mind" (2 Timothy 1:7).

"Those that are with us (*me*) are more than those that are with them" (2 Kings 6:16).

"The Lord is on my side; I will not fear. What can man do to me?" (Psalm 118:6).

"I will not fear though tens of thousands assail me on every side" (Psalm 3:6).

"(*I will*) fear not, then; (*I*) am of more value than many sparrows" (Matthew 10:31, Amplified).

"The Lord is my light and my salvation—whom shall I fear? The Lord is the stronghold of my life—of whom shall I be afraid?" (Psalm 27:1)

"The angel of the Lord encamps around those who fear him and he delivers them (*me*)" (Psalm 34:7).

"(*I will*) have no fear of sudden disaster or of the ruin that overtakes the wicked" (Proverbs 3:25).

"It is (*God*) alone who is to be feared" (Psalm 76:7).

"The Lord Almighty is the only one (*I*) am to regard as holy, He is the only one (*I am*) to fear, He is the only one (*I am*) to dread" (Isaiah 8:13).

"The fear of the Lord is the beginning of wisdom, and knowledge of the Holy One is understanding" (Proverbs 9:10).

"*I* will not fear the terror of night, nor the arrow that flies by day, nor the pestilence that stalks in the darkness, nor the plague that destroys at midday. A thousand may fall at (*my side*), ten thousand at (*my*) right hand, but it will not come near me. (*I*) will only observe with (*my*) eyes and see the punishment of the wicked" (Psalm 91:5–8).

"*I* sought the Lord and He answered me; He delivered me from all my fears" (Psalm 34:4).

"But I will rescue you (*insert your name here*) on that day declares the Lord; you (*insert your name here*) will not be given into the hands of those you fear" (Jeremiah 39:17).

"Fear of man will prove to be a snare, but whoever trusts in the Lord is kept safe" (Proverbs 29:25).

"The Spirit (*I*) received does not make (*me*) a slave, so that (*I*) live in fear again, rather, the Spirit (*I*) received brought about (*my*) adoption to sonship. And by him (*I*) cry 'Abba, Father'" (Romans 8:15).

"I, *(insert your name),* will not be afraid; I will not be put to shame. I will not fear disgrace; (*I*) will not be humiliated" (Isaiah 54:4).

"But now, this is what the Lord says—He who created (*me, insert your name here*), He who formed me (*insert your name here*): 'Do not fear, for I have redeemed you; I have summoned you by name; (*insert your name here*) you are mine'" (Isaiah 43:1).

"So do not fear (*insert your name here*), for I am with you; do not be dismayed, for I am your God. I will strengthen you and help you; I will uphold you with my righteous right hand" (Isaiah 41:10).

The Word of God is the "sword" of the Holy Spirit

"For I am the Lord your God who takes hold of your right hand and says to you, Do not fear; I will help you" (Isaiah 41:13).

"Have I not commanded you (*insert your name here*)? Be strong and courageous. Do not be afraid; do not be discouraged, for the LORD your God will be with you wherever you go" (Joshua 1:9).

This is why the Word of God is referred to in the Bible as the "sword of the Spirit."[21] It is the sword that is used to defeat the spirit of fear and doubt that is trying to destroy you. You need to meditate on these and other similar verses in the Bible and chew on them constantly until they become part of you. Record situations when God has delivered you from fear or from a seemingly enormous mountain, so that you can have confidence of His ability to do the same in the future.

Blowing Away the Residue of Fear

Finally, you can blow away the remaining residue of the flood, which is the spirit of fear, by spending all that time you were using to fill your temple with fear, in praising and praying to God instead!

Praise is a powerful wind that blows away the spirit of fear. Fill your home, your car, and your workplace with music that praises God and puts you in a worshipful mood so that you will always remember that your God is bigger than any situation you may be facing. Read verses in the Bible that deal with praise (see chapter 9, Session 5). "Shout for joy to the LORD, all the earth. Worship the LORD with gladness; come before him with joyful songs. Know that the LORD is God. It is He who made us, and we are His; we are His people, the sheep of His pasture. Enter His gates with thanksgiving and His courts with praise; give thanks to him and praise his name" (Psalm 100:1–4).

"I will call upon the Lord, who is to be praised; so shall I be saved from my enemies" (Psalm 18:3, NKJV). God inhabits the praise from His people—which means He comes down when you praise Him, and when that happens, the atmosphere of fear in your mind and around you has no choice but to change.

"But You are holy, O You who dwell in [the holy place where] the praises of Israel [are offered]" (Psalm 22:3, Amplified). Give it a try and give it consistent time! The flooded rooms will not necessarily be dry overnight and there is a possibility of periodic leaks of fear when you are not on guard. Remember to just continue keeping your focus on your Most Holy Place where God's Spirit of love resides and you will surely overcome. Then go out and help someone else, show unexpected love and kindness to them so that your focus is removed from yourself. May God deliver you from the spirit of fear into the hands of the Holy Spirit of love.

Praise is a powerful wind that blows away the spirit of fear

Pray This Prayer with Me:

Dear God, Thank You very much for your Holy Spirit, the Spirit of love You have poured into me to help others and to enable me to overcome the spirit of fear. Help me to turn off all the faucets of fear in my life that are feeding my Holy Place, and to always turn on all the channels of love that come from focusing my mind on Your Word, and in praising and worshipping You so that my temple is fully activated toward being an agent of Your love. In Jesus' name I pray. Amen.

1. Deuteronomy 7:9.
2. Romans 8:38–39.
3. 2 Corinthians 5:20.
4. Matthew 6:33; John14:21.
5. Luke 5:16.
6. Matthew 7:21, 12:50, 26:39.
7. 1 Corinthians 13.
8. Matthew 18:35.
9. 1 John 4:20; 1 Corinthians 13:5.
10. 1 John 3:23.
11. Matthew 26:39, 42
12. Acts 3:1–10.
13. James 2:8, 9.
14. Luke 6:43–45.
15. 2 Corinthians 2:14–16.
16. John3:5, 6.
17. John 16:14–16.
18. Numbers 13 and 14.
19. 1 John 4:18, KJV.
20. Matthew 4:1–11.
21. Ephesians 6: 17.

CHAPTER 26

Building God's Kingdom on the Temples of God

(Session 13b)

And let us consider how we may spur one another on toward love and good deeds, not giving up meeting together, as some are in the habit of doing, but encouraging one another—and all the more as you see the day approaching.—Hebrews 10: 24–25 (NIV 2011)

Becoming a Fulfilled Temple of God

The fundamental purpose of this book has been to show you how to enable the Spirit of God that is resident within your Most Holy Place to become fully empowered, so that He can have free reign throughout your temple and guide you in fulfilling the full purpose for which God intended when He created you. As you become guided by the Spirit of God, you will take on the very nature of God, complete with the fruit of the Spirit that identifies you with Him, especially love.[1] When you are obedient in doing what God has called you to do, you will live righteously in the eyes of God. Under these conditions, God promises you will flourish: "'The righteous will flourish like a palm tree; they will grow like a cedar of Lebanon; planted in the house of the LORD, they will flourish in the courts of our God. They will still bear fruit in old age, they will stay fresh and green, proclaiming, 'The LORD is upright; He is my rock, and there is no wickedness in Him'" (Psalm 92:12–15).

Empowered by the Spirit, you will be enabled to bring down strongholds of sin that have held you bound in slavery. You will not only be able to activate your God-given talents, but you will also have access to the gifts of the Holy Spirit as you need them, to transform not only your own life, but also the lives of those around you. You will be able to endure the storms in your life with a peace that is confounding to those around you because you know that the school master guiding you through the storm is greater than any storm you may encounter, and His plans for your life are always good in spite of your current situation.[2]

Your life will be a shining example of light to the world that God will use to draw others into His kingdom, so that they too can enjoy the benefits of a full relationship with Him. As your relationship with God is developed daily, especially in the little things, you will learn to trust Him wholly and to never lean on your own understanding. If you never learn to trust God for little things, you will never trust Him for big things. Unless God is the one who builds your temple and everything inside it, all your efforts in life will ultimately be futile. As you determine to trust Him, He will not only build you up but He will stand and watch over you all the time, something impossible for you to do on your own. "Unless the LORD builds the house, the builders labor in vain. Unless the LORD watches over the city, the guards stand watch in vain" (Psalm 127:1, NIV 2011).

With God as your Master and your friend, you will then be ready to take on your role within God's kingdom, and be part of His plan for restoring your family, your neighborhood, your city, and your nation even while you are fully aware of your own inadequacy. I am excited for you!

A Kingdom Made Up of Temples of God

As we noted in previous sessions, Jesus constantly spoke about the kingdom of heaven.[3] Based on what you have learned, you are now ready to take up your position as a key and valued member of God's kingdom. God's kingdom is not made up of a single individual acting in isolation, but consists of a multitude of individuals bringing their skills and love for Him together under a single banner for one unified purpose. In virtually all the situations in which He described the kingdom of heaven, Jesus spoke about a group of people, not one individual.

In addition, He was almost always around people. Indeed, Jesus spent a lot of time alone in prayer and fasting—but this was primarily to stay connected with God the Father. However, there are many more descriptions of times He spent teaching, introducing and building up God's kingdom to His twelve disciples and to small and large groups of Jews and Gentiles (non-Jews). Jesus was modeling for you and me what it means to be part of God's kingdom. You become a more effective member of God's kingdom when you spend time with other members of the kingdom and you help build up the kingdom when you spend time telling and teaching people outside the kingdom about God. We are not called to be secret service, undercover agents in God's kingdom; He does not need our secret admiration or intelligence. He has not called us to become His temple so that we can isolate ourselves from the other members of His kingdom or to retreat from the rest of the world. This was not the approach of the early believers in Jesus.

"Day after day, in the temple courts and from house to house, [the apostles] never stopped teaching and proclaiming the good news that Jesus is the Messiah" (Acts 5:42, NIV 2011).

You are Part of a Body of Believers. God is calling you to be a full participant in His kingdom, so you can play your role and use your gifts to build up His kingdom and complement the gifts of other Christians. This means you need to regularly be in the midst of other believers to utilize the full extent of the gifts God has given you to benefit others; you also are benefited from the gifts of others within the kingdom.

> For just as each of us has one body with many members, and these members do not all have the same function, so in Christ we, though many, form one body, and each member belongs to all the others. We have different gifts, according to the grace given to each of us. If your gift is prophesying, then prophesy in accordance with your faith; if it is serving, then serve; if it is teaching, then teach; if it is to encourage, then give encouragement; if it is giving, then give generously; if it is to lead, do it diligently; if it is to show mercy, do it cheerfully. (Romans 12:4–8, NIV 2011)

You are the hands and feet of Jesus Christ in this world. You are needed as part of a local church or body of believers to help build and use the gifts and talents God has blessed you with for several of His purposes. One purpose is to ensure that other members of the kingdom can be blessed by your gifts so that they can be encouraged. In addition, when you are in the midst of other believers, you will also be encouraged. Another purpose of gathering is to help others who do not yet know about Christ but are seeking the truth to get a glimpse into what His kingdom is about, so you can be part of the greater light that draws them unto God. Jesus wants you to shine your light!

"You are the light of the world. A town built on a hill cannot be hidden. Neither do people light a lamp and put it under a bowl. Instead they put it on its stand, and it gives light to everyone in the house. In the same way, let your light shine before others, that they may see your good deeds and glorify your Father in heaven" (Matthew 5:14–16, NIV 2011).

Making Disciples of Nations

The final command from the Lord Jesus Christ was to make disciples of nations. "Therefore go and make disciples of all nations, baptizing them in the name of the Father and of the Son and of the Holy Spirit, and teaching them to obey everything I have commanded you. And surely I am with you always, to the very end of the age" (Matthew 28:19–20).

Making disciples of nations begins with *one* human being who is wholly committed to being a temple of God and letting his or her light shine to draw others to Christ. When one person brings the talents of his or her temple together with another person who is also a spiritual temple, and then they join with other human temples in the local church and are all willing to use their God-given talents to draw nonbelievers into God's kingdom, the kingdom grows exponentially, and many more people will be saved from eternal condemnation.

Nations will never become disciples of Jesus as commanded without a local body of believers coming together to intercede and be used by God. Every person in every nation around the world is local to some neighborhood, and the primary and most effective means of reach is local. It is also from local churches that missionaries that go out to the ends of the earth must be supported through prayers, finances and other means. God intends us as His temples to be praying for and caring for people from all nations. "For my house will be called a house of prayer for all nations" (Isaiah 56:7b).

In a dramatic scene described in the Gospels, Jesus was so offended that the Jewish temple courts were no longer devoted to serving God but instead were being used by tradesmen to enrich themselves that He began overturning the tables of the tradesmen. He alluded to the verse above in justifying His actions.

"On reaching Jerusalem, Jesus entered the temple courts and began driving out those who were buying and selling there. He overturned the tables of the money changers and the benches of those selling doves, and would not allow anyone to carry merchandise through the temple courts. And as he taught them, he said, 'Is it not written: "My house will be called a house of prayer for all nations"? But you have made it "a den of robbers"'" (Mark 11:15–17).

Since your body as a believer is the temple of God today, Jesus' comments apply to you and me as well. Use of your temple for anything other than the purpose of praying and communicating with God and communicating God's love to others is tantamount to stealing from God's temple and turning it into a den of robbers. God is calling believers to pray for all nations. Since there are hundreds of nations, joining together with other believers will enable more effective prayer as different believers focus on specific nations for which to pray. I encourage you today to pick a few nations of the world to commit to praying for regularly.

Creating an Atmosphere of Heaven on Earth

An added benefit to gathering with other believers is to jointly lift up worship and praise to God, recreating the atmosphere of worship that is found in heaven and encouraging God's overflowing presence. "Then I heard every creature in heaven and on earth and under the earth and on the sea, and all that is in them, saying: 'To Him who sits on the throne and to the Lamb be praise and honor and glory and power, for ever and ever!'" (Revelation 5:13, NIV 2011)

We are not called to be secret service, undercover agents in God's kingdom

When ordinary, imperfect believers gather to praise and worship the perfect God with one heart and to encourage one another, God's Spirit overflows and He is no longer simply within them, but also comes into their midst. Satan is then put to flight because his preferred condition of operation is in the dark, and when the light of God comes, darkness always disappears. I have personally witnessed many miracles of atmospheric changes within homes in turmoil with lives transformed, major illnesses cured and spirits lifted in situations where believers have gathered in unity to praise and worship God. When a body of believers gathers to pray together, Jesus promises fulfillment through the power of the prayer of agreement.

"Again, truly I tell you that if two of you on earth agree about anything they ask for, it will be done for them by my Father in heaven. For where two or three gather in my name, there am I with them" (Matthew 18:19–20, NIV 2011).

This is a very certain promise. As Christians, we do not need to be afraid of confronting challenging situations in our homes, jobs, neighborhoods and nations, even when circumstances appear to be bleak or hopeless. God has promised to do what we jointly ask for, conditional of course—as with all of God's promises—that we are also being obedient to His commands. Gathering to pray to God without obedience in our personal lives, while continuing in *persistent and willful* sin, is a waste of our time and of God's time, and those prayers will not be answered.

God Does Not Require Perfect Temples

Participation in God's kingdom does not require you to be perfect. You should never exclude yourself from serving God or being in His presence or the presence of other believers because you feel inadequate or imperfect; you will be waiting all your life. We are all members of His kingdom by grace, not by perfection, and God can use you more if you recognize your weaknesses. "But He said to me, 'My grace is sufficient for you, for my power is made perfect in weakness.' Therefore I will boast all the more gladly about my weaknesses, so that Christ's power may rest on me" (2 Corinthians 12:9).

As a believer, you are a temple under construction, and buildings under construction are imperfect

No one except Jesus is or has ever been perfect. If your heart is set on following God and has been committed to Jesus, God sees you as perfect through the lens of Jesus Christ. He is honor bound as your Father to treat you as His precious son or daughter.[4] The Holy Spirit deposited within you will then help you on your lifelong journey toward perfection that culminates only when you reach heaven.

Similarly, when you gather together with other believers, recognize that just like you, everyone around you is a temple under construction and any building under construction will have many imperfections. God has not called us into His church or other places of gathering to criticize the current condition of the other temples that are being built, but rather to use our own talents to be a part of the construction of the neighborhood of temples. You will likely find a lot that you can criticize in any gathering of believers. Just remember that a beautiful choir always sounds better than the imperfect individual voices that make it up. While God loves all the individual voices in His kingdom, the collective voice of the whole choir excites Him more.

Temples Transforming Nations

Let us then for one moment imagine what it would be like in America or any other nation when individual Spirit-filled temples of God gather together in a neighborhood to form neighborhood temples and neighborhood temples are linked together into a community of temples and community temples are linked together all over the nation in total devotion to God. If believers gather together for the common purpose of this type of transformation, God is honor-bound to ensure that big things happen.

Repeatedly, there was revival in Judah when the kings and people of that nation repented and collectively decided to follow God, after years of disobedience and following after their own desires and after other gods.[5] Imagine what would happen to the surge of individualism, greed, marriage failures and divisive politics, depression and suicides, addictions and murders, personal bankruptcies and hopelessness when God is brought back into the picture. This can only occur through you and other Christian men and women. We have been commanded to be the salt of the earth, and this requires that we all turn from our outer courts and face the Most Holy Place of our temples so we can be differentiated from the rest of the world. "You are the salt of the earth. But if the salt loses its saltiness, how can it be made salty again? It is no longer good for anything, except to be thrown out and trampled underfoot" (Matthew 5:13).

Salt is a preservative. As salt, you should be helping preserve people for God's kingdom. While the taste of salt is recognizable from an individual grain, the full flavor is more apparent when multiple crystals are applied to the tongue together. Furthermore, a characteristic of salt is that it induces thirst. When you are salt to the earth, there should be greater thirst for Jesus among those who are exposed to you. This is God's desire, and my prayer for you and for America and all nations of the world today, that individual temples of God will come together to transform the world and set the stage for the victorious return of our Lord and Savior, Jesus Christ. You should also make this your desire. There is no condition impossible or too challenging for God. Are you willing and ready?

You can do it as you become a Spiritual temple! We can do it! Let's do it!

Pray This Prayer with Me:

Dear God, my heavenly Father, I thank You very much for everything You have taught me through this book about becoming the type of temple You intended me to be when you created me, a Holy Spirit-filled temple. I willingly and willfully commit myself to the common purpose of being an effective member of your kingdom. Grant me the grace, wisdom, and hunger to be part of a community of temples that can be used to ensure the world knows the value of the gift You have given us in your Son, in ensuring the certainty of their eternal destiny. May I never view myself the same again and always be ready to do my part in helping accomplish Your desire that others will come to know Your loving grace. In Jesus' holy name, I pray. Amen.

Questions to Ponder:

- Why is agape love more reflective of the love of Christ than phileo love?
- Why is love more important to God than faith, hope, or prophecy?
- What aspects of agape love do you struggle with? (Refer to the section beginning in the second paragraph of "How Do You Love God," in Session 13a)
  - Why do you think this is?
  - How do you think you can overcome your struggle with this aspect of agape love?
- Do you struggle with a spirit of fear?
  - Why do you think this is?
  - Can you think of faucets that you have turned on to welcome fear into your temple?
  - How can you overcome your fear?
- Are you a full participant or simply an observer in the kingdom of God?
- Which of your talents can you use toward building God's kingdom?
  - In your neighborhood?
  - In your local church?
  - Around the nation?
  - Around the world?
- Are you ready to take the transformative steps toward becoming a spiritual temple of God? How are you going to do it?

Prayer Points

- Pray that God will instill more of His Spirit of agape love into you each day such that *you* will seek to love others no matter how you may feel toward them.
- Pray that God will help you to recognize how much bigger He is than any spirit of fear that may be aiming to derail your destiny. Ask that He helps you to turn off the faucet of fear, to mop it up, and to blow it out of your temple each time it threatens to rear its ugly head.
- Pray that God will enable you to be a full participant in His kingdom, and that He will enable you to utilize whatever gifts He has blessed you with, no matter how meager they may appear to you.
- Pray that you will never allow satan to convince you your talents pale in comparison with what God can use to build His kingdom.
- Pray that God will instill upon your heart to regularly pray for individuals within your family, your community, your workplace, and your civic leaders.
- Pray that God will give you at least two nations to pray for regularly.
- Finally, pray that all the principles you have learned in the *Real House of God* will take root, sprout, and germinate in you and will bear fruit, transforming you from a carnal or logical temple into a fully loaded Spirit-filled temple of God.

1. Galatians 5:22–23.
2. Isaiah 48:17; Jeremiah 29:11.
3. Matthew 16:9, 18:1, 3, 4, 23; 19:12, 14, 23, 20:1, 22:2, 23:13, 25:1.
4. Hebrews 2:10–13.
5. 2 Kings 23:1–29; 2 Chronicles 14–15, 17:1–20, 1–29, 29:1–3, 2:23, 34–35.

CPSIA information can be obtained at www.ICGtesting.com
Printed in the USA
LVOW080101280213

322022LV00003B/3/P